Gandhi's Philosophy of Action

Prem Anand Mishra

CONCEPT PUBLISHING COMPANY PVT. LTD.
NEW DELHI-110059

ISBN-13: 978-93-88937-51-1

First Published 2020

Published and Printed by

Concept
Since 1974

Concept Publishing Company Pvt. Ltd.
A/15-16, Commercial Block, Mohan Garden,
New Delhi-110059 (INDIA)
T : 91 11 25351460, 91 11 25351794
E : publishing@conceptpub.com; *W* : www.conceptpub.com

Cataloging in Publication Data--Courtesy: D.K. Agencies (P) Ltd. <docinfo@dkagencies.com>

Mishra, Prem Anand, author.
Gandhi's philosophy of action / Prem Anand Mishra.
pages cm
Includes bibliographical references and index.
ISBN 9789388937511

1. Gandhi, Mahatma, 1869-1948—Philosophy. 2. Karma. 3. Act (Philosophy) 4. Knowledge, Theory of. I. Title.

LCC DS481.G3M57 2020 | DDC 128.4 23

Acknowledgements

This book is an extended version of my short study *Epistemological Basis of Gandhian Action* supported by Gujarat Vidyapith. I am grateful to our Vice-Chancellor Prof. Anamikbhai Shah and Registrar Dr. Rajendra Khimani for their constant inspiration from the beginning of the study to its present form. Their continuous support to carry out this academic pursuit has always been a motivating factor for me. I wish to express my deep sense of gratitude to Prof. Sudarshan Iyengar, former Vice-Chancellor of Gujarat Vidyapith and my Ph.D. supervisor, who encouraged and helped me to shape the idea of this study and made valuable comments while discussing the theme of this book. I am also indebted to Prof. M.P. Mathai who discussed crucial points related to this book and enabled me to think of Gandhi's action in the bigger framework of his worldview. Thanks to Prof. Vidyut Joshi, former Vice-Chancellor, Bhavnagar University, for his challenging question and critical comments related to the theme of this book. I am also thankful to Prof. Tridip Suhrud who made me familiar with the Ashramic intellectual tradition of Gandhi. Thanks to Prof. Anil Dutta Mishra for his constant motivation and support. I owe a debt of gratitude to my wife Amita and daughter Utsavi who have tolerated my busy pursuit with utmost patience. Finally, I am obliged to Concept Publishing Company Pvt. Ltd. for its keen interest in publishing this book in record time.

Contents

Acknowledgements v
Introduction ix

1. Conceptualizing Gandhi's Action: Satyagraha and Constructive Programme 1
2. Gandhi's Action and its Relation to his Metaphysics 23
3. Gandhi's Metaphysics and its Epistemological Basis 38
4. Epistemological Basis of Gandhi's Action 56
5. Ethics of Gandhi's Action: Responsibility for One's Self 75
6. Gandhi's Action: Self and its Responsibility to Other 97
7. Esthetics of Gandhi's Action: Unison of Universal Love, Responsibility and Detachment 118
8. Gandhi and Indian Philosophy of Action (Karma) 142

Conclusion 170

Bibliography 176
Index 180

Introduction

> The fact that I have affected the thought and practice of our times does not make me fit to give expression to the philosophy that may lie behind it. To give a philosophical interpretation of the phenomenon must be reserved for men like you.[1]
>
> Well, all my philosophy, if it may be called by that pretentious name, is contained in what I have said. You will not call it Gandhism; there is no ism about it.... All that I have written is but a description of whatever I have done.[2]
>
> I am not built for academic writings. Action is my domain.... All my action is actuated by the spirit of service.[3]

These extracts show that Gandhi was hesitant to designate himself as a philosopher and he was more concerned with action. Indeed, Gandhi was not a philosopher in the sense in which the word is understood today in the academic field. The reason is that he was not concerned with the abstract metaphysical, moral and epistemological questions about reality. He, in fact, defined the function of philosophy only in the context of action. He once noted, "Philosophy to be worth anything has got to be applied in one's own life".[4]

Yet, it does not mean that Gandhi was bereft of an analytical attitude. Rather it was through reasoning and conducting tests in the different fields he developed his own philosophy. His philosophical goal was self-realization or *Moksha* that he wanted to achieve through the service of humankind which inherited the relentless action. He also proclaimed that all his political and other activities are intended for self-realization. Thus he established a unity between action and liberation. In short in Gandhi's philosophical discourse what is striking is: the primacy of action.

Although Gandhian scholars have noted that action plays a pivotal role in Gandhi's philosophy, but they overlook one of the important facts that Gandhi's action has its own philosophy. This study is centred on this overlooked theme, i.e. philosophy of Gandhi's action.

The study intends to illustrate that what elements really 'constitute' Gandhi's action and how Gandhi's action is related to his metaphysics, epistemology, and ethics. On this basis, the study also aims to emphasize that essentially which kind of action or work can be termed as Gandhian. It is important to note that all 'good work' or 'good action' with 'good intention' is not necessarily Gandhian in nature. In fact, any action depends on how we look at the world and our corresponding relation to the subject and objects of the world. In other words, action depends upon our perspective. It is the perspective that defines, refines and gives meaning to any action. Thus, the question of action is primarily metaphysical and epistemological one, and it is not only a matter of 'doing something' in given situation but rather it means how one perceives and infers the existing reality and responds them. Thus, from outside one might see the same action carried by many people but that may well be carried from the different perspectives. The study is about Gandhi's perspective, and it attempts to explore and analyze the metaphysical, epistemological and ethical/ philosophical basis of Gandhi's action.

The philosophy of action has always drawn the scholars to reflect on it. Broadly, the philosophers of action divide action into two groups: action based on 'knowledge without observation' and 'goal-directed action'. Anscombe (1963) informs us about the action which is based on 'knowledge without observation'. In this case, the agent knows 'without observation' that he/she is performing the certain action that means he/she does not know consciously that what purpose is being served by his/her action. On the other hand, we find 'goal-directed action' in which agents normally know what is his/her action is and he/she has a kind of *direct* control or guidance over his/her own behaviour and action. In this regard, David Velleman describes knowledge of one's actions as 'spontaneous' and as 'self-fulfilling' that means 'expectations of acting' that tend to produce 'actions of the kind expected' (Velleman, 1989 : xi). For Velleman, these expectations are themselves intentions and they are chiefly derived from the agent through practical reasoning about what he/she is to perform. However, the most intensely debated topic in the philosophy of action is the explanation of intentional actions in terms of the agent's reasons for acting. Davidson (1963) and other action theorists hold the position that reason explanations are causal explanations, i.e. explanations that cite the agent's desires, intentions, and means-end beliefs as causes of the action. On the other hand, Bratman (1987) provides a more rigorous characterization of the constitutive norms of intention and points out three main norms for action; requirements of *internal consistency*, *means-end coherence*, and *consistency with the agent's beliefs*. This brief discussion leads us to think that one's action is closely linked with one's own belief and knowledge system.

Gandhi's action, personal and public, forms a coherent whole and it was based on his belief and knowledge system. His action was based on his metaphysics, epistemology, and ethics. Generally scholars, for example Borman (1986), relates Gandhi's action with his metaphysics of Truth—Absolute and Relative. The reason is that Gandhi himself accepted that his all action is dedicated to the pursuit of Truth. Elaborating his metaphysics of truth Gandhi wrote, "This truth is not only truthfulness in word, but truthfulness in thought also, and not only the relative truth of our conception, but the Absolute Truth, the Eternal Principle, that is God" (Gandhi, 2008 : xiii). Thus, Gandhi's action was 'truth in action'. Furthermore, most of the scholars, for instance Dalton (1993) and Terchek (1998), view Gandhi's action as 'application of non-violence' in all possible walks of life. In other words, they emphasize that the process of Gandhi's action is *ahimsa* or non-violence. The inseparability of truth and non-violence is well accepted by Gandhian scholars that are based on Gandhi's dictum that "truth and non-violence are two sides of the same coin". In this regard, some scholars, Borman (1986) and Allen (2008) emphasize on the Gandhi's theory of 'purity of means' in the discussion of Gandhi's action. Furthermore, Borman, emphasizes one of the significant aspects of Gandhi's action, i.e. *Anashakt karma* (Selfless action) that Gandhi took from Gita (Borman, 1986 : 36). Recently Gandhi's action has been understood by Anthony Parel (2006) in the framework of four *Purushrath,* namely *Dharma, Kama, Arth*, and *Moksha.* Thus, very little attempts have been made to understand Gandhi's action in its totality by exploring his metaphysics and epistemology. Scholars like Datta (1953) and Iyer (2007) also confine their views by marking out that Gandhi's action is the outcome of his Metaphysics. In this regard, Prof. Mathai makes an important point and goes one step ahead by pointing out the relationship between Gandhi's metaphysics and his epistemology. He argues, "Absolute truth was a metaphysical presupposition for Gandhi....Gandhi had underlined the need for having such a presupposition, as he believed that without such a presupposition no search for truth was possible" (Mathai, 2000 : 46). Quoting Gandhi "if we grant nothing we find nothing", Mathai further observes, "Gandhian philosophy, that truth, as a metaphysical presupposition is an essential precondition for epistemic pursuits" (Mathai, 2000 : 46). On Gandhi's epistemology, its nature and outcome, Prof. Dashrath Singh has devoted a full chapter in his book *Gandhivaad ko Vinoba kee Den*. He argues that Gandhi did not derive his epistemology out of his intellectual curiosity but he thought on it from the larger perspective of life (Singh, 1975 : 71). Furthermore, he mentions that 'this larger perspective includes the development of personal consciousness and its extension to the society' (p. 71). Prof. Singh also points out that Gandhi's epistemology might be termed as 'eclectic' (p. 71). It needs to be pointed out that Prof. Singh does not elaborate how Gandhi's action is based on his metaphysics and his epistemology. Another significant aspect of Gandhi's action 'selfless action' has been discussed by Gandhi's associate Mahadev Desai. In the book *The Gospel of Selfless Action* Or *The Gita according to Gandhi* (1946), which is the translation of Gandhi's *Anasakti Yoga* with a long introduction, Desai tries to elaborate Gandhi's action in terms of teachings of *Gita* particularly its views on 'selfless action'. Prof. Singh also asserts that Gandhi's action and his epistemology are primarily derived from his reading and understanding of *Gita*.

Thus, when we review existing literature on the philosophy of Gandhi's action, we notice that they deal with this issue in a 'fragmented manner' and fail to provide 'a comprehensive view'. In other words, the philosophy of Gandhi's action has not been discussed in its totality and comprehensiveness. Some scholars focus on intention part of the Gandhian action, some on the purity of means and some on Gandhi's gospel of selfless action. However, one significant consensus among all the scholars is that Gandhi's actions are derived from his metaphysics of Truth. It can also be noted from the review of existing literature that there is hardly any substantial study that deals with the epistemological and ethical basis of Gandhian action.

In the light of review of the literature and the gap that we notice in them, the major questions raised in the study are : what are the elements that really constitute an action in Gandhi's view? What is the basis and nature of Gandhi's action? How Gandhi's views on action are related to his ethics and theory of knowledge? From where does Gandhi get inspiration for his views on the action? As action relates the individual to others, how does Gandhi view the relation between self and other? Is there any action or actions needed for oneself before engaging with others? As Gandhi tends to adhere to the Hindu philosophical tradition and of which the law of *karma* is an integral part, then, how does Gandhi get influenced by and reflect on the law of *karma*?

Addressing these questions is essential to develop Gandhi's philosophy of action. As we may note, these questions are interrelated and inseparable from each other. This study basically attempts to examine these questions by investigating Gandhi's original writings as primary sources. In my view, this rather unconventional 'inside-out' approach, studying Gandhi on his own terms, allows us for a serious study on Gandhi's interpretation of his apparently unconventional ideology. The study is limited to analyze Gandhi's action in its totality and does not compare Gandhi's philosophy of action from other philosophies of action.

The study is divided into eight chapters.

The first chapter titled *Conceptualizing Gandhi's Action: Satyagraha and Constructive Programme* attempts to conceptualize Gandhi's action by abstracting Gandhi's praxis *Satyagraha* and Constructive Programme. The chapter attempts to find out as to what actually lies behind the Gandhi's philosophy of *Satyagraha* and Constructive Programme as dimensions of Gandhi's action in the public sphere. It is revealed that Gandhi's *Satyagraha* and Constructive Programmes are derived from his metaphysical presupposition of Truth. It is further shown that the *Satyagraha* and Constructive Programme are not merely the desire to see Truth, but *an insistence* on Truth in the personal and public life. Thus, *Satyagraha* and Constructive Programme are motivated by the commitment and action to Truth, i.e. Truth-in-action.

The second chapter is titled as *Gandhi's Action and its Relation to his Metaphysics*. It emphasizes how Gandhi's action is directly related to his views on Truth and non-violence. The chapter demonstrates that Gandhi's actions are concrete implications of his metaphysical viewpoints. It is also shown that his notion of Truth— both Absolute and Relative, is not for academic interest or scholastic discussion but it strongly conveys one to engage in action. His Absolute truth serves as the guideline for the action; relative truth provides space for action in the form of experimentation. It also explains how Gandhi's non-violence or *ahimsa* denotes activity and action. Moreover, his metaphysics that implies brave action is not restricted to personal exercise in good faith but it incorporates community and group action too. It calls for a social and political action.

The third chapter, *Gandhi's Metaphysics and its Epistemological Basis*, views the sources and methods of knowledge by which Gandhi reaches to his metaphysical notion of Truth. The chapter tries to reconstruct Gandhi's epistemology in relation to his metaphysics of Truth. It is shown that epistemologically, Gandhi's source of Absolute truth is Hindu scripture, however, he elaborated it in his own fashion during his time and context. As examined, for Gandhi, the Absolute truth which is known by faith is beyond our empirical grasp. The corollary of this notion, as explained in the chapter, is that we must *act* in the knowledge that we are holding on to such truth, as we are able to apprehend in this world. This indicates to his view on the relative truth which is empirical in nature. The chapter explains the nature and implications of Gandhi's epistemological basis in relation to his metaphysics.

The fourth chapter is titled as *Epistemological Basis of Gandhi's Action.* It examines the knowledge base and nature of Gandhi's action. It also attempts to know the sources from that Gandhi get inspiration for his views on the action. It attempts to explain that how Gandhi's views on action are related to his theory of knowledge. It is shown that Gandhi views on the relation between action and knowledge are deeply influenced by his understanding of *Gita*. It is argued that for Gandhi there are three things that inspire action: knowledge, the object of knowledge and the knower. The most striking aspect of his definition is its inclusiveness/integration of action in relation to knowledge. The chapter also highlights that the concept of action that Gandhi borrowed from the *Gita* makes knowledge just one component of the totality of action. Thus, the need for knowledge was itself to be understood only in terms of its impact on action.

The chapter five *Ethics of Gandhi's Action: Responsibility for One's Self* highlights the relation between his ethics and action for oneself. It has been shown that Gandhi's ethics begins with realizing oneself and it calls for certain personal actions. The personal action includes the process of self-observation, self-examination, and self-correction. It is also marked that Gandhi's action, fundamentally, invites one to take responsibility for one's self. The chapter examines the Indian and Western notion of self and elaborates on Gandhi's notion of self and individual's responsibility to it. The chapter also discusses the action as the responsibility of one's self in the form of methods of self-purification/self-realization. Gandhi's methods for self-purification, as the chapter shows, include traditional Hindu methods of self-purification but their new interpretation and practice by Gandhi in the given context of time and space.

The chapter six *Gandhi's Action : Self and its Responsibility to Other. Other* examines Gandhi's action in response to the critical question of the relation between self and others. The chapter first explores the basis on which self is related to other in Gandhi's worldview. Arguing that in Gandhi's worldview self and other is related to each other with the notion of responsibility, the chapter discusses the nature of responsibility in Gandhi's worldview and examine on *what ground* Gandhi fixes the responsibility of self towards others. It also addresses the question as to how to act responsibly. The chapter also explains the relationship between freedom and responsibility in Gandhi's worldview and argues that in Gandhi's worldview freedom does not only mean freedom from coercion and domination, but it also means self-regulation through self-restraint. The chapter also highlights that in Gandhi's worldview the self and other are not two different categories but the other is one's extended self.

The chapter seven *Esthetics of Gandhi's Action: Unison of Universal Love, Responsibility and Detachment* argues that the core of Gandhi's philosophy of action can be summarized in three words; universal love, responsibility, and detachment. The chapter shows that Gandhi's philosophy of love is closely linked with his paradigm of 'essential unity of all that exists' and its related notion of 'interdependence'. His notion of love inherently involves the notion of responsibility which is not only limited to the personal level but it goes beyond oneself and encompasses other or the public sphere also. It is argued that Gandhi's notion of responsibility is 'radical' and 'infinite' in nature but not 'unrestricted'. It is demonstrated that his notion of responsibility is not confined only to structural analysis and intervention, but equally, it offers a philosophy of self-transformation. It is also shown that Gandhi's view of detachment does not mean a passive disinterest or cold indifference but active state of conscious awareness of the unity of life. Although love and detachment seem contradictory but Gandhi resolved it by redefining both love and detachment.

The chapter eight *Gandhi and Indian Philosophy of Action (Karma)* examines Gandhi's philosophy of action in the broader context of Indian philosophy of action (*Karma*). Tracing out the commonalities and differences among the different school of thought of Indian philosophy, the chapter argues that like the traditional Indian philosophical thinkers, Gandhi believed in the existence of the law of *Karma*. This can be marked out through his views on re-birth, incarnation, fate, destiny, and death. The chapter argues that Gandhi's belief in the law of *karma* does not imply that he considers man's life and activities to be completely determined. For him, there is no antithesis between the law of *karma* and the freedom of will. In his view, the law of *karma* implies freedom, for it lays down that the man is the architect of his own destiny. It shows that Gandhi gives a moral interpretation of the law of *karma* emphasizing the pragmatic and ethical values of this belief. Finally, *Conclusion* summarizes the arguments made in the previous chapters.

Notes

1. Gandhi, M.K. to S. Radhakrishnan, 16 September 1934, cited in S. Gopal, Radhakrishnan: A Biography (Delhi: Oxford University Press, 1989), p. 138.
2. "Speech at Gandhi Seva Sangh Meeting-III", 3 March, 1936, *CWMG*:68: 260.
3. *Harijan*, 3 March, 1946, CWMG: 90:1
4. CWMG:45:226

References

Allen, Douglass (ed.). (2008). *The Philosophy of Mahatma Gandhi for the 21st Century.* Lanham: Lexington Books.

Anscombe, G.E.M. (1963). *Intention.* Oxford: Blackwell.

Borman, William. (1986). *Gandhi and Nonviolence.* New York: State University of New York Press.

Bratman, M. (1987). *Intention, Plans, and Practical Reason.* Cambridge, MA: Harvard University Press.

Dalton, Dennish. (1993). *Mahatma Gandhi: Nonviolent Power in Action.* New York: Columbia University Press.

Datta, Dhirendra Mohan. (1961). *The Philosophy of Mahatma Gandhi.* Madison: The University of Wisconsin Press.

Davidson, D. (1963). 'Actions, Reasons, and Causes' in *Essays on Actions and*

Events. Oxford: Oxford University Press.
Desai, Mahadevbhai. (1946). *The Gospel of Selfless Action Or The Gita according to Gandhi.* Ahmedabad: Navajivan.
Gandhi, M.K. (2013). *An Autobiography or My Experiments with Truth.* Ahmedabad: Navajivan.
Iyer, Raghavan N. (2007). *The Moral and Political Thought of Mahatma Gandhi.* New Delhi: Oxford University Press.
Mathai, M.P. (2000). *Mahatma Gandhi's World View*. G.P.F: New Delhi.
Parel, Anthony. (2006). *Gandhi's Philosophy and the Quest for Harmony.* New York: Cambridge University Press.
Singh, Dashrath. (1975). *Gandhivaad ko Vinoba Kee Den* (Hindi). Patna: Bihar Hindi Granth Akadami.
Tercheak, Ronald J. (1998). *Gandhi: Struggling for Autonomy.* New Delhi: Vistaar Publication.
Velleman, J.D. (1989). *Practical Reflection.* NJ: Princeton University Press.

1
Conceptualizing Gandhi's Action
Satyagraha and Constructive Programme

Gandhi's action incorporates his individual action in the form of personal 'experiments', community action carried in his various *ashrams* with the co-workers, and mass scale social and political actions followed by millions of Indians. Thus, any reader of Gandhi's action finds that his actions have a wide spectrum that embraces almost everything that life offered him in his time. The accounts of his personal action in the form of 'experiments' may be found in his *Autobiography*, while his community action can be perceived in his small booklet *Ashram Observances in Action*. Gandhi's *Autobiography* depicts that the actions of his life were in the form of 'experiments' based on his understanding of truth at a particular moment. On the other hand, his community activities in the Ashram, as we are informed, commenced everyday with the congregational morning worship generally at 4:15 a.m. to 4:45 a.m. and closed with the evening prayer at 7 p.m. to 7:30 p.m (Gandhi, 2010: 74). The whole day activities of the Ashram was rigorous that included sanitary service, sacrificial spinning, agriculture, dairy, tannery, national education and Khadi production. We are also informed that all members of his Ashram, whether permanent or otherwise, were supposed to 'use every minute of their time to good account' (Gandhi, 2010: 90). Not only this 'every word and every act were to be well thought out'. Moreover, we are reminded that the centre of all the activities of the members of Ashram was the truth. The scope and intensity of Gandhi's personal and community action, as his *Autobiography* and *Ashrama Observance in Action* suggest, demonstrate that indeed he was the man of action or *karmyogi* who was in a relentless quest for truth. The descriptions of these two books further convey to us that he tried to conceptualize truth not as a static entity but as always in the process of becoming and widening through action.

Interrelated to these personal and community actions, Gandhi's action, especially in the public sphere, holds two significant but inseparable apparent dimensions—resistance and reconstruction. While resistance is known as Satyagraha in Gandhi's paradigm; reconstruction is recognized in the term of the Constructive Programme. These two actions in the public sphere are not two separate categories but in Gandhi's opinion, they are 'complementary' to each other. This chapter, essentially, deals with the theme as to what actually lies behind the Gandhi's philosophy of Satyagraha (resistance) and Constructive Programme (reconstruction).

The root of Satyagraha is *Satya* or truth. For Gandhi, Truth and *ahimsa* are closely interlinked like two sides of the coin so are *ahimsa* and Satyagraha interrelated. The interrelatedness of Gandhi's views on *satya*, *ahimsa*, and satyagraha is such that it is difficult to separate them analytically. To analyze one, it is necessary to include the other. Satyagraha, as Gandhi repeatedly argued, is a direct corollary of truth and non-violence and it is the way in which non-violence is put in the public action.

As far as the historical evolution of Gandhi's Satyagraha is concerned, the idea behind the Satyagraha existed before the term was coined. Initially, Gandhi used the term 'passive resistance' for Satyagraha when he was engaged in a political struggle in South Africa. The idea surfaced when he was fighting against the Asiatic Law Amendment Ordinance introduced into Transvaal Legislative Council in 1906. However, it was Gandhi's dissatisfaction with the phrase 'passive resistance' that compelled him to search a more suitable and accurate term that propound the principle he wanted to describe.[1] During the struggle in South Africa one of his followers suggested the term *sadagraha* to demonstrate the nature of struggle that Gandhi was waging there and that 'was generating a new force' among Indians.[2] *Sadagraha* literally meant 'firmness in a good cause'. Gandhi modified the term *sadagraha* into Satyagraha. The change signifies two things. First, it made his principle more explicit and at the same time linked it more closely with his concept of Truth and non-violence. Second, the ethical connotation of the method of action he proposed was being made clear by the choice of Satyagraha rather than *sadagraha*. Gandhi himself explained the reason of modification of the term *sadagraha* in his book *Satyagraha in South Africa*, "I liked the word, but it did not fully represent the whole idea I wished it to connote. I, therefore, corrected it to '*satyagraha*'. Truth (satya) implies love, and firmness (*agraha*) engenders and therefore, serves as a synonym for force. I thus began to call the Indian movement '*satyagraha*', that is to say, the Force which is born of Truth and Love or non-violence and gave up the phrase 'passive resistance' in connection with it, so much so that even in English writing we often avoided it and used instead the word '*satyagraha*' itself or some other equivalent English phrase. This then was the genesis of the movement which came to be known as satyagraha, and of the word used designation for it"(Gandhi, 1954: 109).

Gandhi's Satyagraha has been interpreted in many ways by the scholars. For Bondurant, it is 'Gandhian method of conducting conflict without violence' (Bondurant, 1954: v), while for Diwaker, it is 'a new way of life as well as a unique technique of using the soul- force in man' (Diwaker, 1969: 2). It has also been portrayed as 'War without violence' and for many western thinkers it is considered as 'moral equivalent of war'. In recent time, Satyagraha has been interpreted as the Gandhian method of conflict resolution. These interpretations, of course, have their own value in Gandhian literature; however, I wish to explain Gandhi's Satyagraha in the term of his philosophy of action.

The term Satyagraha renders practical expression to the ethical notions of Gandhi's truth and non-violence in the public sphere[3]. As an action in the public sphere, Satyagraha is Gandhi's direct non-violent action to eliminate injustice prevailed in the social, economic, and political reality of everyday life. In his words, "With Satya combined with ahimsa, you can bring the world to your feet. Satyagraha in its essence is nothing but the introduction of truth and gentleness in the political, i.e. the national life" (Prabhu and Rao, 2002: 167). On the *nature* of Satyagraha, he pointed out, "Satyagraha is utter self-effacement, greatest humiliation, greatest patience and brightest faith. It is its own reward" (CWMG: 26: 200). As a *form of action*, it excludes the use of violence in any shape or form, whether in thought, speech, and deed. The reason is, as Gandhi mentioned, "In the application of Satyagraha, I discovered, in the earliest stages, that pursuit of Truth did not admit of violence being inflicted on one's opponent, but that he must be weaned from error by patience and sympathy. For, what appears to be truth to the one may appear to be error to the other. And patience means self-suffering. So the doctrine came to mean vindication of Truth, not by infliction of suffering on the opponent but one's own self" (Prabhu and Rao, 2002: 167). For Gandhi, Satyagraha is the *art of living and dying*. "The fight of satyagraha is for the strong in spirit, not the doubter or the timid. Satyagraha teaches us the art of living as well as dying. Birth and death are inevitable among mortals. What distinguishes the man from the brute is his conscious striving to realize the spirit within" (Prabhu and Rao, 2002: 168).

As a form of action, the *goal* of Satyagraha is the conversion of opponents, not coercion. It is a dialectical search for truth which strives at winning over the adversary by the force of love through stimulating in him a sense of justices. In its application, it distinguishes between people and system. It is based on the premise that the system may be evil but people are never beyond redemption. Thus, Satyagrahi may dislike the system but not the people who are connected with the system. In fact, the Satyagrahi empathizes with the people he opposes and tries to see things from their point of view. This creates an understanding and opens up the way to conversion through a constant appeal to the head and the heart of the opponent.

It is important to note that Gandhi recognizes the limit of an appeal to the reason solely as a way of stirring a person's sense of justice. Gandhi argues that it is through patient persuasive reasoning together with voluntary suffering by which the satyagrahi can seek to melt the heart of his opponent and open his eyes to the truth. He notes, "I have found that mere appeal to reason does answer where prejudices are ageless and based on supposed religious authority. Reason has to be strengthened by suffering and suffering opens the eyes of the understanding" (Bose, 1948: 222). Thus, as an action, Satyagraha is an appeal to morality and reason of human being.

Satyagraha: Truth as a Force in Public Life; Truth-in-Action

As noted, the term 'Satyagraha' was coined by Gandhi in South Africa. Gandhi himself wrote about the implications of the word and it is interesting to note that when he writes on satyagraha he uses the term 'force'. For insistence, he mentioned: "The term `Satyagraha' was coined by me in South Africa to express *the force* that the Indians there used for full eight years, and it was coined in order to distinguish it from the movement then going on in the United Kingdom and South

Africa under the name of passive resistance" (CWMG: 16: 368). Again he mentioned that Satyagraha is 'a force that works silently and apparently slowly' and further argues that 'in reality there is no force in the world that is so direct or so swift in working' (Prabhu and Rao, 2002: 167).

Again, in the Satyagraha Leaflet No. 6, April 25, 1919, Gandhi notes that the literal meaning of Satyagraha as 'insistence on truth, and *force* derivable from such *insistence*' (CWMG: 15: 248). In the same leaflet, Gandhi also observes that Satyagraha is a 'binding force'. Behind this notion, it was Gandhi's belief that every truth is *self-acting*, and possesses an inherent *strengths*'. He further mentioned that Truth is 'self-evident' and carries the 'seed of self-propagation'.

One may well argue: what is the nature of the force that Gandhi mentions which flows from Truth? Gandhi's writings suggest that the force he mentions is a not the material force but spiritual force. Gandhi called it 'spirit-force' or *'dharmabal'*(the force of Dharma), as opposed to physical force or 'brute force' or *'pashubal'*. The equivalent of 'Satyagraha', he noted, 'rendered into English means Truth Force. I think Tolstoy called it also Soul Force or Love Force' (Bose, 1948: 182).

We, thus, see four terms Gandhi interchangeably uses for the force that exists in Satyagraha—the force of Dharma, Truth force, Soul force and Love force. To Gandhi, Truth force, love force and the force of Dharma were the same because Dharma included Truth and Love. It was named as 'soul force' to demonstrate that it is entirely different from the force that originates from the body. The force that comes from body Gandhi calls it *'pashubal'* or brute force. Thus, Gandhi makes an ethical difference between the soul force and physical force.

Why does Gandhi perceive the Truth force as Spirit force and why does he consider love-force to be 'spirit force'? He comes to this conclusion by examining the meaning of Satyagraha. In *Satyagraha Leaflet No. 6,* April 25, 1919, Gandhi wrote, "I feel that the time has now arrived to examine the meaning of Satyagraha. The word was newly coined some years ago, but the principle which it denotes is as ancient as time.... One of the axioms of religion is, there is no religion other than truth. Another is, religion is love. And as there can be only one religion it follows that Truth is love, and love is truth. We shall find too, on further reflection, that conduct based on truth is impossible without love. Truth force then is love force" (CWMG:15: 248).

Thus, Gandhi's truth force has the basis of religion which preaches love. Consequently, he does not make any distinction between love and truth. We also note that Gandhi adds the term 'force' with truth and love. It means truth and love are not the passive concepts but they are active and acting as the force. It is necessary here to have a brief look at Gandhi's perception of force to grasp his notion of soul force or love force which is the basis of Satyagraha.

Even a cursory look at Gandhi's writings on this subject convinces us to recognize that Gandhi's notion of force comes from his metaphysical views on God. He did not view God as a person but 'the force among all forces'. Moreover, "All other forces are material. But God is the vital Force or spirit which is all-pervading, all-embracing and therefore, beyond human ken" (Ptd. in Varma, 2001: 45). Gandhi's writings on the God suggest that he has used many qualifying words for the God. He mentioned God as an Unseen Power, a living force, the sovereign Law that governed the Universe, the Power or Force that informed everything and held the world together; God is Truth, love, conscience, Dharma, the Lawmaker, the Law and Executor, indefinable mysterious power, greatest democrat, hardest taskmaster, guide and protector, and Supreme Alchemist.[4]

In a more philosophical form, once he wrote, "I do dimly perceive that while everything around is ever changing, ever dying, there is underlying all that changes, a *living power* that is changeless, that holds all together, that creates, dissolves and recreates. That informing power or spirit is God" (Prabhu and Rao, 2001: 47). It is also important to note that Gandhi interpreted God in an experimentally definable concept. In 1926, he changed his position from 'God is Truth' to 'Truth is God'. This can be called a fundamental shift in his metaphysical outlook. The reason for such a shift shows Gandhi's deep thinking process of the idea. On this shift, he himself noted, "God is Truth, but God is in many other things also. That is why I say Truth is God.... Only remember that Truth is not one of the many qualities that we name. It is the living embodiment of God, it is the only Life, and I identify Truth with the fullest life, and that is how it becomes a concrete thing, for God is His whole creation, the whole Existence, and service of all that exists—Truth—is service of God" (Prabhu and Rao, 2001: 47).

We noted above, for Gandhi, Truth or God is 'the force of all forces'. The reason, he provides, is 'Truth is what exists and prevails'.

A close reading of these statements leads us to perceive the relationship between Truth and Force. Gandhi seems to argue that, to exist or prevail, Truth has to overcome forces that may be unconducive or opposing. It means: Truth prevails because there exists a powerful force in it that overcomes all other forces. In other words, Truth has *inherent* forces.

He also suggests that Truth or *Dharma* is a force of cohesion, and not of disintegration. His writings give an impression that in his view what is consistent with the Law of Truth leads to cohesion and it is positive, and what is inconsistent with the Law of Truth leads to erosion and disintegration and it is negative. Thus, Gandhi seems to assign a particular nature to force that can be called negative and positive forces. It is on this metaphysical belief of negative and positive forces in reference to the inconsistency and consistency with Truth, Gandhi makes the ethical category of forces of evil and the forces of good.

Gandhi's notion of 'force' in truth force or soul force may be examined to comprehend his overall philosophy of Satyagraha in action. In this regard, Ravindra Varma's observation is worth discussing. He locates the whole discussion of Satyagraha in the context of sources of force. Varma argues there are many sources from which force originates that can be classified into two broad groups: gross sources (physical or material source) and subtle sources (non-material, like the mind or intellect, or the soul or the spirit) (Varma, 2001: 48). He also argues that forces originating from gross or material sources are subject to decline, depletion, and extinction with time, while the forces that emanate from subtler sources like the intellect and the soul or spirit do not suffer such rapid reduction as material forces suffer. In other words, the subtle force that arises from subtle sources does not have the weakness of gross or material sources have. Thus, Varma's discussion leads him to conclude that the nature of any kind of force depends upon the source which generated it. He also provides three criteria- scale, speed and durability—by which material force and subtle force/soul force can be differentiated. In this context, he points out, "Gandhi believed that the more subtle the force, the greater its impact in terms of scale, speed and durability" (Varma, 2001: 49). Within this framework, Varma attempts to explain the use of force in Gandhi's truth force or soul force which is the basis of Satyagraha.

Varma further argues that Gandhi was convinced of the superior effectiveness of soul force/spiritual force even in mundane matters and situations. The reason is Gandhi believed that the sovereign or superior Law was valid in the mundane field as well. Moreover, the superior Law also held the superior force. Varma quotes Gandhi, "Soul force or spiritual force (Truth Force) is the highest and most powerful force available to man. Since this force (Soul Force) *arises* from the higher realm of the spirit, it must be effective in the lower realms as well" (Varma, 2001: 49). Extending these arguments, one may find a corollary which validates that material force, especially when it operates through human beings, can, therefore, be overcome by spiritual force. It is not surprising that Gandhi wrote, "My purpose in life is to demonstrate that the strongest physical force bends before moral force when it is used in defence of truth" (CWMG:16: 13).

Gandhi was equally convinced about the *speed* with which spiritual or moral forces operate in the mundane world. He mentioned, "The human voice can never reach the distance that is covered by the still small voice of conscience" (CWMG: 15: 257). Again, "I would content myself with saying that when once the forces of truth and ahimsa are set in motion, the speed as they move becomes so accelerated that they take no time in permeating millions" (CWMG:15: 256).

Besides, the *power* of material forces has definite limitations. Material forces are conditioned by degrees of proximity or the effectiveness of the instruments of transmission. On the other hand, the spiritual force has no such *obstructions* that material force has to confront. Thus, spiritual force can exert its power, and achieve results even from a distance, and even without dependence on physical proximity or a material medium.

The reason is, as Varma argues, spiritual force communicates and operates at the spiritual level. It means, spiritual force communicates on a trans-physical, trans-verbal, trans-intellectual level with another human being. However, the experience of such communication becomes possible only when ego-centrism declines and fades. Thus, in Varma's view, "Satyagraha or the spiritual force that it deploys, therefore, is a vehicle that transports or elevates both persons involved to a higher plane above ego-centrism or ego-consciousness, where differences and intransigence melt in the warmth of the sense of oneness" (*ibid.*, p. 50). This perspective of Satyagraha or the use of soul-force can be well recognized when one closely examines Gandhi's fast for justice or truth.

In Gandhi's Satyagraha, thus, the person who offers Satyagraha does not take help of the material force or to the lower realm to fight with the evil doer, but, believes in his/her soul force and tries to convert the evil-doer. Gandhi seems to convey that since Satyagraha is a spiritual force, it cannot be used in conjunction with physical force. The reason is that the effect of one cancels the effect of the other. Thus, Satyagrahi has to avoid all forms of physical force or violence that would frustrate and negate the effect of soul force/spiritual force.

What we notice from these discussions is that Satyagraha as an action is a struggle between material forces and spiritual forces. It is also remarkable that Gandhi does not negate the force or its significance. Rather, he wants to change the social-political *status quo* by exercising soul force/spiritual force instead of material force. This position can be adequately illustrated by one of the Gandhi's writings.

Writing a letter to the Viceroy Lord Irwin on the eve of the Salt Satyagraha, on 2 March, 1930, Gandhi mentioned,"....The matter resolves itself into one of the matching forces. Conviction or no conviction, Great Britain would defend her India's commerce and interest by all the forces at her command. India must consequently evolve force enough to free herself from that embrace of death.... My experience, limited though it undoubtedly is, shows that non-violence can be an intensely active force. It is my purpose to set in motion that force as well against the organized violent force of the British Rule as (against) the organized violent force of the growing party of violence. To sit still would be to give in to both the forces above-mentioned. Having an unquestioning and immovable faith in the efficacy of non-violence as I know it, it would be sinful on my part to wait any longer...." (CWMG: 43:6).

On this account, Varma observes, "This shows that as a strategist, Gandhi was aware of the determinant nature of the parity or superiority of the forces that were in the confrontation. To him, a 'matching force' did not mean an equal or higher quantum of the force of the same kind, but some form of countervailing force powerful enough to overcome the other force" (Varma, 2001: 52).

In Satyagraha, there is a possibility of action at three levels—physical, intellectual and spiritual. The physical action includes meetings, demonstrations, picketing and so on. The intellectual action includes persuasion, joint surveys, offers of mediation or arbitration. While the spiritual or moral action includes the undergoing of 'voluntary suffering' to induce introspection and transformation in the mind of the person or group on the other side. For Gandhi, in every case, whether physical, mental or intellectual, satyagrahi's activity must be consistent with the code of the soul force/spiritual force or non-violence.

It might be argued: why is Satyagrahi's action to be non-violent? The reason is non-violence is the only means by which one can vindicate Truth or bring about true or enduring transformation. Moreover, if Satyagraha is based on the higher law, then, it must be consistent with the higher value of non-violence, otherwise, it will be self-contradictory if it uses the lower values of violence.

In Satyagraha, the motivation of the Satyagrahi is not to achieve his/her own dominance over other, but to see that Truth prevails. Most importantly, Satyagraha is not merely the desire to see Truth, but the insistence on Truth. The Satyagrahi is, therefore, motivated by the commitment and action to Truth. In short, Satyagraha is Truth-in-action

A little elaboration seems to be required to clarify the phrase Truth-in-action. Analytically, Satyagraha includes three inseparable aspects: first, seeking and identifying Truth, second living in accordance with Truth, and third, endeavouring to see that Truth prevails. Thus, there becomes three inseparable dimensions of Satyagraha in the form of action. The first one involves action that relates to an internal relentless quest of one's self,[5] the second involves action to ordering one's way of life by observing vows to become consistent with the quest for Truth,[6] and the third engages action to change the society/environment/conditions and institutions that affect one's life.[7] Gandhi also set the special qualifications for Satyagrahi in the given Indian context.[8]

Thus, a Satyagrahi is not an academic or a philosopher concerned merely with identifying Truth, but he/she has to do the specific action for himself/herself to be consistent with Truth and he/she has also to take action to make his social-political context conducive to Truth. In short, action, therefore, becomes an integral or inescapable part of Satyagraha.

In short, Satyagraha is an active direct non-violent action in the public sphere that is based on the force of Truth or soul. It is an unending, relentless, dialectical quest for truth both at the personal and social level. The beauty of Satyagraha lies in its creativity based on non-violence and moral persuasion. The satyagrahi adopts

Satyagraha as a method of action and insists on truth being established. That is why, interlinked with the way of life, Satyagraha in the form of non-violent action resists all unjust authority and source of evil prevailed in the public sphere.

Constructive Programme: Truth-in-Service

Like Satyagraha, one of the most significant dimensions of Gandhi's action is his Constructive Programme.[9] Gandhi coined the term Constructive Programme after he returned to India in 1915 from South Africa. His Constructive Programme was a social movement based on his own distinctive social philosophy. As a grassroots social movement, Constructive Programme aimed at national reconstruction and reorientation that was an integral part of Gandhi's nationalist movement. It must be mentioned that Gandhi viewed Constructive Programme more important than his non-violent campaigns against injustice and exploitation. For practical purposes, it refers to a range of programmes and practices by which he wanted to radically reorient Indians physically, psychologically, socially, economically, politically, and spiritually to achieve 'true freedom' not only from British Rule but from modernity as well.

Although Gandhi's Satyagraha has received serious attention from academicians and activists worldwide, his Constructive Programme has not got the serious attention as it deserves. I wish to present a brief review of the literature on Gandhi's Constructive Programme before arguing how it serves as a form of action. Scholars have treated Gandhi's Constructive Programme in such a way that undermines its significance as a powerful non-violent action. For instance, Peter Ackerman and Jack Duvall describe the Constructive Programme as having a support role. Their argument is that, "For Gandhi, social regeneration [the constructive programme] was not an end in itself; it was the groundwork for non-violent action" (Peter and Duvall, 2000: 72). Gene Sharp, a well-known scholar of non-violent action, also undermines the significance of the Constructive Programme as non-violent action by limiting its role to politics. In his 1979 book, *Gandhi as a Political Strategist: With Essays on Ethics and Politics*, Sharp provides a limited description of the constructive programme from Gandhi's perspective (Sharp, 1979: 77-86). Similarly, Anthony Parel characterizes the Constructive Programme in ways that undermine its power as forceful non-violent action. For example, he refers to Gandhi's Constructive programme as areas of work "particularly suitable for the action of NGOs" (Parel, 2006: 62). Parel creates further confusion by stating but not explaining, "Freedom is maximized and violence minimized when the state and NGOs work in harmony" (*ibid.*, p. 62). Parel's brief statements about the relationships amongst the state, NGOs, satyagraha, and civil society do not explain the non-violent mechanisms through which the Constructive Programme maximizes freedom and minimizes violence.

In this sequence, Allwyn Tellis's research focuses directly on the Constructive Programme. He interprets it as integral to Gandhi's nationalist movement, but not as a non-violent action. Tellis examines the Constructive Programme 'as a body of discourse' (Tellis, 2006: 7). He also explains that Gandhi recognized the 'power of symbols', he 'not only invented and used them but was himself symbolic of the culture he was striving for'. On the other hand, John Bondurant places Gandhi's Constructive Programme within the context of the explanations of non-violence as interpreted by Gandhi. Bondurant states "The constructive programme was an essential component of the Gandhian revolutionary struggle for Indian independence" (Bondurant, 1957: 180). She describes it as a positive form of non-violent action, as opposed to the resistance forms of non-cooperation and civil disobedience. In this sequence, Michael Nagler's work provides the most recent contributions to understanding non-violent constructive programme in the Gandhian tradition (Nagler, 2014: 1-6). His focus is the practice of non-violence. He contends that the Constructive Programme used in conjunction with non-violent struggle offers the best prospect of liberating people from injustice. Nagler articulates what he refers to as five principles of Constructive Programme. They encompass building continuity and community into society, using the creative force for good, providing the means by which people can meet their basic needs themselves, returning control to the people, and training in non-violent living.

This brief review of the literature draws our attention to two significant characteristics. First, Gandhi's Constructive Programme has been observed by the scholars in a very inadequate manner. Scholars view Constructive Programme either in a very isolated and fragmented way or they extend it in the sort of supportive role of Satyagraha. They miss the point that Gandhi's Constructive Programme was not a project and it cannot be limited to the pamphlet (of the same title) which he wrote in 1941. In fact, Gandhi's Constructive Programme, as Tellis points out, should be recognized as a 'body of discourse' for action that comprises Gandhi's speeches, correspondence, interviews, editorials, and pamphlets addressed to various audiences, at different times, and for different purposes. Joining Tellis, what I wish to suggest and add here is that Gandhi's Constructive Programme must be examined in his overall 'experiment with the truth'. It seems unfair to acknowledge Constructive Programme as a 'strategy' to make India free from British yoke or only as a method of national regeneration, as many scholars have depicted.

Second, what we discover from the review of the literature on Gandhi's Constructive Programme is that the latter has been reviewed in the context of liberal society and liberal democratic system. Scholars fail to appreciate that Gandhi had a different vision of society and his design of democracy was also different from the liberal democracy.

To perceive the philosophy of Gandhi's Constructive Programme in its entirety and to recognize it as a form of action, it seems necessary to examine his model of society, social development and his critique of the liberal state. Gandhi's writings suggest that he regarded the society inherently and unconsciously nonviolent. He argues that "We find the general work of mankind is being carried on from day to day by the mass of people acting as if by instinct. If they were instinctively violent the world would end in no time. It is when the mass mind is unnaturally influenced by wicked men that the mass of mankind commit violence. But they forget it as they commit it because they return to their peaceful nature immediately the evil influence of the directing mind has been removed" (CWMG:31:100).

Thus, he affirmed that the society is essentially based on the law of non-violence, while violence is a temporary deviation from it. In fact, Gandhi viewed the society as a 'larger family' and sought to organize it through the conscious force of non-violence or the law of non-violence. He rejected the notion that society cannot be organized on the basis of non-violence. He once mentioned, "It has become the fashion these days to say that society cannot be organized or run on non-violent lines. I join issue on that point. In a family, when the father slaps his delinquent child, the latter does not think of retaliating. He obeys his father not because of the deterrent effect of the slap but because of the offended love which he senses behind it. That, in my opinion, is an epitome of the way in which society is or should be governed. What is true of the family must be true of the society which is but a larger family" (CWMG: 68:102).

Gandhi's notion of society as a 'larger family' recognizes the society in the form of 'oceanic circle' not as a 'pyramid'. He also argued that instead of imitating the western model of organizing the society India must have its own form and structure of society and the state. In 1936, he wrote that 'They [Western] have system suited to their genius. We must have ours suited to our genius'. Further, in Gandhi's view, organizing the society on the basis of non-violence is possible only in the small unit and that small unit is the village in India. He wrote, "Society based on non-violence can only consist of groups settled in villages in which voluntary co-operation is the condition of dignified and peaceful existence" (CWMG: 71:95).

Through Constructive Programme, Gandhi attempted to initiate a non-violent but radical transformation of the life of ordinary Indians making structural changes possible and visible. In its totality, the Constructive Programme visualizes a society that begins at the level of the 'individual' and moves into 'ever-widening' social formations. He argued that in such form of social organization, life would not be a 'pyramid' with the apex sustained by the bottom, but it would be an 'oceanic circle' whose centre would be the individual. The individual, as he argues, would be always ready to perish for the village, and the latter ready to perish for the circle of villages, till at last the whole becomes one life composed of individuals. He further argues that in such a model of social organization, "the outermost circumference will not wield power to crush the inner circle but will give strength to all within and derive its own strength from it" (CWMG: 85: 33). Although Gandhi understood that his proposal would be 'never realizable in its completeness' and it might be 'taunted as all Utopian', however, he argued that "we must have a proper picture of what we want before we can have something approaching it"(CWMG: 85: 33).

Juxtaposing his proposal of social organization with his overall social philosophy, it can be noticed that the root of this proposal is not politics or economics but his ontology. To quote him, "This society must naturally be based on truth and non-violence which, in my opinion, are not possible without a living belief in God, meaning a self-existent, all-knowing living Force which inheres every other force known to the world and which depends on none and which will live when all other forces may conceivably perish or cease to act"(CWMG: 85: 33). It is on this grounding of ontology, Gandhi launched a stark critique of all the prevailing forms of the state and government also.

He argued that prevailing forms of government took the modern state for granted and represented different ways of organizing it. He also argued that they were inherently incapable of tackling its structural defects. Even liberal democracy, the least objectionable of them, did little to integrate state and society, decentralize political power, involve citizen in the conduct of public affairs, and reduce the extent and depth of internal and external violence. Extending a sharp critique of the Western liberal capitalist state, he considered British parliament a 'sterile woman' for not having 'done a single good thing' and a 'prostitute' because 'it is under the control of a minister who changes from time to time' (Gandhi, 2008: 27). In a similar way, Gandhi criticized Communism also. Certain aspects of Marxism were agreeable in theory, but Gandhi detested the fashion by which Communism was imposed and, moreover, its propagation of atheism. In practice, it was also criticized for its tendency to concentrate power in the hands of the few. Thus, ideally, Gandhi rejected the institution of the modern state as it represented the hierarchical power structure in which, he found, violence is in-built. But for practical purpose, Gandhi accepted the state as 'necessary evil' until society regulates itself non-violently.

Above discussion lead us to recognize the fact that the core of Gandhi's social philosophy is the primacy of the individual in the society. However, Gandhi's consideration of the individual is different from the idea of individual, liberalism or Marxism has characterized. For Gandhi individual is not the impersonal and mechanistic object that the modern liberal state takes for granted. Moreover, Gandhi did not view the individual as social and economic *laissezfaire* what modern liberal states tend to argue. Similarly, Gandhi did not see the individual as an agent of the state worship as Marxist accepts. Moreover, for Gandhi, the individual is not merely the result of heredity and environment, of cause and effect. The guiding principles, which in his view should regulate the life of the individual existing as a social being, are the supreme and eternal values of truth and non-violence. Gandhi's individual is 'self-disciplined' who considers 'others'. In this regard, it may be pointed out that Gandhi's notion of the individual is derived from the concept of *dharma* or natural obligations disseminated by ancient Indian civilization.

It is the overall perspective, although mentioned very briefly, from which Gandhi's Constructive Programme can be viewed. The central objective of the Constructive Programme is to create a society by means of truth and non-violence. In the preface of his booklet, *Constructive Programme*, Gandhi also notes that "The constructive programme may otherwise and more fittingly be called construction of Poorna Swaraj or complete Independence by truthful and non-violent means" (Gandhi, 2015: 7).

It may be argued: what is the basis to say that the Constructive Programme can be called "more fittingly the construction of Poorna Swaraj or complete Independence?" The answer lies in the method of action that he proposes. He argued that Poorna Swaraj or complete independence would be complete only to the extent the people would practice truth and non-violence in their personal and social life. In his view, Complete Independence through truth and non-violence meant the independence of every unit without distinction of race, colour or creed. This kind of independence, as one may perceive, is never exclusive and, therefore, wholly compatible with inter-dependence within or without. To put the philosophy of Constructive programme into the practice, we are informed, Gandhi provided a list on the duty of Gram Sevak to reveal how service can be rendered in the Indian context.[10] To realize the philosophy of Constructive Programme in Indian village he also described how all-round village service can be performed.[11] What is here significant to note is that Gandhi's Constructive Programme is purely a moral action and intervention in the society which strengthens morality in man and society. However, if Gandhi's Constructive programme is an action and intervention in the existing social political and economic reality of the society, what is the root of such an action/intervention?

It can be argued that Gandhi's Constructive Programmes is derived from his metaphysical presuppositions. To support the argument, I wish to put a piece of Gandhi's writings that summarizes his metaphysical position. "Man's ultimate aim is the realization of God, and all his activities, social, political, religious, have to be guided by the ultimate aim of the vision of God. The immediate service of all human beings becomes a necessary part of the endeavour simply because the only way to find God is to see Him in His creation and be one with it. This can only be done by the service of all. I am a part and parcel of the whole and I cannot find Him apart from the rest of humanity. My countrymen are my nearest neighbours. They have become so helpless, so resourceless, so inert that I must concentrate myself on serving them. If I could persuade myself that I could find

Him in a Himalayan cave, I would proceed there immediately. But I know that I cannot find Him apart from humanity" (CWMG: 63: 240).

This piece of writing suggests that the God can be found only through serving his Creation. Juxtaposing this writing with Gandhi's Constructive Programme, we may deduce that the Constructive Programme is not a separate, state-centric or goodwill gesture activity but it is an action to serve the God or spiritual activity. It becomes more obvious when one observes that Gandhi did not see the difference between the spiritual and the mundane. In his words, "I do not believe that the spiritual law works on a field of its own. On the contrary, it expresses itself only through the ordinary activities of life. It thus affects the economic, the social and the political fields" (CWMG: 28: 148).

Thus, it is not surprising that he views God or Truth in the action carried out through different Constructive Programmes. To quote him, "My God is myriad-formed and, while sometimes I see Him in the spinning-wheel, at other times I see Him in communal unity; then again in the removal of untouchability and that is how I establish communion with Him according to as the spirit moves me" (Prabhu and Rao, 2002: 225). Serving and caring the Creation of God, as the axiom of the Constructive Programme, he once claimed, "I claim to know my millions. All the 24 hours of the day I am with them. They are my first care and last because I recognize no God except the God that is to be found in the hearts of the dumb millions. They do not recognize His presence; I do. And I worship the God that is Truth or Truth which is God through the service of these millions" (Prabhu and Rao, 2002: 197).

Above discussion lead us to conclude that, Gandhi's Constructive Programme, like Satyagraha, emerged out of his metaphysical conviction. In other words, Gandhi's notion of truth is central to his Constructive Programme. As we may note, his notion of truth recognizes the essential unity of all that exists as well as oneness with all the fellow human and sub-human forms of life.

Summing up

The details of Gandhi's action includes his individual action in the form of 'experiments', community action conducted at his different Ashram, and action carried out at the mass level in the form of

Satyagraha and Constructive Programme. These three levels of action were not separate for him and there was an inherent unity among them as his all actions were derived from his metaphysical supposition of truth.

His action, at the mass level, has two significant but interrelated dimensions—Satyagraha and Constructive Programme. His Satyagraha provides practical expression to the metaphysical and ethical ideas of his Truth and non-violence in the public sphere. Satyagraha is based on 'Truth' force and we examined that Gandhi believed that the more subtle the force, the greater its impact in terms of scale, speed and durability. In fact, Satyagraha, as an action, is a struggle between material forces and spiritual forces in the public sphere. We have also noted that Gandhi does not negate the force or its significance but he wants to change the social-political *status quo* by employing soul force or spiritual force not by using material force. Further, for Gandhi, Satyagraha is not merely the desire to see Truth, but *the insistence* on Truth. The Satyagraha is, therefore, motivated by the commitment and action to Truth, i.e. Satyagraha is, in fact, Truth-in-action. In other words, Satyagraha is not an academic or a philosophical issue concerned merely with identifying Truth, but one has to do the certain action for oneself to be consistent with Truth and simultaneously one has also to take action to make one's social-political context conducive to Truth. In short, the action is an integral or inescapable part of Satyagraha. Like Satyagraha, Gandhi's Constructive Programme is also a significant dimension of his action. It is based on his view on society as 'larger family', his model of society and social development in the form of 'oceanic circle', and his critique of the liberal state. The Constructive Programme aims to create a society by means of non-violence and truth. His Constructive Programmes is also derived from his metaphysical presuppositions of Truth. His notion of Truth recognizes the 'essential unity of all that exists' as well as 'oneness' with all the fellow human and sub-human forms of life. Gandhi argues that truth has to be realized through the service of mankind, thus, his conception of truth is not a static entity but a process of becoming and widening through action.

Notes

1. Gandhi wrote, "None of us knew what name to give to our movement. I

then used the term 'passive resistance' in describing it. I did not quite understand the implication of 'passive resistance' as I called it. I only knew that some new principle had come into being. As the struggle advanced, the phrase 'passive resistance' gave rise to confusion and it appeared shameful to permit this great struggle to be known only by an English name. Again, that foreign phrase could hardly pass as current coin among the community. A small prize was therefore announced in Indian Opinion to be awarded to the reader who invented the best designation for our struggle. We thus received a number of suggestions. The meaning of the struggle had been then fully discussed in Indian Opinion and the competitors for the prize had fairly sufficient material to serve as a basis for their exploration". (Gandhi, M.K. (1954) *Satyagraha in South Africa,* Ahmedabad: Navajivan: 109)

2. In his journal, *Indian Opinion*, he asked his readers to suggest the name for the struggle he was waging against the British in South Africa. He mentions, "Shri Maganlal Gandhi was one of the competitors and he suggested the word 'sadagraha', meaning 'firmness in a good cause'. (*Ibid.,* p. 109)
3. The source of Gandhi's Satyagraha is the teachings of many eminent personalities and philosophies. The idea of Lord Krishna preached in the *Gita* had the tremendous influence upon Gandhi. Besides the *Gita*, Jesus' Sermon on the Mount, the writings of Thoreau, Tolstoy and Ruskin influenced him a lot to frame the idea of Satyagraha.
4. Compiled by author from *The Mind of Mahatma Gandhi* by R.K. Prabhu, and U.R. Rao. (2002). Ahmedabad: Navajivan.
5. Prayer, observing silence, Fasting may be cited as the form of action in this context.
6. Eleven vows: Truth, non-violence, *brahmacharya*, fearlessness, control of the palate, non-possession, and non-stealing, bread-labour equality of religions, anti-untouchability, and *Swadeshi*, may be cited in this context.
7. Non-cooperation and Civil disobedience may be cited in this context.
8. Qualifications of a Satyagrahi as Gandhi mentioned:

   "...The following qualifications.... I hold are essential for every Satyagrahi in India:

   1. He must have a living faith in God, for He is his only Rock.
   2. He must believe in truth and non-violence as his creed and, therefore, have faith in the inherent goodness of human nature which he expects to evoke by his truth and love expressed through his suffering.
   3. He must be leading a chaste life and be ready and willing, for the sake of his cause, to give up his life and his possessions.
   4. He must be a habitual Khadi-wearer and spinner. This is essential for India. He must be a teetotaler and be free from the use of other intoxicants in order that his reason may be always unclouded and his mind constant.
   5. He must carry out with a willing heart all the rules or discipline as may be laid down from time to time.

6. He should carry out the jail rules unless they are specially devised to hurt his Self-respect.
7. The qualifications are not to be regarded as exhaustive. They are illustrative only." (Prabhu and Rao, 2002: 171)
   It needs to be recalled that Satyagraha requires no material assistance and physical aid and it is capable of being exercised by men, women, and children. It is open, voluntary, that involves self-sacrifice. It has to be exercised by well-prepared and trained people.

9. The constructive programme aimed to make political independence more meaningful. There were certain weaknesses in the Indian social structure which needed to be eliminated. For examples, conflicts between different religious groups (mainly Hindus and Muslims), untouchability, fear arising out of ignorance, economic disparities, the decaying condition of our villages, the plight of *adivasis*, *kisans* and the labourers, and the position of women were areas of major concern. In a small booklet, entitled Constructive Programme: its meaning and place, which he wrote on the train from Sevagram to Bardoli, he appealed to all Congressmen and others engaged in the freedom struggle to address these issues. The 18 points constructive programme thus became his framework for the new India he wished to see after *Swaraj*. It needs to be pointed out that Gandhi's pamphlet, *Constructive Programme: Its Meaning and Place* (1941, revised in 1945), was his last major publication in response to the insistent demands of his supporters for a manual that would encapsulate the principles and prescriptions of his constructive programme. The content of Constructive Programme, however, was hardly novel—it was a compilation of issues and initiatives that Gandhi had promoted in one way or another throughout his public career beginning in South Africa in the late nineteenth century.
10. Duties of *Gram Sevak* (CWMG: 90: 528):
    1. Every worker shall be a habitual wearer of Khadi made from self-spun yarn or certified by the A.I.S.A. and must be a teetotaler. If a Hindu, he must have abjured untouchability in any shape or form in his own person or in his family and must be a believer in the ideal of inter-communal unity, equal respect and regard for all religions and equality of opportunity and status for all irrespective of race, creed or sex.
    2. He shall come in personal contact with every villager within his jurisdiction.
    3. He shall enroll and train workers from amongst the villagers and keep a register of all these.
    4. He shall keep a record of his work from day-to-day.
    5. He shall organize the villages so as to make them self-contained and self-supporting through; their agriculture and handicrafts.
    6. He shall educate the village folk in sanitation and hygiene and take all measures for prevention of ill health and disease among them.
    7. He shall organize the education of the village folk from birth to death

along the lines of Nayee Talim, in accordance with the policy laid down by the Hindustani Talimi Sangh.

8. He shall see that those whose names are missing on the statutory voters' roll are duly entered therein.
9. He shall encourage those who have not yet acquired the legal qualification, to acquire it for getting the right of franchise.

11. *All-round Village Service*

"A Samagra Gramasevak must know everybody living in the village and render them such service as he can. That does not mean that the worker will be able to do everything single-handed. He will show them the way of helping themselves and procure for them such help and materials as they require. He will train up his own helpers. He will so win over the villagers that they will seek and follow his advice. Supposing I go and settle down in a village with a ghani, I won't be an ordinary ghanchi earning 15-20 rupees a month. I will be a Mahatma ghanchi. I have used the word 'Mahatma' in fun but what I mean to say is that as a ghanchi I will become a model for the villagers to follow. I will be a ghanchi who knows the Gita and the Quran. I will be learned enough to teach their children. I may not be able to do so for lack of time. The villagers will come to me and ask me: "Please make arrangements for our children's education." I will tell them: "I can find you a teacher but you will have to bear the expenses." And they will be prepared to do so most willingly. I will teach them spinning and when they come and ask me for the services of a weaver, I will find them a weaver on the same terms as I found them a teacher. And the weaver will teach them how to weave their own cloth. I will inculcate in them the importance of hygiene and sanitation and when they come and ask me for a sweeper, I will tell them: "I will be your sweeper and I will train you all in the job." This is my conception of Samagra Gramaseva" (CWMG: 83: 46).

References

Bondurant, J. (1957). *Conquest of Violence*. Princeton. Princeton University.

Bose, Nirmal Kumar. (1948). *Selections from Gandhi*. Ahmedabad: Navajivan

Diwaker, R.R. (1969). *Saga of Satyagraha*. New Delhi: GPF.

Gandhi, M.K. (1954). *Satyagraha in South Africa*. Ahmedabad: Navajivan.

Gandhi, M.K. (2008). *Hind Swaraj or Indian Home Rule*. Ahmedabad: Navajivan.

Gandhi, M.K. (2010). *Ashram Observances in Action*. Ahmedabad: Navajivan.

Gandhi, M.K. (2015). *Constructive Programme: Its Meaning and Place*. Ahmedabad: Navajivan.

Nagler, Michael. (2014). *The Principles of Constructive Programme*. The Metta Center for Nonviolence.

Parel, Anthony. (2006). *Gandhi's Philosophy and the Quest for Harmony*. New York: Cambridge University Press.

Peter Ackerman, and Jack Duvall (2000). *A Force More Powerful: A Century of Nonviolent Conflict*. New York: Palgrave.

Prabhu, R.K., and U.R. Rao (2002). *The Mind of Mahatma Gandhi*. Ahmedabad: Navajivan.

Sharp, Gene (1979). *Gandhi as a Political Strategist: With Essays on Ethics and Politics*. Boston. MA: Porter Sargent.

Sri Darnai, Krishnalal (1939). *War Without Violence. A Study of Gandhi's Method and its Accomplishments*. New York: Harcourt.

Tellis, Allwyn (2006). "*Mahatma Gandhi's Constructive Programme: Building a New India*". (Ph.D. Thesis, the University of Illinois at Urbana-Champaign, ProQuest.)

The Collected Works of Mahatma Gandhi (*CWMG*). Vol. 1-100, New Delhi: Publications Division Government of India. Retrieved from https://www.gandhiheritageportal.org.

Varma, Ravindra (2001). *The Spiritual Basis of Satyagraha*. Ahmedabad: Navajivan.

2

Gandhi's Action and its Relation to his Metaphysics

It is explicitly maintained that Gandhi was essentially a *Karmyogi* (man of action) with no concern or little concern for metaphysics or philosophical speculations. However, as we have noted in the previous chapter, Gandhi's actions have the substantial metaphysical basis and in no way, they are only contextual. In fact, the unity of Gandhi's thought and the interrelatedness of the various aspects of his social-political action emerge out of his firmly-held metaphysical beliefs. It becomes apparent when Gandhi reveals what he meant by Truth. It can be argued that whenever Gandhi attempted to explain what he meant by Truth he was certainly engaged in metaphysical speculations. However, it does not mean that he arrived at the meaning of Truth as the result of strict philosophical or metaphysical exercise like other philosophers. Gandhi's case is entirely different. Gandhi did not first learn to define Truth and then applied it to the various aspects of life, rather the various aspects of life revealed its truth before him.

We have discussed in the previous chapter, although very briefly, that scholars have generally observed Gandhi's action—both Satyagraha and Constructive Programme- in the terms of forms, details, features, philosophy, and significance but they have not considerably elaborated that what really constituted Gandhi's action. For example, Satyagraha is a non-violent direct *action* and one can find out its details, features, and philosophy but it is hardly discussed what is underneath the non-violent direct *action* that Satyagraha claims and what is the structure and nature of the non-violent direct *action*. This inevitably leads us to examine first the basis of Satyagraha. If Satyagraha is holding truth, as discussed earlier, then, questions come up as to how Gandhi views Truth and how it can be held. This chapter deals with Gandhi's views on the truth, which is his metaphysics and examines its relation to his views on the action.

In fact, the concept of Truth or *Satya* is fundamental and central to the thought of Gandhi. It is not without significance that the subtitle of his autobiography is "*The Story of my Experiments with Truth*". However, it needs to be pointed out at the very outset that Gandhi's interpretation of Satya or Truth has multifarious implications. His writings on Truth suggest that he gives multiple meanings to the truth on different occasions. In fact, instead of using the term Truth in its conventional meaning, he has added various new meanings to it. Even a cursory look on his writings on Truth suggests that, for him, the term Truth has metaphysical, ontological, moral and mystical significance. For instance, he notes in his small booklet *From Yervada Temple*, '*Satya* is derived from *sat* which means being' (Gandhi, 2014: 7). This is the ontological connotation of Gandhi's Truth. His writings on the Truth also shows that for him Truth means 'truthfulness in word, thought and deeds' (Gandhi, 2014: 8). Thus, Gandhi's truth has ethical connotations also. Gandhi also observes Truth in its absolute form. He also argues that absolute Truth cannot be fully realized as long as we are mortal (Prabhu and Rao, 2002: 45, 54). This provides a mystical element to Gandhi's notion of Truth.[1] What is more significant in Gandhi's notion of Truth is that he views Truth not only as the necessary basis of all life and therefore of all human society, but it also implies that every man should be a truth seeker. He repeatedly mentions that the only objective of human life is to realize Truth (Prabhu and Rao, 2002: 46). Thus, in Gandhi's worldview, Truth is a dynamic concept and an ideal that has to be realized.

Before we unpack Gandhi's notion of truth in detail, it is essential to note that Gandhi's approach to Truth was not of an intellectual and philosopher. It was rather that of a man who tried ceaselessly 'to be' and 'to do good'. Secondly, as demanded by his essentially practical attitudes, he was more concerned with the pragmatic application of the truth than intellectual discussion.

Truth as Metaphysical Foundation of Gandhi's Action

On Gandhi's view on truth, the most significant and perhaps most systemic writing amidst his voluminous writings is the introduction to his *Autobiography*. Gandhi notes in the introduction to his *Autobiography,*

> "...for me Truth is the sovereign principle, which includes numerous other principles. This truth is not only truthfulness in word, but truthfulness in thought also, and not only the relative truth of our conception, but the Absolute Truth, the Eternal Principle, that is God. There are innumerable definitions of God, because his molestations are innumerable. They overwhelm me with wonder and awe and for a moment stun me. But I worship God as Truth only.... But as long as I have not realized this Absolute Truth, so long must I hold by the relative truth as I have conceived it. That relative truth must, meanwhile, be my beacon, my shield and buckler" (Gandhi, 2013: xiii).

To have an explicit view of Gandhi's Truth, we may analyze this important piece of Gandhi's writings on Truth. Claiming that Truth is 'Sovereign principle', Gandhi seems to signify two important points. First 'Sovereign' means independent and self-governing, thus, the truth is not dependent on anything, hence, it is self-determining. Second, by the word 'principle', Gandhi seems to convey further two meanings; first, truth as the overriding 'principle' of the conduct; and second as the ontological reality. These two meanings are, however by no means separate. For as a principle of conduct as well, truth is valid and binding. Further, his notion that truth 'includes numerous other principles' suggest Gandhi's genuineness of efforts and sovereign nature of truth again. Further, 'not only truthfulness in word but also in thought' signifies that common perception of speaking truth is not enough but one should be truthful in 'thought' also. By truthful in 'thought' Gandhi emphasizes 'purity' of thought that needs self-restraint and finally to the purification of one's self.

From the above piece of writing, it is also evident that he makes a distinction between the 'Absolute truth' and 'Relative truth'. This distinction has much importance in Gandhi's overall philosophy.[2]

The significance of Gandhi distinction between 'absolute Truth' and 'relative truth' is that it accepts both universal and particular at the same time. But, what is relative truth and absolute Truth? Analysis of his writings on this subject suggests that anything that is objectively true or true on the basis of human experience can be taken as relative truth. In other words, what is empirically true can be considered as relative truth. On the other hand, absolute Truth transcends human experience. Absolute truth is the sum total of all that is there in the universe. Gandhi seems to attribute an ontological status to the truth calling it absolute. He takes truth in the sense of ultimate existence or Reality or God. What is called Absolute, Substance, Brahman or the principle of Being in metaphysics is characterized as Truth by Gandhi.

However, it is 'relative truth', Gandhi is chiefly concerned with. Relative truth provides much space for Gandhi to make experimentation with own experiences or contextual truths. The beauty of 'relative truth' is that it presupposes our readiness to admit openly our errors and to learn from them. It may be noted that Gandhi firmly declared that the right to err and the freedom to experiments constitute the universal and indispensable condition to all progress. In other words, he felt that a man of truth must ever be confident and diffident at the same time, confident in his vision of devotion to the truth but humble because of his consciousness of fallibility.

Second work that throws significant light in a systemic way on Gandhi's notion of Truth is his small booklet *From Yervada Mandir*. In this small booklet, he also presents the practical viewpoint how truth can be practiced in our everyday life. He noted in *From Yervada Mandir*,

> Devotion to this Truth is the sole justification for our existence. All our activities should be centered in Truth. Truth should be the very breath of our life. When once this stage in the pilgrim's progress is reached, all other rules of correct living will come without effort, and obedience to them will be instinctive. But without Truth it is impossible to observe any principles or rules in life.
>
> Generally speaking, observation of the law of Truth is understood merely to mean that we must speak the Truth. But we in the Ashram should understand the word Satya or Truth in a much wider sense. There should be truth in thought, truth in speech, and *truth in action*. To the man who has *realized this truth* in its fullness, nothing else remains to be known, because all knowledge is necessary included in it. What is not included in it is not truth, and so not true knowledge; and there can be no inward peace without true knowledge. If we once learn how to apply this never failing test of Truth, we

will at once able to find out *what is worth doing*, what is worth seeing, what is worth reading (Gandhi, 2014: 8).

This is precisely, Gandhi suggests, what is the nature of truth. Truth is not an intellectual exercise but a matter of 'realization' that needs some action. Moreover, Truth is directly linked with true knowledge and also in Gandhi's view one should learn 'how to apply never-failing test of truth'. Thus, Gandhi's Truth is dynamic in nature and requires applications. In the first part of the above quote what is remarkable is 'law of truth'. Gandhi's writings, although scattered on this subject, constantly mentions the 'law of Truth' with some other terms. It needs elaboration as to what does Gandhi mean by 'law of truth'. It will also throw some light on the nature of Truth he envisioned.

For Gandhi, Truth is the Law of the Universe or the Law that governs the Universe. He also observes that this Law is not a Law of Annihilation or Destruction, but one that governs formation, cohesion, and transformation.[3] "If it had been one of destructions, the world would have come to an end long ago" (Prabhu and Rao, 2002: 416). He further mentioned that "My own experience has led me to the knowledge that the fullest life is impossible without an immovable belief in a Living Law in obedience to which the whole Universe moves"(Prabhu and Rao, 2002: 417). As noted earlier, Gandhi considers the Law of Truth as 'sovereign'. The corollary of these assumptions, as we may deduce, is that there cannot be two sovereign Laws that are parallel. Further, it also means all other laws are subsidiary and supplementary or complementary to the Law of Truth or the sovereign law; they cannot be parallel or contrary to the sovereign Law.

It is from this point of view Gandhi argues that the 'Law of Truth' that rules in the higher realm must, therefore, be valid in the lower realm as well. Thus, he notes, "I do not believe that the spiritual law works in a field of its own. On the contrary, it expresses itself only through the ordinary activities of life. It thus affects the economic, social and political fields" (CWMG:28:148). In other words, because the Law is sovereign, the same sovereign Law, therefore, rules over the spiritual and mundane spheres; the individual and society; the part and the whole. Suppose, if separate laws governed the part and the whole, the part would cease to belong to the whole, and the whole would also lose its identity without the part or parts. Thus, for him, whatever we see in the world, animate as well as inanimate, is subject to the Law. In his view, every part of the universe is subject to the Law even if it is unaware of the Law. In Gandhi's view, the Law, the law-giver and the executor (the power that enforces the Law) are all one, or 'rolled into'one.[4] He also argues that there is no question of the revision of the Law and exemption or immunity being granted by the Law or its effects (Gandhi, 1961: 273). On the level of action, the practical implication of this view is that if any law made by man, conflicted with the higher Law, he should ignore the lower law to conform to the higher law. However, this is not only the matter of intellectual understanding. He argues that one must live according to the Law. Thus, it is not surprising that Gandhi proposes the vow of truth. However, he recognized that this highly exalted and exacting conception of truth could be comprehended and practiced only by few. The vow of truth, in the practical sense, implies that there is no place for prejudice, evasion, deception, secretiveness or distortion. Further, the vow of truth cannot be taken without also taking the other vows.

The third writing that throws a condensed view of Gandhi on Truth is the definition that he himself gives. In his journal *Young India*, dated 31-12-'31, Gandhi answers the question; 'What ....is Truth and how it can be realized ?' He responds, "A difficult question, but I have solved it for myself by saying that *it is what the voice within tells you.*" But one might argue that 'the voice within' might be different from the different people. Then, how will the truth be understood? Gandhi answers,

> "Well, seeing that the human mind works through innumerable media and that the evolution of the human mind is not the same for all, it follows that what may be truth for one may be untruth for another, and hence those who have made these experiments have come to the conclusion that there are certain conditions to be observed in making those experiments. Just as for conducting scientific experiments there is an indispensable scientific course of instruction, in the same way strict preliminary discipline is necessary to qualify a person to make experiments in the spiritual realm. *Everyone should, therefore, realize his limitations before he speaks of his Inner Voice.* Therefore, we have the belief based upon experience, that those who would make individual search after Truth as God, must *go through several vows*, as for instance, the vow of truth, the vow of *Brahmacharya* (purity)—for you cannot possibly divide your love for Truth

> and God with anything else, the vow of non-violence, of poverty and non-possession. Unless you impose on yourselves the five vows you may not embark on the experiment at all. There are several other conditions prescribed, but I must not take you through all of them. Suffice it to say that those who have made these experiments know that it is not proper for everyone to claim to hear the voice of conscience, and it is because we have at the present moment everybody claiming the right of conscience without going through any discipline whatsoever and there is so much untruth being delivered to a bewildered world, all that I can, in true humility, present to you is that truth is not to be found by anybody who has not got an abundant sense of *humility*. If you would swim on the bosom of the ocean of Truth you must *reduce yourself to a zero*. Further then this I cannot go along this fascinating path (Prabhu and Rao, 2002: 42).

This inner voice, according to Gandhi, is the voice of God, the final judge of the rightness of every deed and thought. In the matter of inner voice, the law of majority has no place. It needs to be pointed out that this concept of conscience led him to respect the conscience of those who disagreed with him. The test of the presence and power of individual conscience, as he suggested, is the willingness to suffer for one's belief to the point of public ridicule, and if necessary political martyrdom and even physical death.[5]

This concept of conscience can be traced both in Western as well in Indian tradition. Kant also argued that conscience proves God when reason cannot. In Indian tradition notion of *'vidhi'* or Moral imperative is like that. Gandhi's significance is that he identified it with the infallible of Truth or God in man. Moreover, he tried to employ the notion of conscience in the social-political field. Although this idea seems influenced by West, however, Gandhi made the bolder and wider use of it. The crucial and practical significance of this conscience is that it gives men the courage to say 'no', in the face of injustice and exploitation. In other words, the concept of conscience or Truth is not a theoretical one or only of intellectual interest. In fact, the supremacy of the individual and his view of conscience emphasize action in society. Thus, Gandhi insists on heroic and even rebellious action in society. As we may observe, this conscience necessitates acts of sacrifice and fearlessness.

Further, Gandhi's plea for heroism, based on conscience or truth, in society involves him the recognition of the need for inspired leadership in political and social activity. It also emphasizes the role of small groups as pioneers and pathfinders. According to Gandhi, a leader is useless when he acts against the prompting of his conscience. Thus, Gandhi aims to combine the individual conscience with a programme of mass action in the form of Satyagraha and Constructive Programme.

One may argue that God, inner voice, conscience, justice are all very abstract concepts. They can be differently interpreted and their conceptual boundary can be made distinct from each other. To identify all of them with the truth is bound to create a lot of confusion and ambiguity. Thus, Gandhi's identification of Truth with these ideas makes truth conceptually ambiguous. There is substance in these arguments, however, this ambiguity disappears when we recognize that Gandhi viewed his metaphysics as a guideline for his action not as abstract formulation for intellectual discourse. Moreover, he did not claim that he has found the truth but claimed that he has found the method to achieve it. He notes, "I am but a seeker after Truth. I claim to have found a way to it. I claim to be *making a ceaseless effort to find it*. But I admit that I have not yet found it. To find Truth completely is to realize oneself and one's destiny, i.e. to become perfect. I am painfully conscious of my imperfections, and therein lies all the strength I possess, because it is a rare thing for a man to know his own limitations" (Prabhu and Rao, 2002: 18, *italics mine*).

We may note that making *a 'ceaseless effort'* to find truth moved Gandhi to action both in the personal and public realm. At the personal level, Gandhi sets the criteria by which one can realize the truth. He notes, "For the quest of Truth involves *tapas* (self-suffering), sometimes even unto death. There can be no place in it even a trace of self-interest. In such selfless search for Truth nobody can lose his bearings for long. Directly he takes to the wrong path he stumbles and is thus redirected to the right path. Therefore, the pursuit of Truth is true *bhakti* (devotion). It is the path that leads to God. There is no place in it for cowardice, no place for defeat. It is the talisman by which death itself becomes the portal to life eternal" (Gandhi, 2014: 8).

We noted that Gandhi tried to employ Truth in politics and society. For him, to tread the path of truth implies an active life in the world. It means the realization of truth in action. Thus, against the Western maxim 'might is right', Gandhi presents Eastern one that is '*Satyameva Jayte*' that means truth alone conquers. The significance of Gandhi's truth is that it was developed in an effort to undermine external authority as well as it reaffirmed the moral autonomy and authority of individual as an agent to take part in politics and society.

Truth-in-action invited Gandhi to develop an inseparable category what he called *ahimsa* or non-violence. Once he noted that "non-violence is the first article of my faith. It is also the last article of my creed" (Prabhu and Rao, 2002: 23). He holds that without *ahimsa* it is not possible to seek and find Truth. In his view, they are so intertwined that it is practically impossible to unravel and separate them. They are like the two sides of a coin. Again, for Gandhi, the non-violence is not a matter of philosophy or intellectual inquiry that can be discussed and learned by deliberations but it involved enterprise. In order to test non-violence, he argued, one must learn to dare danger and death, mortifies the flesh, and acquires the capacity to endure all manner of hardships.

Gandhi's writings on non-violence are fascinating. He describes it in exalted terms in his writings. He argues that '*rishis* who discovered the law of non-violence in the midst of violence were greater geniuses than Newton'. He mentions, non-violence is the 'law of the human race' and is 'infinitely greater than and superior to brute force'. It is an 'unchangeable creed'. It requires "a living faith in God,' it is 'soul force' or the power of Godhead within you". It is 'active force of the highest order', 'greatest force at the disposal of mankind', 'supreme law', 'one of the world's great principles', 'highest ideal' and in its dynamic condition it means 'conscious suffering'.[6]

Relating non-violence to action, he observes, "Non-violence is like radium in its action. An infinitesimal quantity of it embedded in a malignant growth acts continuously, silently and ceaselessly till it has transformed the whole mass of the diseased tissue into a healthy one. Similarly, even a little of true non-violence acts in a silent, subtle, unseen way and leavens the whole society" (Prabhu and Rao, 2002: 122). Gandhi noted that his whole life is an endevour to apply non-violence in different walks of life. He wrote, "I have been practicing with scientific precision non-violence and its possibilities for an unbroken period of over fifty years. I have applied it in every walk of life, domestic, institutional, economic and political. I know of no single case in which it has failed. Where it has seemed sometimes to have failed, I have ascribed it to my imperfections. I claim no perfection for myself. But,

I do claim to be a passionate seeker after Truth, which is but another name for God. In the course of that search, the discovery of non-violence came to me. Its spread is my life mission. I have no interest in living except for the prosecution of that mission" (CWMG: 72: 230-31).

What is important to note is that Gandhi attempted to make the personal virtue of non-violence social and he also showed the way that how non-violence can also be 'organized' for action in mass scale in the form of Satyagraha and Constructive Programme. To quote him, "I hold that non-violence is not merely a personal virtue. It is also a social virtue to be cultivated like the other virtues. Surely society is largely regulated by the expression of non-violence in its mutual dealings. What I ask for is an extension of it on a larger, national and international scale" (CWMG: 68:278).

Yet, it might be questioned: how non-violence and truth are inseparable as Gandhi argued? Gandhi declared that it was in the course of his pursuit of truth that he discovered non-violence. He did not conceptually derive non-violence from the truth but got to know about it because of the course of the pursuit. Not truth, but seeking the truth, may reveal the means to the goal. Before we deal with the issue of the relation between truth and non-violence let us ask that it is possible to peruse one without another in the general sense of the term truth and non-violence. In other words, is it possible to pursue truth (relative truth) without non-violence?

We may note that indeed it is possible. For example, nations go to war believing truth is on their side, or that they are on the side of truth. In the same way, non-violence is also possible without pursuing truth. For example, most of the religious practices are generally non-violent but they do not peruse truth. They are confined only to the practices. It is, thus, possible to pursue truth without regard to non-violence, and non-violence without regard to truth. But, we may perceive the result, the pursuit of truth on its own makes one self-righteous and even capable of killing in its name. Thus, truth without non-violence may turn to absolutism. Similarly, non-violence pursued on its own, without truth, could simply be used as a cover to countenance passivity, even cowardice, and degenerate into a form of self-indulgence. In short, one without the other tends to make the exercise of the pursuit of each on its own potentially reckless. It is in this context one might observe Gandhi's views on the relation between Truth and non-violence. We have noted above that for Gandhi *ahimsa* and truth are like two sides of the same coin. To quote him,

> "Ahimsa and Truth are so intertwined that it is practically impossible to disentangle and separate them. They are like the two sides of a coin, or rather of a smooth unstamped metallic disc. Who can say, which is the obverse, and which is the reverse? Nevertheless *ahimsa* is the means: Truth is the end. Means to be means or later. When once we have grasped this point, final victory is beyond question. Whatever difficulties we encounter, whatever apparent reverses we sustain, we may not give up the quest for Truth which alone is, being God Himself" (Gandhi, 1958: 224-225).

Thus, for Gandhi non-violence is the means, and truth, or God, is the end. This engages us in of the most significant aspects of Gandhi's philosophy; the relation between means and end. This aspect might be discussed briefly here.

Back in 1909, Gandhi noted in *Hind Swaraj*, "The means may be likened to a seed, the end to a tree; and there is just the same inviolable connection between the means and the end as there is between the seed and the tree. I am not likely to obtain the result flowing from the worship of God by laying myself prostrate before Satan" (Gandhi, 2008: 71). In fact, for Gandhi, there is 'no wall of separation between means and end' (CWMG:24:396). He also noted that there is 'an inexorable' relation between means and ends, as there is an inexorable relationship between cause and effect. In the light of this relationship, Gandhi looked upon means and ends as 'convertible terms' like two sides of the same coin. It means one can reach an end only through means consistent with the end. Conversely, the end that one reaches will depend on the means one adopts. For Gandhi, means determine the nature of what we achieve. Wrong means, therefore, can lead us astray or result in the distortion of our ends. Here we may reflect that how this idea is related to Gandhi's action, especially to his Constructive Programme and Satyagraha. If one wants to create a non-violent society that is objective of the Constructive Programme, one cannot do so by maintaining violence or a reign of terror. One must adopt non-violent means to establish a non-violent society. In the same way, Satyagraha also attempts to build a peaceful and non-violent society through the peaceful and non-violent means. In its fullest implication, it can be argued that there is no greater assurance of democracy and equality than a regime of non-violence. Thus, the means that one adopts is, therefore, imperative. In fact, Gandhi emphasizes more on means than the end. The reason is that means is always within our reach. In his words, "Indeed, the Creator has given us control (and that too very limited) over means, none over the end" (CWMG:24:396). Thus, he holds that if we care about the means, we reach the end promptly. It logically takes him to argue for 'purity of means'. He maintains, 'Our progress towards the goal will be in exact proportion to the purity of our means'. 'This is a proposition that admits of no exception'(CWMG:24:396).

Finally, it might be argued that what is the role of men in Gandhi's metaphysical scheme and why one should do the action? Gandhi argues that the individual is a part who is conscious, thus, he/she can understand the Law of Truth which is whole. Moreover, he/she has the ability, and the duty to understand the symbiotic relationship between the part and the whole. He/she can also understand that any departure from the conditions of this relationship will be untenable and ruinous. As Gandhi believed that the higher law revealed itself in all spheres, and governed every sphere, one must realize one's self and one's role in this world through taking part in all possible fields and act in conformation with the higher law. Gandhi's emphasis on the worldly existence is significant as it engages human being in action.

We notice that Gandhi does not make any difference between the spiritual world and practical world or mundane. Thus, his action is not divided into two separate domains. He notes "If any action of mine claimed to be spiritual is proved to be impractical, it must be pronounced to be a failure. I do believe that the most spiritual act is also the most practical act in the true sense of the term" (Prabhu and Rao, 2002: 8). In fact, Gandhi did not believe in withdrawing from the world of everyday life to devote himself to spiritual practices like other *yogis*. To him, there was only one world, and Truth had to benefit human beings in this world.

There was still another philosophical reason that convinced Gandhi that he could not disengage from the mundane world. He believed that the Law that governed the Universe was sovereign. It had, therefore, to hold good in every realm, the realm of the spirit as well as the realm of the mundane. One who wanted to find the law and live by it could not, therefore, ignore or withdraw from any field of human activity. In every field, he had to look for, and apply the spiritual law. He could not do this if he withdrew from everyday life or the problems or activities of everyday life if he thought that any field was extraneous to the pursuit of the Law or Truth.

Yet, why one should act and what should be the course of action? Gandhi argues that one must act in this world because the human being has no escape from the action. Gandhi's view of the action, which we will see in more detail in the next chapters, is derived from his reading and understanding of *Gita.* A wonderful verse in the *Gita* (III-5) pronounces "No one can remain even for a moment without doing work. Work here means motion of inanimate as well as animate beings. It is characteristic of human beings that they may obey this law in a selfless spirit." Thus every moment human being confronts with the need to act and every action has its consequences. No human being, therefore, can escape the consequences of his action. Even inaction has its consequences. He, therefore, needs a code that could help him to determine his course of action. As discussed earlier, in Gandhi's framework, this code flows only from the identification of the Supreme Law that governs the Universe or Truth. One had to recognize the Law because the Law was unalterable, and its effect was inexorable.

For Gandhi, in every action, there is a challenge as well as an opportunity. The human being can either act according to the Supreme Law or act in defiance of it. If he/she chooses to act according to the Law he/she will make progress, and the results he/she achieves will endure. If he/she does not, he/she will fail and regress; the edifice that he/she erects will be shaky, and will eventually crash. Thus, in Gandhi's view, every mundane act should be made a spiritual act by conforming to the Supreme Law. Thus, Gandhi's metaphysics implies that a seeker after Truth or one who seek spiritual progress cannot afford to ignore or exclude any aspect of life from his field of concern and action.

Summing up

Having discussed different aspects of Gandhi's metaphysical belief system in relation to his action, let us summarize the arguments. We observed that Gandhi's action is an extension of his metaphysical belief system. In other words, his actions are implications of his metaphysical viewpoints. His notion of Truth, both Absolute and Relative, is not for academic interest or dry scholastic discussion but it strongly conveys one to engage in action. His absolute Truth serves as a guideline for the action; relative truth provides space for action in the form of experimentation. We have also noticed that non-violence plays the pivotal role in his metaphysical scheme. Non-violence or *ahimsa* implies activity and action and it is by means of *ahimsa* Gandhi develops his philosophy of temporal action. We also noted that his notion of truth as inner voice or conscience also invites one for heroic action. Moreover, his metaphysics that implies brave action is not restricted to personal exercise in good faith but it incorporates community and group action too. We have also found that his metaphysics is not the static description of reality but it is dynamic and evolving in nature which provides space for new avenues of action for people. In his words, "Truth is like a vast tree, which yields more and more fruit the more you nurture it. The deeper the search in the mine of truth the richer the discovery of the gems buried there, in the shape of openings for an even greater variety of service" (Prabhu and Rao, 2002: 43).

Notes

1. The Gandhian notion of Satya is conceptually more in accord with the views of the ancient Greek. However, in practice, it is closer to modern existentialism rather than the classical notion of truth.
2. In a sense, he was both a pragmatist and Platonist, a difficult combination but one that he did not regard as impossible.
3. Gandhi notes, "The fact that mankind persists shows that the cohesive force is greater than the disruptive force, centripetal force greater than centrifugal". (see Prabhu and Rao, 2002: 416).
4. Gandhi notes, "He is the Law-maker, the Law and the Executor" (CWMG: 83:141). He also mentioned that 'He and His Law are one. There is nothing outside His Law' (CWMG: 83:379). He further mentions, "God may be called by any name so long as it connotes the living Law of life in other words, the Law and the Lawgiver rolled into one" (CWMG: 83:373).
5. We may recall Gandhi's notion of conscience is close to Socratic Daemon.
6. Compiled from *The Mind of Mahatma* by the author himself.

References

Gandhi, M.K. (1958). *Hindu Dharma*. Ahmedabad: Navajivan.

Gandhi, M.K. (2008). *Hind Swaraj or The Indian Home Rule*. Ahmedabad: Navajivan.

Gandhi, M.K. (2013). *An Autobiography or My Experiments with Truth*. Ahmedabad: Navajivan.

Gandhi, M.K. (2014). *From Yervada Mandir*. Ahmedabad: Navajivan.
Gandhi, M.K. (1961). *In Search of the Supreme*. Vol. I. Ahmedabad: Navajivan.
Prabhu, R.K., and U.R. Rao. (2002). *The Mind of Mahatma*. Ahmedabad: Navajivan.
The Collected Works of Mahatma Gandhi, (*CWMG*), Vol. 1-100, New Delhi: Publication Division. Government of India.
Retrived from https://www.gandhiheritageportal.org.

3

Gandhi's Metaphysics and its Epistemological Basis

In the previous chapter, we have noted, Gandhi's action is essentially based on his metaphysics of Truth. We have also perceived Gandhi defined truth in the form of absolute truth, relative truth and as an inner voice. How does Gandhi reach to these notions of truth? In other words, what are the sources from them Gandhi reach to these conceptions of truth? This question compels us to examine the source and method of knowledge by which Gandhi reaches to his metaphysical notion of truth. This chapter seeks to explore Gandhi's theory of knowledge or epistemology in relation to his metaphysics or notion of truth. Gandhi did not write systematically on his epistemology, thus, what is first required, is to reconstruct his epistemology on the basis of his writings.

In an endeavour to reconstruct Gandhi's epistemology in relation to his metaphysics, we need to be informed about two important points as a background. First of all, he was deeply influenced by the Indian philosophical tradition and its idea of universality of Truth. In fact, the recognition of the universality of Truth, the presence of Truth in each and every individual, and the possibility of reawakening it through spiritual discipline, that Gandhi invokes in his metaphysical notion, have been the essence of Indian Philosophy right from the Vedic times to the contemporary period. Unlike the Western tradition, Indian philosophy focuses on self-discipline also which has been systematically and elaborately explained and practiced in India. Gandhi simply adopted it to demonstrate its power in contemporary time. He spared no aspect of life from its application and no individual from its practice. Thus, he has proved himself to be the best believer and practitioner in the principle of Truth. As he noted "I do not claim to have originated any new principle or doctrine. I have simply tried in my own way to apply the eternal truths to our own daily life and problems" (Prabhu and Rao, 2002: 25).

The second point that has to be kept in mind is that he claimed that he was a *Sanatani* Hindu.[1] Here the term *Sanatani* Hindu refers: a Hindu with roots in ancient tradition. He himself noted, "Believing as I do in the influence of heredity, being born in a Hindu family, I have remained a Hindu. I should reject it if I found it inconsistent with my moral sense or my spiritual growth" (CWMG:35: 166). Bondurant also argues that Gandhi was very much influenced by the Hindu religion (Bondurant, 1957: 108). She observes, '*satyannnastiparo dharma*', i.e. there is no religion or duty greater than truth is one of the essentials of Hinduism. Further, she notes that Truth always figured out in the traditional Hindu stories of India; like stories of Harishchandra or Prahalad. The emphasis on truth is paramount in the writings of early philosophers also. She observes, "The vast body of philosophic commentary, the network of dialectic, the complex systems of logic and disputation which characterize Hindu philosophical and religious literature bear eloquent evidence to the lack of dogma and attest to a passion for truth arrived at through speculation" (Bondurant, 1957: 108). Further, she notes, "In India, the Hindu tradition holds out to man the possibility of ultimate realization of the absolute: the consummation of man's striving with the Godhead and such is the meaning of man's realization" (Bondurant, 1957: 16). She locates Gandhi's views of absolute Truth in this Hindu philosophical tradition and explicitly states "His [Gandhi] acceptance of the absolute followed the Hindu understanding, and his personal view on God was the Hindu view of the all-pervading Brahama" (Bondurant, 1957: 16). Thus, as she remarks, "Gandhi did not deny the orthodox Hindu philosophical position identifying truth with being or reality" (Bondurant, 1957: 111).

Keeping these features of Hindu philosophy in mind, it can be argued that Gandhi adopted the notion of Absolute truth from Hindu scripture and elaborated in his own frame. Further, affirming the isomorphism of Truth (*Satya*) and Reality (*Sat*) Gandhi seems to remain faithful to his tradition of Hinduism. We have already noted in the previous chapter that he viewed reality as Absolute Truth. Considering reality as Absolute Truth, Gandhi preserved the metaphysical and ethical connotation of such traditional Hindu terms as *dharma*, universal law, the sovereign principle and cosmic moral law. Moreover, as previously noted, for him 'nothing is, or nothing exists, except Truth and where Truth is there also is true Knowledge (*cit*) and where true knowledge is, there also is bliss' (*anand*). This is a conventional Hindu philosophical position which Gandhi accepted entirely. As Glyn Richard points out, "... he sought to live his life in the spirit of Truth and in accordance with the religious and ethical ideals of the Hindu way of life" (Glyn Richard, 1982: 157). He further mentions how Gandhi's conception of truth is near to Hindu philosophy. "The early Hindu tradition refers to ultimate reality as Brahaman, the substratum of existence, which in Advaita or non-dualist tradition is identified with Atman, the innermost Self and principle of life, and it refers to the eternal law and the moral law, which man is required to live in accordance with as the Sanatana Dharma and *rta*. Gandhi preserves the metaphysical and ethical connotations of these Hindu terms by his use of Satya or Truth" (Glyn Richard, 1982: 157). He further argues, "for him, Truth is the essence of reality since nothing is except Truth and, like Brahman of the earlier tradition, Truth is *Sat -Cit- Anand*, Being-Consciousness, Bliss. Gandhi claimed to have had glimpses only of absolute truth is understandable since, like Brahman, it is the ideal beyond prediction, the *neti neti*, (not this, not this) which cannot be embodied in concrete particulars" (Glyn Richard, 1982: 157). Thus, Gandhi acquired his understanding of truth as a participant in the Hindu way of life.

The second point that needs to be discussed is that Gandhi accepts it is impossible for mortal man to lay claim to attain or to possess Absolute Truth. This, as we noted, is also a Hindu position. Gandhi writes, "We can visualize it in our imagination. We cannot through the instrumentality of this ephemeral body, see face to face Truth which is eternal. That is why in the last resort one must depend on faith" (Gandhi, 2014: 9).

Gandhi's reference to 'faith' explains why he describes the absolute truth as God. It is, indeed, an affirmation of faith. When he claims 'Truth is God', he is actually making a declaration in 'faith' rather than a statement in the indicative mood. Such a declaration of faith requires no external verification. Gandhi argues that it is logical to use reason, but he insists that ultimately the absolute Truth or existence of God defies all proof and has to be based on 'faith' which transcends reason.

Thus, for him, Absolute Truth, which is known by faith, is beyond our empirical grasp which means we must act in the knowledge that we are holding on to such truth as apprehend in this world. This indicates to his view on relative truth. He notes in his *Autobiography*, "That relative truth must, meanwhile, be my beacon, my shield and buckler. Though this path is straight and narrow and sharp as the razor's edge, for me it has been the quickest and easiest. Even my Himalayan blunders have seemed trifling to me because I have kept strictly to this path. For the path has saved me from coming to grief, and I have gone forward according to my light. Often in my progress I have had faint glimpses of the Absolute Truth, God, and daily the conviction is growing upon me that He alone is real and all else is unreal" (Gandhi, 2013: xiii).

Without relative truth, it can be argued, the absolute truth which is a matter of faith would be nothing but empty utopianism. It is only through particular instances of truth by which one can understand absolute Truth. Thus, relative truth is necessary to convey the meaning of absolute truth which affirms in faith. Relative truth, as Gandhi states, is our 'beacon' in the sphere of the empirical.

Therefore, epistemologically he reaches to his notion of absolute truth by faith, while his notion of relative truth is empirical. When Gandhi discusses that he had the only 'glimpse' of absolute truth, it does not mean that he was caught in some kind of hypnotized Ultimate entity, but rather through his participation in relative truth that is empirical in nature, Gandhi could sense the absolute.

From the psychological and action point of view, Gandhi's analysis of the absolute truth and relative truth has remarkable significance. It is based on the nature of the human mind, its effectiveness, and its fallibility. Ravindra Varma has made an interesting analysis in this connection. He argues that all minds are not at the same intellectual level or the spiritual level. They are also not at the same level of freedom from the temptations and distortions arising from the senses and the ego. Thus, "the perception one gains from mind may, therefore, be incomplete and erroneous, or faulty" (Varma, 2001: 33). Besides, as he mentions, the perception at any given moment is conditioned or determined by the effectiveness, the mind has acquired or possesses at that moment. Thus, "perception at a given moment is related to the effectiveness of the mind at that moment" (Varma, 2001: 33). Varma observes that the vision of Truth that arises at that moment is Gandhi's relative Truth. As the human being suffers from limitations as long as he is in the body, thus, the

Truth that one perceives is always bound to be affected by these limitations and only be relative in nature. Nevertheless, the human being needs to proceed from this relative version of the truth to the absolute truth.

Although Gandhi's relative truth is empirical in nature, it does not mean the knowledge of relative truth is possible only through sense perception. In fact, Gandhi provided a very limited role to the sense perception while discussing the realization of Truth of any kind. He noted that sense perceptions can be, often are, false and deceptive, however real they may appear to us.[2]

It does not mean that Gandhi objected to any scientific investigation or empirical knowledge or to empirical methods themselves. His methodological insight; the collection of data, its verification, logical reasoning for reaching to the correct statement can be found in his most of activities including his Satyagraha.

As Varma notes, "Gandhi did not believe in any creed that would not or could not subject itself to scientific investigation and verification through the processes of observation and experimentation, logical analysis or the use of reason, and the clinching test of evidence, —empirical or experiential" (Varma, 2001: 29-30). Then, what about the knowledge gained from sense perception that Gandhi calls deceptive?

In this regard, Unto Tahtinen makes an interesting analysis of Gandhi's view on knowledge and his methods. In Gandhi's case, he observes, "The heart of the matter is the position, meaning and value of the knowledge in question with regard to synthetic Truth" (Unto Tahtinen, 1979: 25). Unto Tahtinen further notes that Gandhi "stresses that there is a higher Truth which lies beyond countless partial truths and factual knowledge" (Unto Tahtinen, 1979: 25). Thus, for Gandhi, empirical and factual knowledge can be valid in its own field; it may even be necessary and useful. Nevertheless, we must recognize its limited character. Facts cannot replace the absolute Truth, nor can they take its place. Facts, however true they may be, only have values when they have the proper place in the context of Absolute Truth.

Like sense perception, Gandhi attributes limited value to rationality and reason also. He noted that "Experience has humbled me enough to let me realize the specific limitations of reason. Just as matter misplaced becomes dirt, reason misused becomes lunacy" (Prabhu and Rao, 2002: 63). He further mentions, 'rationalists are admirable beings' but 'rationalism is a hideous monster when it claims for itself omnipotence'. Moreover, "attribution of omnipotence to reason is as bad a piece of idolatry as is worship of stock and stone believing it to be God" (Prabhu and Rao, 2002, 63). But he also reminds that "I plead not for the suppression of reason, but for a due recognition of that in us which sanctifies reason" (Prabhu and Rao, 2002: 63).

Gandhi's writings on knowledge confirm that he is less concerned about its value in the term of mundane and he seems to be more concerned about its spiritual significance or applicability. In a letter to Bhagwanji Pandya, he conveys his meaning of knowledge, "Knowledge means the realization of the self. One who has fully realized truth and non-violence is a perfect *jnani* in spite of being unlettered" (CWMG: 55: 44). Further, in a Letter to Naran Das, he again mentioned the meaning of knowledge, ".... we may consider the definition of knowledge contained in Chapter XIII of the *Gita*. We are there told that humility, *amanitvam* etc., constitute knowledge and that all the rest is ignorance. If this is true—and there is no doubt that it is true—much that we hug today as knowledge is ignorance pure and simple, and therefore only does us harm instead of conferring any benefit. It makes the mind wander and even reduces it to a vacuity, and discontent flourishes in endless ramifications of evil"(CWMG:44: 104).

Gandhi's epistemology is based mostly on his reading and interpretation of *Gita* that we will examine in detail in the next chapter. What is to be noted here is that Gandhi's views on knowledge defy those forms of Western epistemology that exclusively believes on empiricism or rationalism as the only source of valid knowledge.[3] We have noted Gandhi criticizes the 'omnipotence to reason' and consider it 'as bad a piece of idolatry'. At another place, he convincingly notes that 'rational explanation' has own significance but taking it as 'only one' to understand the life and world is problematic. He argues that 'reason' cannot be given 'highest place' when we think about beyond the mundane. He noted,

> "...if you say that nothing is beyond rational explanation, you will certainly run into difficulties. If we give the highest place to reason, we shall be faced with serious difficulties. Our own *atman* is beyond reason. People have indeed tried to prove its existence with logical arguments...Reason may be a useful instrument of knowledge at one stage. But

> anybody who stops there will never enjoy the benefits of true spiritual knowledge, in the same way that intellectual knowledge of the benefits of eating food does not by itself help one to enjoy those benefits. God or the atman is not an object of knowledge. He Himself is the Knower. That is why we say that He is above reason. There are two stages of knowledge of God. The first is faith, and the second and the last is the first-hand experience to which faith leads. We know from experience that reason can be all too easily deceived. But, we have not known anybody, howsoever mighty he may be, who could deceive true faith" (CWMG: 49: 399-400).

Thus, in Gandhi's view reason is only 'an instrument of knowledge' and it should be taken only as 'an instrument' and not as the final authority of everything. It is helpful but not the omnipotent. For him, one must use reason where it is applicable but there are areas where reason cannot work. On that occasion, it is 'faith' that works. He noted, "There are subjects where reason cannot take us far and we have to accept things on faith. Faith then does not contradict reason but transcends it. Faith is a kind of sixth sense which works in cases which are without the purview of reason" (Prabhu and Rao, 2002: 63).

Thus, when reason does not work Gandhi invokes faith. Moreover, for him, faith is a kind of 'sixth sense'. Most important to mark out is that Gandhi does not see reason and faith contradictory to each other. In fact, he suggests that 'faith transcends reason' when intellect fails. In an interview with Mott, he spoke, "Intellect takes us along in the battle of life to a certain limit but at the crucial moment it fails us. Faith transcends reason. It is when the horizon is the darkest and human reason is beaten down to the ground that faith shines brightest and comes to our rescue. It is such faith that our youth require and this comes when one has shed all pride of intellect and surrendered oneself entirely to His will" (CWMG:44; 60).

Nevertheless, for Gandhi faith does not mean dogmatic religious belief. He defines faith as 'a living, wide-awake consciousness of God within'. He considers the power of faith in term of spirituality, "It is faith that steers us through stormy seas, faith that moves mountains and faith that jumps across the ocean. That faith is nothing but a living, wide-awake consciousness of God within. He who has achieved that faith wants nothing. Bodily diseased, he is spiritually healthy; physically poor, he rolls in spiritual riches" (Prabhu and Rao, 2002: 63). Gandhi's writings on faith suggest that he perceives it in a very unconventional way. He did not view faith only in the form of 'living consciousness of God within', as mentioned above, but also noted that it is fundamental nature of the world. In his words, "Without faith, this world would come to naught in a moment. True faith is the appropriation of the reasoned experience of people whom we believe to have lived a life purified by prayer and penance. Belief, therefore, in prophets or incarnations who have lived in remote ages is not an idle superstition but a satisfaction of an inmost spiritual want" (Prabhu and Rao, 2002: 63).

Gandhi takes faith to a very deeper level and locates individual faith in the whole scheme of universe or God. Man is not alone he/she is the part of God. By the example of a 'little drop' and 'ocean' Gandhi shows how faith works. In his journal *Harijan* dated 3 June, 1939, he noted,

> Everyone has faith in God though everyone does not know about it. For, everyone has faith in himself and that multiplied to the nth degree is God. The sum total of all that lives is God. We may not be God but we are of God—even as a little drop of water is of the ocean. Imagine it torn away from the ocean and flung millions of miles away. It becomes helpless torn from its surroundings and cannot feel the might and majesty of the ocean. But if someone could point out to it that "it is of the ocean, its faith would revive, it would dance with joy and the whole of the might and majesty of the ocean would be reflected in it.
>
> Gandhi also argues that knowledge must be combined with faith. "I know it from experience that where knowledge has not been combined with faith, faith has quickly evaporated, and glorious beginnings have ended in smoke (CWMG: 34: 352).

These discussions lead us to recognize the fact that for Gandhi 'reason' and 'sense perception' is not the only faculty through which one gains knowledge. They have a limited role in our life.[4] They play a significant role in our physical world but for the spiritual world, one needs to rely on faith. He developed even a formula on 'Faith *versus* Reason', "The formula, therefore, I have humbly suggested for guidance is rejection of every demand for faith where a matter is capable of present proof, and unquestioned acceptance on faith of that which is incapable of proof except through personal experience" (CWMG: 33:232).

It might be argued: how does Gandhi reach to his notion of faith? Does he come to this by scripture? Gandhi repeatedly mentions the Hindu Holy Scripture *Gita* when he remarks about knowledge. As scripture as the source of valid knowledge is well accepted in Hindu philosophical tradition, does he completely follow it as a source of valid knowledge? In other words, does Gandhi believe that Hindu scripture is divine composition, or they are limited by time and space? How does he interpret scripture and, moreover, who has the right to interpret the scriptures? Does he accept scripture in its totality or in part in his epistemological formulations? These questions may be attempted by his response to the questions related to faith, scripture, and reason asked by either his followers or some other.

Although Gandhi believes in 'divine knowledge', however, he wrote that it cannot entirely be borrowed from 'books' or 'scriptures'. In his words, 'It [knowledge] has to be realized in oneself'. Further in his view, "Books are at best an aid, often even a hindrance" (CWMG:24:402). Gandhi acknowledges the scripture as an authority but with certain limitations. In his view, scripture should not be in 'conflict with reason' or 'the dictates of hearts'. It should also not 'supplant reason'. In his words, "I would reject all authority if it is in conflict with sober reason or the dictates of the heart. Authority sustains and ennobles the weak when it is the handiwork of reason, but it degrades them when it supplants reason, sanctioned by the still small Voice within" (CWMG: 19:85).

Thus, the primacy of reason plays a key role in Gandhi's views on scripture as the source of knowledge. He argues that scriptural texts are 'inspired book', nevertheless, they cannot be taken as the final source of knowledge. His argument is 'divine knowledge' does not come 'directly from the God' and they are mediated by the process of 'double distillations'. To quote him, when he was asked about the place of authority as the source of knowledge:

> "I exercise my judgment about every scripture, including the *Gita*. I cannot let a scriptural text supersede my reason. Whilst I believe that the principal books are inspired, they suffer from a process of double distillation. Firstly they come through a human prophet, and then through the commentaries

> of interpreters. Nothing in them comes from God directly. Mathew may give one version of one text and John may give another. I cannot surrender my reason whilst I subscribe to divine revelation. And above all, "the letter killeth, the spirit giveth life." But you must not misunderstand my position. I believe in faith also, in things where reason has no place, e.g. the existence of God. No argument can move me from that faith, and like that little girl who repeated against all reason "yet we are seven" I would like to repeat, on being baffled in argument by a very superior intellect, "Yet there is God" (CWMG:64:75).

Thus, Gandhi gives primacy of reason, but at the same time, he also gives a significant place to faith in a situation 'when reason has no place, e.g. the existence of God'.

Gandhi had also developed his own method to interpret the scripture. He did not interpret the scripture 'literally' but tried to get 'the spirit' of it. Moreover, he applied the 'test of Truth and Ahimsa' for 'interpretation of the scripture'. As he noted,

> "I am not a literalist. Therefore, I try to understand the spirit of the various scriptures of the world. I apply the test of Truth and Ahimsa laid down by these very scriptures for interpretation. I reject what is inconsistent with that test, and I appropriate all that is consistent with it. The story of a Shudra having been punished by Ramachandra for daring to learn the Vedas I reject as an interpolation. And in any event, I worship Rama, the perfect being of my conception, not a historical person facts about whose life may vary with the progress of new historical discoveries and researches. Tulsidas had nothing to do with the Rama of history. Judged by historical test, his Ramayana would be fit for the scrap-heap. As a spiritual experience, his book is almost unrivalled at least for me. And then, too, I do not swear by every word that is to be found in so many editions published as the Ramayana of Tulsidas. It is the spirit running through the book that holds me spell-bound" (CWMG:28:111).

Thus, we find, Gandhi does not recognize scripture for its historical significance or factual point of view but looks at it as 'a spiritual experience'. It is in this sense Gandhi gives importance to scriptures because they may serve as 'a spiritual guide'. The words of scripture are not important but its spirit running through it.

Now it might be argued: who has the right to interpret scripture? For Gandhi, interpreting scripture is not an academic exercise and if it is so it is of no value.[5] A learned person can make learned interpretation of scriptures, but according to Gandhi, that will not be the 'true interpretation'. For Gandhi, logic and rational analysis are not so important in interpreting a scripture but it is the 'prayerful study' of scriptures and 'experiences' of the interpreter that makes interpretations really true. Gandhi mentions that one must have the right capacity for correct interpretations of scripture. This right capacity includes; spiritual discipline and practice of Yamas and Niyamas. To quote him,

> "A prayerful study and experience are essential for a correct interpretation of the scriptures. The injunction that a Shudra may not study the scriptures is not entirely without meaning. A Shudra means a spiritually uncultured, ignorant man. He is more likely than not to misinterpret the Vedas and other scriptures. Everyone cannot solve an algebraical equation. Some preliminary study is a *sine qua non*. How will the grand truth "I am Brahman" lie in the mouth of a man steeped in sin! To what ignoble purposes would he turn it! What a distortion it would suffer at his hands! A man, therefore, who would interpret the scriptures must have the spiritual discipline. He must practice the Yamas and Niyamas—the eternal guides of conduct. A superficial practice thereof is useless. The Shastras have enjoyed the necessity of a *Guru*. But a *Guru* being rare in these days, a study of modern books inculcating *bhakti* has been suggested by the sages. Those who are lacking in *bhakti*, lacking in faith, are all qualified to interpret the scriptures. The learned may draw an elaborately learned interpretation out of them, but that will not be the true interpretation. Only the experienced will arrive at the true interpretation of the scriptures. But even for the inexperienced, there are certain canons. That interpretation is not true which conflicts with Truth. To one who doubts even Truth, the scriptures have no meaning. No one can contend with him" (Gandhi, 1959: 11).

Gandhi seems to fix certain criterion to interpret scriptures. First, for him, any interpretation of scripture that is in conflict with Truth is not the true interpretation. Truth is fundamental to him and every other thing is secondary even the scripture and its interpretations. Second, even in interpreting scripture, one must have faith in Truth otherwise 'the scriptures have no meaning'. Third, 'For understanding the meaning of Shastra one must have a well-cultivated moral sensibility and experience in the practice of their truth' (CWMG:28:314). Fourth, in determining the meaning of a text in a Shastra, one should not stick to the letter but its spirit, its meaning in the total context" (CWMG: 28:318).

Finally, it might be discussed from which source of knowledge, Gandhi claims an inner voice as Truth. This includes a serious question raised by many; how can Gandhi claim inner voice as Truth as an inner voice is subjective while Truth must be objective?

Before we deal with the above question, let us examine Gandhi's notion of it as closely as possible. We noticed in the previous chapter that Gandhi answered the question, what is Truth, by saying that "it is what the voice within tells you". At face value, this idea refers to the method, how one may get the required insight. But, if we go deeper we notice that the answer also includes the idea, that it is a person, an individual, who is the authority of this knowledge. It is not the cultural tradition, a Holy Book nor any social or state organization to determine the content of Truth. It is an individual and he alone, in the final analysis, after discussion with others and seriously pondering, makes the decision. In this case, the source of understanding the nature of truth is neither analytic nor synthetic reasoning, at least not that alone. As Gandhi mentioned, "put all your knowledge, learning and scholarship in one scale and truth and purity in the other and the latter will by far outweigh the other" (CWMG: 39:430). We have also noted that Gandhi does not give value to the mere intellectual conception of the things of life. It is the spiritual conception which eludes the intellect. In his view, God must rule the heart and transform it. Thus, Gandhi argues that it is purity of thought or mind and heart that makes one fit to listen to his inner voice. For such an inner voice one should have the patience to acquire the necessary qualifications.

As hinted earlier, there is an argument that inner voice is a subjective feeling as it is grounded on subjectivity. And if an inner voice is taken as truth, as Gandhi argues, then the truth will be rooted in subjectivity. In that case, there will be no common standard of applying the truth. Then, it is possible that there will be conflicting inner voices of different people. Thus, in the absence of explanatory value or objective standard, inner voice cannot be the basis of truth. As we will see, for Gandhi this is a simplistic argument against the inner voice.

For Gandhi, an inner voice is not a 'subjective matter' as many argue. Also, it is not a 'hallucination' as many people believe. For him, an inner voice is a 'scientific truth' that can be tested only with essential qualifications'. Interestingly Gandhi suggests that 'Inner Voice' can also be expressed as 'dictates of reason'. On Inner Voice, in his one of the valuable writings, he mentioned,

> "There is no question of hallucination. I have stated a simple scientific truth, thus to be tested by all who have the will and the patience to acquire the necessary qualifications, which are again incredibly simple to understand and easy enough to acquire where there is determination. I can only say: "You have to believe no one but yourselves. You must try to listen to the Inner Voice, but if you won't have the expression "Inner Voice", you may use the expression "dictates of reason", which you should obey, and if you will not parade God, I have no doubt you will parade something else which in the end will prove to be God, for fortunately, there is no one and nothing else but God in this universe." I would also submit that it is not everyone claiming to act on the urge of the Inner Voice (who) has that urge. After all, like every other faculty, this faculty for listening to the still small Voice within requires previous effort and training, perhaps much greater than what is required for the acquisition of any other faculty, and even if out of thousands of claimants only a few succeed in establishing their claim, it is well worth running the risk of having and tolerating doubtful claimants. A person falsely claiming to act under the divine inspiration of the promptings of the Inner Voice without having any such, will fare worse than the one falsely claiming to act under the authority of an earthly sovereign. Whereas the latter on being exposed will escape with an injury to his body the former may perish body and soul together. Charitable critics impute no fraud to me but suggest that I am highly likely to be acting under some

> hallucination. The result for me, even then, will not be far different from what it would be if I was laying a false claim. A humble seeker that I claim to be has need to be most cautious and, to preserve the balance of mind, he has to reduce himself to zero before God will guide him. Let me not labour this point" (Prabhu and Rao, 2002: 32).

Thus, Gandhi warns, "Everyone should, therefore, realize his limitations before he speaks of his Inner Voice. Therefore, we have the belief based on experience, that those who would make individual search after truth as God, must go through several vows, as for instance the vow of truth, the vow of *brahmacharya,* — for you cannot possibly divide your love for Truth and God with anything else — the vow of non-violence, of poverty and non-possession. Unless you impose on yourself the five vows, you may not embark on the experiment at all" (Prabhu and Rao, 2002: 42).

Thus, in Gandhi's view, an Inner Voice is not something 'mystic' but it is 'a scientific truth' that can be tested. As scientific inquiry needs some training and preconditions, Gandhi argues that one must go through some training and follow preconditions needed to listen to one's own inner voice. He wrote, "Just as for conducting scientific experiments there is an indispensable scientific course of instruction, in the same way, strict preliminary discipline is necessary to qualify a person to make experiments in the spiritual realm."

This precondition, as discussed, includes Yamas and Niyamas. One also requires determination to listen to inner voice. Moreover, one also has to 'reduce himself to zero before God will guide him' and he/she could listen to the inner voice. Gandhi also seems to suggest that the inner voice is irrespective of religion and one can listen to it even by following the reason, what he calls 'dictates of reason'. The explanation is that as he mentions, "if you will not parade God, I have no doubt you will parade something else which in the end will prove to be God, for, fortunately, there is no one and nothing else but God in this universe."

Lastly, it might be argued; how are Gandhi's metaphysics and epistemology related to his notion of action? We have noted, Gandhi believed that every human being had the ability to know the Truth. This capacity also casts a task on the human being to make an effort to realize the Truth. It requires faith in Absolute Truth and experimenting with partial truths what he calls relative truth. For relative truth, one must use empirical evidence and use reason like scientists. Thus, in the field of inquiry on external phenomena, for Gandhi, empirical evidence and reason are supreme, and cannot be ignored or substituted by anyone who wanted to identify Truth. However, one must realize that it is not enough, there are domains where reason and empirical truth cannot work and at that time one needs faith. The human being needs efforts even for faith. The efforts call for total commitment and constant endeavour. In realizing the truth, one has to be prepared to renounce or steer away from all that distracts, to consecrate one's mental and physical energy. As we have noted, Gandhi believed that the quest for truth had to follow the scientific method. It is not surprising that he described religion as the 'science of the soul'. As in the case of other sciences, this science too had its own discipline and its own system of training for the seeker. This inevitably leads one to perform an action based on deep metaphysics and epistemology.

Summing up

Let us summarize the argument discussed in this chapter. Epistemologically, Gandhi's source of Absolute Truth is Hindu scripture. He took the idea of Absolute Truth from Hindu scripture and elaborated it in his own style. For him, Absolute Truth, which is known by faith, is beyond our empirical grasp. The corollary of this notion is that we must act in the knowledge that we are holding on to such truth as we are able to apprehend in this world. This indicates to his view on the relative truth which is empirical in nature. However, it does not mean the knowledge of relative truth is possible only through sense perception. In fact, Gandhi assigned a very limited role to the sense perception when he discussed the realization of Truth of any kind and regarded sense perception as 'deceptive'. Gandhi acknowledged 'reason' as 'an instrument of knowledge' to realize the truth but he also showed its limitations. He argued that reason cannot be given 'highest place'. He also criticized the 'omnipotence to reason' and considered it 'as bad a piece of idolatry'. Gandhi seems to suggest that empirical or factual knowledge or knowledge through reason can be valid in its own field; it may even be necessary and useful. Nevertheless, we must recognize its limited character. Facts cannot replace the Absolute Truth, nor can they take its place. Facts, however true they may be, only have values when they have the proper place in the context of Absolute Truth. For Gandhi, empirical knowledge and reason are applicable in certain areas but there are areas where they cannot work. On that occasion, it is 'faith' that works. Gandhi recognizes faith as 'sixth sense' and most importantly he does not see reason and faith 'contradictory' to each other. He suggests that 'faith transcends reason' when intellect fails. He defines faith as 'a living, wide-awake consciousness of God within' and viewed it as 'a satisfaction of an inmost spiritual want'. However, in Gandhi's epistemology, faith does not entirely come from scripture. Gandhi acknowledges the scripture as an authority but scripture is not final. In his view, scripture is 'best aid' or 'spiritual guide' for spiritual progress but it should not be in 'conflict with reason' or 'the dictates of hearts' or 'supplant reason'. For him, scriptural texts are 'inspired book' and they cannot be taken as the final source of knowledge as they 'suffer' from 'a process of double distillations'. Moreover, Gandhi also developed his own criterion to interpret the scripture. He applied the 'test of Truth and Ahimsa' for 'interpretation of the scripture'. Further, he argued that interpreter of scripture must follow Yama and Niyamas and have a living faith in Truth otherwise 'the scriptures have no meaning'. Finally, on the issue of inner voice as Truth, we notice that Gandhi points out that inner voice is not something mystic or 'a kind of hallucination' but it is 'a scientific truth' that can be tested. As scientific inquiry needs some training and preconditions, Gandhi argues that one must go through some training and follow preconditions needed to listen to one's own inner voice. His metaphysics and epistemology, in its dynamics and power, convince one to perform an action for oneself and others.

Notes

1. He also called himself Santani Hindu. He wrote, "I call myself a Sanatani Hindu, because,
   (i) I believe in the Vedas, the Upanishads, the Puranas and all that goes by the name of Hindu scriptures, and therefore in Avataras and rebirth;
   (ii) I believe in the Varanshrama Dharma in a sense, in my opinion, strictly Vedic but not in its present popular and crude sense;
   (iii) I believe in the protection of the cow in its much larger sense than the popular; and
   (iv) I do not disbelieve in idol-worship." (CWMG: 35: 166).

2. Gandhi noted, "Sense perceptions can be and often are false and deceptive, however real they may appear to us. Where there is realization outside the senses it is infallible. It is proved not by extraneous evidence but in the transformed conduct and character of those who have felt the real presence of God within. Such testimony is to be found in the experiences of an unbroken line of prophets and sages in all countries and climes. To reject this evidence is to deny oneself. This realization is preceded by an immovable faith. He who would in his own personal test the fact of God's presence can do so by a living faith and since faith itself cannot be proved by extraneous evidence the safest course is to believe in the moral government of the world and therefore in the supremacy of the moral law, the law of truth and love. The exercise of faith will be the safest where there is a clear determination summarily to reject all that is contrary to truth and love". (CWMG: 37: 349-50).
3. Here lays a difference of opinion between the Western Natural Law-scholars and Gandhi. According to the Western tradition, the higher law is discoverable by reason alone. This is so because Natural Law ideology has grown up in opposition to the positive law. But Gandhi calls to fasting and prayer to purify the mind. The moral requirements are self-purification and inward search. Gandhi claims that truth is by nature self-evident. It shines clear as soon as you remove the cobwebs of ignorance that surround it. It appears that knowledge of truth has primarily moral and spiritual requirements; reasoning is secondary and cannot succeed without those primary conditions.
4. Intuition, love, forgiveness etc. are also the instruments of knowledge. Though for modern rationalists all these aspects of human personality do not play any role as far as knowledge (the instrumental one) is concerned, Gandhi in contrast thought that role of emotions, which we gained through experience, have their own importance.
5. He writes on who is really eligible to study Gita. He notes, 'While it is open to all to revel in the poetry of the *Gita*' (CWMG: 32: 233, 292), the 'earnest seeker should observe *yama* and *niyama* and other rules of discipline, should acquire *adhikara* or fitness, before taking up the study of the *Gita*' (CWMG: 32:vii). He further noted "We should study and understand the *Gita* not merely to satisfy our curiosity but with the aim of putting its teaching into practice.... We should leave alone what we cannot put into practice. It is a misuse of our intellectual energy and a waste of time to go on reading what we cannot put into practice" (CWMG: 32: 227-8).

References

Bondurant, J. (1957). *Conquest of Violence*. Princeton: Princeton University.
Gandhi, M.K. (1959). *Message of Gita*. Ahmedabad: Navajivan.

Gandhi, M.K. (2013). *An Autobiography or My Experiments with Truth*. Ahmedabad: Navajivan.

Gandhi, M.K. (2014). *From Yervada Mandir.* Ahmedabad: Navajivan.

Glyn Richards. (1982). The Philosophy *of Gandhi*. London: Curzon Press.

Prabhu, R.K. and U.R. Rao. (2002). *The Mind of Mahatma* Gandhi. Ahmedabad: Navajivan.

Unto Tahtinen, (1979). *The Core of Gandhi's Philosophy.* New Delhi: Abhinav Publication.

The Collected Works of Mahatma Gandhi, (*CWMG*), Vol. 1-100, New Delhi: Publication Division Government of India. Retrirom https://www.gandhiheritageportal.org.

Varma, Ravindra. (2001). *The Spiritual Basis of Satyagraha*. Ahmedabad: Navajivan.

4

Epistemological Basis of Gandhi's Action

Gandhi's views on Truth provided direction to his thought and action; and we noticed in the previous chapter that those views were organically linked with his views on reason, faith, and experiences. These two inseparable philosophical categories, his metaphysics and epistemology, provided bedrock to his engagement with active action in personal/public life. It is not surprising to note that Gandhi claimed, "Truth and Life in a sense are one and the same. I should give the same definition for Truth as I have given for Life" (qtd. in Sethi, 1994: 6). In regard to the guiding principle of his life, he mentioned, "The doctrine that has guided my life is not one of inaction but of the highest action" (CWMG: 76:232). Thus, Truth, Life, and Action are interrelated in Gandhi's worldview and they are inseparable.

Yet, for analytical purpose, it might be asked: what are the elements that really constitute an action in Gandhi's view? Or, what is the basis and nature of Gandhi's action? From where does Gandhi get inspiration for his views on the action? And finally, how his views on action are related to his theory of knowledge? This chapter chiefly attempts to respond to these questions.

To begin with, consider the nature and basis/criterion of Gandhi's action. Taking sustenance from his metaphysical position of Truth, Gandhi argues that our action should be moral and corresponding to the broad value of Truth. In fact, Gandhi viewed the action in terms of morality and he saw morality as 'basis of things' which is a corollary of truth and just knowledge. As he noted in his *Autobiography*, "Morality is the basis of things and truth is the substance of all morality" (Gandhi, 2013: 32). Thus, Gandhi's action is moral action in nature.

Gandhi makes a difference between 'moral action' and 'conventional action or behaviour'. In his small booklet *Ethical*

Religion, he observes, "Most of our actions are probably non-moral; they do not necessarily involve morality. For the most part we act according to the prevailing on conventions. Such conventional behaviour is often necessary. If no such rules are observed, anarchy would be the result, and society-social intercourse would come to an end. Still the mere observance of custom and usage cannot properly be called morality" (Gandhi, 2014 a: 11).

The moral action in Gandhi's worldview is not only directed by his metaphysics but it is also based on his view that action should be volitional. He observed, "A moral act must be our own act; it must spring from our own will. If we act mechanically, there is no moral content in our act" (Gandhi, 2014 a: 11). In fact, volition is the nucleus of moral action, and voluntary actions by individuals, in Gandhi's paradigm, are to be performed knowingly and intelligently by self-conscious individuals who have a choice of ends and means. In other words, for Gandhi individual should have control over their actions, otherwise they cannot be held responsible for them. Thus, in Gandhi's view, moral action must be the product of a voluntary will. The corollary of this argument is that, as he argues, the moral action must be free from compulsion, fear, and coercion. He noted, "...an act to be moral it has to be free from fear and compulsion" (Gandhi, 2014a: 13). The reason is that fear and coercion obstruct the growth of human personality and he/she cannot reach to the truth that he/she desires for. Moreover, the action of a man under compulsion is not free and voluntary, thus, cannot have moral worth.

Secondly, for Gandhi, 'good intent' is another criterion of moral action. We have examined that Gandhi sees an organic relation among the thought, speech, and action of the individual. For him, it is not enough that the action performed by us is in itself good, but it should inevitable arise out of good intention. An action is moral when it is morally right without any reference to any personal benefit that may accrue from it. In his words, "It is not enough that an act done by us is in itself good; it should have been done with the intention to do good. That is to say whether an act is moral or otherwise depends upon the intention of the doer" (Gandhi, 2014a: 12). He clarifies this point by an illustration that how an action may look same from outside but its content may be different. He notes, "Two men may have done exactly the same thing, but the act of one may be moral, and that of the other contrary. Take, for instance, a man who out of great pity feeds the poor and another who does the same, but with the motive of winning prestige or with some such selfish end. Though the action is the same, the act of the one is moral and that of the other non-moral" (Gandhi, 2014a: 12).

Third, related to it, in Gandhi's paradigm, an action is morally good if it is done in the spirit of Kantian dictum; 'Duty for duty's sake'. In his words, 'That action is moral which is done only for the sake of doing good'. He further noted in his booklet *Ethical religion*, "If a man does some good deed, he does not do it to win applause; he does it because he must" (Gandhi, 2014a: 8). It implies a person should 'act without self-interest'. However, he observes that "This is not to say that actions prompted by self-interest are all worthless, but only that to call them moral would detract from the [dignity of the] moral idea" (Gandhi, 2014a: 13-14). Thus, in his view, "...all that we need to see is that the act is good and is done with a good intention. The result of an action is not within our control. God alone is the giver of fruit" (Gandhi, 2014a: 12). Thus, one must act without expecting reward or result. He categorically states that "The result of an action is not within our control." Thus, the action that arises from self-interest or initiated by the hope of happiness, mundane or otherworldly, has no moral worth because the intent is not pure. As we will see later on this was the result of Gandhi's reading of *Gita*.

Fourth and that is the most significant criterion of Gandhi's action is the 'universality' of action. He writes, "....the higher morality must be comprehensive; it must embrace all men. Considering our relation to mankind, every man has claims over us, as it is our duty to serve him" (Gandhi, 2014 a: 27). What Gandhi seems to suggest is that action must be universal in a sense that that could be performed by all men under similar circumstances, irrespective of place and time. If an action is motivated by selfish ends it becomes subjective and lacks universality which is a prime requirement in Gandhian paradigm. Thus, for Gandhi, an action can have moral worth only when it serves a universal end, i.e. a moral action must be universalized.

The fifth feature of Gandhi's views on an action is its practicability. Gandhi tried to introduce moral value in public life. Thus, to him, moral ideals had value only if they could control 'the practical ordering of our lives'. He wrote in his booklet *Ethical religion,* "And mere knowledge is not enough, it should be followed by appropriate action. An ethical idea is like an architect's plan. The plan shows how the building should be constructed, but it becomes useless if the building is not raised accordingly. Similarly, an ethical idea is useless so long as it is not followed by suitable action" (Gandhi, 2014a: 7). It does not mean that Gandhi's views on action are utilitarian. In fact, it goes beyond 'benefit' and 'harm'. He does not equate 'good act' as 'beneficial' and 'bad act' as 'harmful'. In his words, whether a certain act is good or bad does *not* depend upon whether it is beneficial or harmful to us.

Thus, in short, for Gandhi, action should be moral and it can be called moral if it volitional, intentional, universal, practical, selfless and free from fear and compulsion simultaneously. If anyone of the above factors is lacking it would not be a moral action in the Gandhi's sense. Furthermore, 'a moral action should be performed consciously, deliberately with the determined will, regardless of gain and loss, of life or death, without turning to look back, ready to sacrifice themselves' (Gandhi, 2014a: 20).

Having examined the nature of Gandhi's action, let us examine, from where does Gandhi get inspiration for his views on the action. Before we deal with this question, we need to remind that Gandhi saw the spiritual life as inseparable from the action in this mundane world. In fact, he tried to unify spiritual life with 'action in this world' which included the active life in the fields of politics, economics, and social reform. This was path-breaking because in Hindu tradition spiritual tradition and engaging with the world are two un-unifiable separate category. The inseparability of the spiritual life and mundane life, in Gandhi's paradigm, originates from his reading and understanding of *Gita*. We have also noted, he argues, that one should act without expecting any results as the result of the action is not in the hands of its doer. Gandhi adopted these views on the action from *Gita* that teaches *Karm yoga* and *anasakt karma*.[1]

It needs to be pointed out that no other book or scripture influenced Gandhi and transformed his life as profoundly and permanently as did the *Bhagavad Gita*. Among the many books he read, *Gita* alone became an unfailing source of strength and solace to him in the darkest hours of his life. As a 'spiritual reference book' (CWMG:41:91), the *Gita* was not only his constant companion; it was his 'eternal mother' whom he esteemed even more than his earthly mother.

Thus, it will be relevant to assess Gandhi's interpretation of Gita to know his views on the action.[2] In this context, it will be also substantially useful to analyze Gandhi's re-defined and expanded view of *Gita's* '*Yajna*' that he employed for an 'act' or 'action'.[3]

Of the three paths of *moksha* mentioned in the Gita—those of action, knowledge, and devotion—Gandhi favoured the path of action.[4] It does not mean that others were ignored but he focused on the primacy of action. The metaphor he employed to show the primacy of action is revealing; 'action is the sun, and contemplation and devotion were its satellite'. Thus, in preferring action to contemplation and devotion, Gandhi was not undermining the importance of these paths that the *Gita* recognized. What is remarkable is that contemplation and devotion were to move around the action. As Parel argues 'The reason was that the other two if given undue emphasis, had a tendency to promote a world–abandoning sort of spirituality" (Parel, 2006: 190). Moreover, "Such spirituality did not do justice to human existence in time. It did not encourage work or action—socially and politically necessary work" (Parel, 2006: 190).

On the other hand, for Gandhi, action or work was essential for the regeneration of the nation and the spiritual re-awakening of the Indian. Thus, the philosophy of action or *Gita's karmayoga* became the core of Gandhi's interpretation of *Gita*.[5]

Gandhi was, in fact, inspired by a very significant notion that *Gita* peaches: *Karm-falyaga* or *Nishkaam-Karma*.[6] He views it in the form of *Anasakti*. Therefore, he notes that *Anasakti* or non-attachment to the fruits of one's actions is the principal message of the *Gita*.[7] For him, an action or work has to be done in the spirit of *Karm yoga*. To meet the standard of *Karm yoga* several conditions had to be met. First, it had to be done in the spirit of detachment; "action or work alone is your proper business, never the fruits thereof; let not your motive be the fruit of works", was the injunction of *Gita II:47* that Gandhi approved. He was also heavily influenced by the verse *Gita II: 51* that read, "those who have renounced the fruit that is born of works, these will be freed from the bondage of re-birth."

Guided by *Gita*, Gandhi observes that it is impossible for a human being to get rid of any action. There must be an action where there is a body. Action, physical or mental, is bound to occur. It is inherent in human nature. It is, in Gandhi's view, 'law of nature'. He notes, "Our very nature impels us to action. Such being the law of nature, one who sits with folded hands but lets his mind dwell on the objects of sense is a fool and may even be called a hypocrite" (CWMG:49:117).

Thus, Gandhi argues that if we are bound to be busy in action, then, why we should not be careful and engage in some productive action. "Rather than indulge in such senseless inactivity, is it not better that a man should control the senses, overcome his likes and dislikes, and engage himself in some activity or other without fuss and in a spirit of detachment? Do your allotted duty, restraining the organs of sense, for that is better than inaction. An idler will only meet his end the sooner for his idleness. But while acting, remember that action leads to bondage unless it is performed in a spirit of sacrifice" (CWMG: 49:117).

Gandhi's reading of *Gita* also implicates us on how we should perform our action. He tells us that one should act with knowledge and wisdom. Here knowledge does not mean scholarly or academic knowledge. He writes, "It is therefore necessary that all actions should be performed intelligently. This wisdom *(jnana)* is not mere book learning. In it, there is no room for doubt. It begins with faith and ends in experience. It enables a man to see all beings in himself and to see himself in God so that everything appears to him to be actually informed by God. Such wisdom affects the salvation of the worse of sinners. It releases the seeker from the bondage of action so that he is not affected by its results. There is nothing else in the world so holy as this wisdom. Therefore try to obtain it with a heart full of faith in God and with the senses under control, so that you will enjoy perfect peace of mind" (CWMG: 49:123).

But the problem is, as Hindu philosophy informs us, all action bind human being, then, what can be done? On the basis of his reading of *Gita*, Gandhi writes in the 'Preface' of his own interpretation of *Gita*, what is known as *Anasakti Yoga*, "By desireless action; by renouncing fruits of action; by dedicating all activities to God, i.e., by surrendering oneself to Him body and soul" (CWMG: 41:94-5).

Elaborating it, he further writes, "While on the one hand, it is beyond dispute that all action binds, on the other hand, it is equally true that all living beings have to do some work, whether they will or no. Here all activity, whether mental or physical, is to be included in the term action. Then how is one to be free from the bondage of action, even though he may be acting? The manner in which the *Gita* has solved the problem is, to my knowledge, unique. The *Gita* says: 'Do your allotted work but renounce its fruit—be detached and work—have no desire for reward and work'" (CWMG: 41:97).

Anasakti does not mean 'indifference' to result as many think. "In no way it means indifference to result," clarifies Gandhi and explains, "Renunciation means the absence of hankering after fruit, because attachment, worry, haste affect our nervous system and upset the balance of our mind" (CWMG: 41:98). He notes that it is reasonably natural that people feel contentment or disappointment in regard to the outcome of their action. But one should not 'invest all one's energy in fretting over the result', instead of that he notes that one should focus on 'perfecting the work'. Thus, he suggests, "It is not unnatural to feel happy about the good outcome of one's hard work, but it is wasteful, both spiritually and psychologically, to invest all one's emotions and energy in fretting over the results instead of focusing on perfecting the work" (Reference).

The most significant aspect of Gandhi's interpretation of *Gita* is his assertion that *Anasakt karm* is possible only through full observance of Truth and non-violence. It was Gandhi's original interpretation based on his personal experimentation and experience. He wrote, "After 40 years of unremitting endeavor fully to enforce the teaching of the *Gita* in my own life, I have in all humility felt that perfect renunciation is impossible without perfect observance of *satya* and *ahimsa* in every shape and form" (Gandhi, 1945: 11).

Why did Gandhi say that "genuine detachment is possible only through complete truth and non-violence?" In order to understand his bold statement, we need to follow his line of reasoning; it is the desire for the fruit of action that causes a person to get attached to whatever he/she is desiring; and attachment leads to all kinds of erratic or indiscreet behaviors such as lying, cheating, stealing, killing and so on. The underlying cause behind almost all acts of indiscretion, untruth, and violence is the lack of control over one's mind, senses and desires. This lack of self-control leads one to form a strong, irrational attachment to the desired fruit of action (*Gita*, Ch. 2, vs. 62-63). On this basis, Gandhi claimed that although the Gita does not directly preach or endorse *ahimsa*, the idea of non-violence is implicit in its major theme of *Anasakti* or non-attachment. Thus, he notes, "The overall teaching of *Gita* is not violence but non-violence is evident from the argument which begins in Chapter II and ends in Chapter XVIII. The intervening chapters propound the same thing. Violence is simply not possible unless one is driven by anger, by ignorant love and by hatred. The *Gita*, on the other hand, wants us to be incapable of anger and attain to a state unaffacted by the three *gunas*" (CWMG: 28:319).

It is on this philosophical interpretation of *Gita*, Gandhi formulated his idea of action in the form of re-interpreting and expanding the terms *Yajna* and *sacrifice*. In his view, *Yajna* means 'an act directed to the welfare of others, done without desiring any return for it, whether of a temporal or spiritual nature' (Gandhi, 2014b: 38). Gandhi also defines the term 'an act' and 'other' in his writings. He notes, "'Act' here must be taken in its widest sense and includes thought and word, as well as the deed" while "'Others' embraces not only humanity but all life." (Gandhi, 2014b: 38).

In the same manner, Gandhi also redefines the term sacrifice described in *Gita* and relates it to a universal kind of action. "Again, a primary sacrifice must be an act which conduces the most to the welfare of the greatest number in the widest area, and which can be performed by the largest number of men and women with the least trouble. It will not, therefore, be a *yajna*, much less a *mahayajna*, to wish or to do ill to anyone else, even in the order to serve a so-called higher interest. And the *Gita* teaches and experience testifies that all action that cannot come under the category of *yajna* promotes bondage" (Gandhi, 2014b: 39).

Gandhi provides a metaphysical connotation to the term *Yajna*. He places *yajna* or action in the very nature of the Creation and creature. He notes that '*yajna* came with the Creation itself' and argues that this body is not ours but it has been 'given us only in order that we may serve all Creation with it'. Not only this but, he also argued that 'the world cannot subsist for a single moment without *yajna*'. In his words, "The world cannot subsist for a single moment without *yajna* in this sense, and therefore, the *Gita*, after having dealt with true wisdom in the second chapter, takes up in the third the means of attaining it, and declares in so many words that *yajna* came with the Creation itself. This body, therefore, has been given us only in order that we may serve all Creation with it. And therefore, says the *Gita*, he who eats without offering *yajna* eats stolen food. Every single act of one who would lead a life of purity should be in the nature of *yajna*"(Gandhi, 2014b: 39).

We may perceive here that Gandhi takes 'action' to the very nature of Creation and Creator. In other words, action has a metaphysical basis and doing any act or action one must keep the higher objective in mind. Thus, he deduces that an action is a primary 'duty of individual' because 'he is debtor', and he is bound to serve the universe. Moreover, whatever one receives in reward or as the outcome of one's own action should be accepted as a 'gift' by the Lord of the universe.

He states, "*Yajna* having come to us with our birth, we are debtors all our lives, and thus for ever bound to serve the universe. And even as a bond slave receives food, clothing and so on from the master whom he serves, so should we gratefully accept such gifts as may be assigned to us by the Lord of the universe. What we receive must be called a gift; for as debtors we are entitled to no consideration for the discharge of our obligations. Therefore, we may not blame the Master, if we fail to get it. Our body is His to be cherished or cast away according to His will" (Gandhi, 2014b: 39-40).

Extending this argument he further states that the individual should understand one's place in the scheme of God. It is the faith in the God that brings Gandhi into action which he further relates to *Anasakti*. In that case, there will be no 'complaint' or 'pity', if one does not get the desired result from one's action. Thus, in his view, one must understand the whole phenomena of cause and effect and place oneself within the chain of cause and effect and also understand one's own limit to comprehend the totality of cause and effect. In his words, "This is not a matter for complaint or even pity; on the contrary, it is a natural and even a pleasant and desirable state if only we realize our proper place in God's scheme. We do, indeed, need strong faith if we would experience this supreme bliss. "Do not worry in the least about yourself, leave all worry to God,"—this appears to be the commandment in all religions" (Gandhi, 2014b: 40).

But what should be the central motive behind individuals' action? We have noted earlier that for Gandhi Truth or the God is the prime mover. And he sought to realize it through service of others. Thus, for Gandhi, the central motive behind the action is service to others. He also affirms that although many times we act unconsciously and render service to others, we must do it consciously. In his view, this will bring happiness not only to oneself but also to the world at large. He argues, "He who devotes himself to service with a clear conscience will day by day grasp the necessity for it in greater measure, and will continually grow richer in faith. The path of service can hardly be trodden by one who is not prepared to renounce self-interest and to recognize the conditions of his birth. Consciously or unconsciously, everyone of us does render some service or other. If we cultivate the habit of doing this service deliberately, our desire for service will steadily grow stronger and will make not only for our own happiness but that of the world at large" (Gandhi, 2014b: 40).

Gandhi also relates his notion of service to *yajna* and argues that

"*Yajna* as an action is the duty to be performed, or service to be rendered, all the twenty-four hours of the day" (Gandhi, 2014b: 41). A person who does the action from this point of view, Gandhi considers him as *yogi*. He mentions, 'For the *yogi* in terms of the *Gita* is neither a dry-as-dust man of knowledge, nor a devotee carried away by his own enthusiasm, but a selfless performer of action imbued with the spirit of wisdom as well as devotion' (CWMG: 49:131). He also notes, "He who would practice *yoga*, i.e. evenness of temper *(samatvam)*, cannot but perform action" (CWMG: 49:125). "But a man who has purified himself by means of selfless action, who has his mind and his senses under control and who has identified himself with all beings, loving them as himself,— such a man stands apart from action a0lthough he is acting all the time, and is not bound by it" (CWMG:49:123).

For the practical purpose, on the basis of his reading of *Gita*, Gandhi also makes difference among the different kind of action performed by the human being. He notes, "Some actions are motivated by desire. Various activities are indulged in by men with a view to fulfil various desires. These are called *kamya* actions. Then again there are certain necessary and natural actions such as —breathing, eating, drinking, lying down, sitting etc., with a view to keep the body a fit instrument of service. And thirdly, there are actions done with a view to serve others. Giving up *kamya* actions is *Sannyasa*, and renunciation of fruits of all actions is *tyaga* as recommended to you all along" (CWMG:49:145-6). These discussions lead us to recognize that, in Gandhi's view, action should not be mechanical in nature but it must be done consciously, deliberately, with the view to renounce self-interest, and should be performed as duty in the form of rendering service to others. Now consider what Gandhi observes about the outcome of an action.

Gandhi's writings on this issue seem to suggest, as noted earlier, that a man can never have command over the fruit of his action, as the nature of the fruit is determined by a number of independent factors. In his words, "Every action is a resultant of a multitude of forces even of a contrary nature. There is no waste of energy. So we learn in the books on mechanics. This is equally true of human actions. The difference is that in the one case we generally know the forces at work, and when we do, we can mathematically foretell the resultant. In the case of human actions, they result from a concurrence of forces of most of which we have no knowledge. But our ignorance must not be made to serve the cause of disbelief in the power of these forces. Rather is our ignorance a cause for greater faith" (CWMG: 68: 277). He continues, "And non-violence being the mightiest force in the world and also the most elusive in its working, it demands the greatest exercise of faith. Even as we believe in God in faith, so have we to believe in non-violence in faith" (CWMG: 68: 277). Thus, for Gandhi, the primacy of action was more than a way of life, and it was an article of faith. The above statement of Gandhi also serves as an important clue for understanding Gandhi's theory of action and its relation to his theory of knowledge. Although Gandhi does not mention any such relation in a direct way, however, his writings on this theme convincingly and amply suggest to us that he viewed such relation in the light of the teaching of *Gita*.

To understand Gandhi's views on action and its relation to knowledge we need to know the three gunas—*sattva, rajas* and *tamas*, that are in Chapter XIV of the *Gita*. He notes that how these three *gunas* become the basis of corresponding knowledge, action, and intellect. In Gandhi's interpretation (letters on the Gita), the three *gunas* born of nature, viz. *sattva* (goodness), *rajas* (passion) and *tamas* (ignorance) bind the soul down. They may be described respectively as the highest, the middling and the lowest. Of this *sattva* is pure and unsullied and gives light; it is, therefore, the source of happiness. *Rajas* arises from attachment and craving and makes a man indulge in all manner of activities. *Tamas* is rooted in ignorance and delusion and makes one negligent and indolent.

Gandhi makes a difference between three types of knowledge and its corresponding action. He notes. "To realize the essential unity that underlies all diversities is *sattvika* knowledge. In *rajasa* knowledge one holds that there are different souls in different creatures, while in *tamasa* knowledge a man does not know a thing and imagines that everything is mixed up without rhyme and reason" (CWMG:49:146-7). On this basis Gandhi makes a threefold distinction in the form of action. "Similarly there are three kinds of action. Action in which there are no likes and dislikes and no desire for personal gains is *sattvika.* That in which there are a desire for enjoyment, egoism and restlessness is *rajasa* action. And *tamasa* action is one in which no thought at all is given to personal capacity and consequential injury or violence and which is undertaken through delusion" (CWMG:49:147). He also refers to three kinds of intellect *sattvika, rajsaik* and *tamsik.* The *sattvika* intellect is able properly to distinguish between action and non-action, "What must be done, and what must not be done, What should be feared, and what should not be feared, What binds and what emancipates the soul." The *rajasa* intellect tries to draw these distinctions but generally fails to do so correctly, while the *tamasa* intellect "looks upon wrong as right and sees all things contrariwise of truth" (CWMG: 49:147).

He recognizes that action without knowledge has no meaning. Moreover, it is through these two, action and knowledge, the devotion appears. "The *Gita* rightly says that action without knowledge is of no worth. I have had experience of this many times and many others too will have had the experience. If action is informed by knowledge devotion comes on its own. To do this one must always take one's stand on truth. If one has come to realize truth nothing else remains to be done. As we look into a mirror and discover the lightest spots on our faces, so must we look into our hearts" (CWMG: 90:343). Thus, we note is that in Gandhi's worldview *Gyan*, *bhakti* and *karma* merge with each other and they are inseparable in the practical sense.

Yet it might be argued: how does Gandhi view the role of knowledge in the totality of action? On this matter, Gandhi again accepts and interprets the position of *Gita*. The most significant verse, by which Gandhi seems to be influenced by on this issue, is in chapter 18 of the *Gita*. According to *Gita*, "Knowledge, the object of knowledge and knower compose the threefold urge to action; the means, the action and the doer compose the threefold sum of action" (BG, 18:18).[8] Gandhi interprets this verse as; there are three things that inspire action: knowledge, the object of knowledge and the knower. And there are three constituents of action—the organ, the deed and the doer. The thing to be done is the object of knowledge; the method of doing it is knowledge and he who knows it is the knower. After he has thus received an impulse to action, he performs an action in which the senses serve as instruments. Thought is thus translated into action (CWMG:49:146-7).

This view of Gandhi points out his explanation of action in relation to knowledge. The most striking aspect of this explanation is its inclusiveness of action and knowledge. This integration also ensures that the analysis is not confined to the objective elements, but also captures the subjective dimension reflected in the knower and the doer. Secondly, as we may note from the above explanation the concept of action that Gandhi borrowed from the *Gita* makes knowledge just one component of the totality of action. The need for knowledge was itself to be understood only in terms of its impact on action.

Thus, for Gandhi knowledge is only an instrument to action. However, it makes its own demand of the concept of knowledge in Gandhi's worldview. As action cannot be deferred till perfect knowledge is achieved the concept must allow for functioning with less than perfect knowledge. In seeking such a concept of knowledge, Gandhi returned to the *Gita* again; relying quite heavily on Chapter XIII of it. What is striking in the concept of knowledge in this chapter is the explicit acknowledgment of the role of the subjective. The very contention that knowledge continuously changes as a result of the interaction between the understanding of the specific and the understanding of the general reflects a belief that the subjective elements of knowledge cannot be ignored. The *Gita*, in fact, goes further and makes quite explicit, "Knowledge of the field and knower of the field, I hold is true *knowledge*" (BG, c13: v3).

The inclusion of knower in the field of knowledge is revealing. It has many implications. First, it introduces the role of subjective in the concept of knowledge. Second, it shows that subjective knower may co-exist with objective facts. Third, the differentiation between knowledge of field and knower of the field in the system of knowledge demonstrates that knowledge cannot be either entirely subjective or entirely objective. The concept of knowledge that Gandhi borrowed from the *Gita* allows for the field to have an objective truth even as the knower of the field introduces a subjective interpretation of that truth.

As we may deduce, the perception of this dividing line would then vary from person to person. In this case, the *Gita* prescribes that one should have greater knowledge (*Gyan Chakchu*) to see this demarcation. Those who, with the eyes of knowledge, thus, perceive the distinction between the Field and the knower of the Field... they attain to Supreme.

But what is real Knowledge, according to Gandhi? Following *Gita*, Gandhi states that "Real knowledge means discrimination between the Field and the knower of the Field" (CWMG: 49:138). But, what is this field? Gandhi notes, "The five great elements, namely, earth, water, fire, air and ether, individuality (*ahamkara*), intellect, the unmanifest, the ten senses,* mind, the five sense objects, desire and hatred, pleasure and pain, *sanghata* (the power of combination inherent in the constituents of the body), consciousness and cohesion,—these constitute the Field with its modifications" (CWMG:49:138). Gandhi prescribes that knowledge of these is essential, as they have to be renounced. Wisdom is the foundation on which such renunciation can be based. "Wisdom here means and includes humility, unpretentiousness, non-violence, forgiveness, rectitude, service of the teacher, purity, steadfastness, self-restraint, indifference to sense objects, absence of egoism, insight into the evil of birth, death, old age, disease and pain, detachment from wife and children, hearth and home, friends and relations, equimindedness to good and bad fortune, whole-hearted devotion to God, love of solitude, dislike for the enjoyment of sensual pleasures in company with others, thirst for knowledge of the soul, and at last the beatific vision. And the reverse of this is ignorance" (CWMG:49:138).

Thus, Gandhi's action is the outcome of his unified metaphysics, epistemology, and his ethics of truth as well as non-violence. This can be well recognized by juxtaposing one of his writings mentioned in *From Yervada Mandir*. He writes, "Thoughts, which turn us away from God, or do not turn us towards Him, constitute impediments in our way. In this connection we may consider the definition of knowledge contained in the 13th chapter of the *Gita*. We are there told, that humility (*amanitvam*) etc., constitute knowledge, and all the rest is ignorance. If this is true,—and there is no doubt that it is true, much that we hug today as knowledge is ignorance pure and simple, and therefore only does us harm, instead of conferring any benefit. It makes the mind wander, and even reduces it to a vacuity, and discontent flourishes in endless ramifications of evil. Needless to say, this is not a plea for inertia. Every moment of our life should be filled with mental or physical activity, but that activity should be *sattvika*, tending to Truth. One who has consecrated his life to service cannot be idle for a single moment. But we have to learn to distinguish between good activity and evil activity. This discernment goes naturally with a single-minded devotion to service" (Gandhi, 2014: 23).

So far we have discussed Gandhi's views on the action in relation to his metaphysics, epistemology and his reading of *Gita* as *Anasakti yoga*. But his view on the action is not confined to only these. In fact, in his writings, he has used a particular Indian philosophical term *Karma* instead of action. The term *Karma* is a more comprehensive concept than action. Action. whether physical or mental, is only one component of *Karma*.[9] Although the detailed analysis of Gandhi's views on karma in the framework of Indian philosophical system has been discussed in the Chapter 8 of this study, however, some of his important import from Indian Philosophy, in regard to *Karma*, might be considered here briefly. The source of these insights, beyond doubt, is his reading of *Gita*.

First of all, Gandhi accepts the Indian philosophical notion of the law of *karma* that means 'everything that happens is the effect of *Karma*'. Second, he also recognizes that *karma* is 'an unfathomable mystery'. He mentions, "It is perfect logic to say that everything that happens is the effect of *karma*. But the true nature of *karma* is an unfathomable mystery. We mortals are so utterly ignorant that we cannot know all the *karmas* which are the cause of even the most ordinary event. It is, therefore, true to say that everything happens through the grace of God. Really speaking, that is the perfect truth" (CWMG: 49:328).

It is on this grounding Gandhi views human fate in relation to his *karma*. In his view, fate is 'fruition of *karma*'. But he is not deterministic; he argues that human being may act in a way that he could get rid of adverse fate or reduce its impact. He states, "Fate is the fruition of *karma*. Fate may be good or it may be bad. The human effort consists in overcoming adverse fate or reducing its impact. There is a continuous struggle between fate and human effort. Who can say which of the two really wins? Let us therefore continue effort and leave the result to God" (CWMG: 79:258). He firmly argues that one must act at any cost and should not leave everything on destiny. "Between destiny and human endeavour there is an incessant struggle. Let us continue to endeavour and leave the result to God. Let us not leave everything to destiny, nor be vain about our endeavour. Destiny will take its own course. We should only see where we can intervene or where it is our duty to do so, whatever be the result" (CWMG:79:433). As a true *karm yogi* he regrets that "The pity is that even while knowing what our duty is, we fail to perform it! For this, let every man answer to himself" (CWMG:79:433).

Accepting the Indian philosophical position of the law of *Karma* Gandhi believes in rebirth also. He notes what we are today is the result of our *prarabdha Karma*, yet we can not/should not give up action. He mentions, "What we call *prarabdha* is nothing but the fruit of deeds in our previous births. Human efforts mean our attempts to make desirable changes therein. Sometimes one acts in opposition to the other, while at other times they run together harmoniously.

Hence it cannot be said that one is always stronger than the other. We cannot disregard *prarabdha*; we cannot give up human effort. This explains the importance attributed to effort free from attachment (CWMG:32:66). In short, Gandhi believes in the law of *karma* and accepts the role of fate or destiny in human life but he is not deterministic; he strongly favours action. He believes in re-birth also and sees the present birth as the result of deeds of the previous birth, yet, he argues that we cannot give up our human effort.

Summing up

Gandhi's action is the outcome of his metaphysics, epistemology and the ethics of Truth and non-violence. These three are inseparable in his overall philosophy and form a dynamic coherent whole. Thus, his action is logically moral in content, form and nature. Differentiating between 'moral action' and 'conventional action', he argues that moral action is 'moral' because it is volitional, intentional, universal, practical, selfless and free from fear and compulsion simultaneously. He further argues that a moral action should be performed consciously, deliberately with the determined will, regardless of gain and loss, of life or death, without turning to look back, and ready to sacrifice themselves.

Epistemologically, the source of Gandhi's views on the action is primarily *Gita* especially its notion of *Karm-faltyaga* or *Nishkaam-Karma*. In his view, *Anasakti* or non-attachment to the fruits of one's actions is the principal message of the *Gita*. Besides, his views on action are based on his re-interpretation and expansion of the notion *Yajna* mentioned in *Gita*. He viewed *Yajna* as 'an act directed to the welfare of others, done without desiring any return for it, whether of a temporal or spiritual nature'. He also defined it as 'an action', as a 'duty to be performed', and as a 'service to be rendered all the twenty-four hours of the day' for 'others'. Mentioning that action should be 'in the spirit of the Creation and creature', he took the notion of action to its metaphysical level.

His view on the relation between action and knowledge is also deeply influenced by his understanding of *Gita*. He saw knowledge as one component of the totality of action and argued that there are three things that cause action: knowledge, the object of knowledge and the knower. The most striking aspect of his philosophy of action is inclusiveness of action and knowledge. In his illustration, the need for knowledge is itself to be understood only in terms of its impact on the action, thus, the action is the test of the validity of knowledge.

Notes

1. The scholars of Indian philosophy have elucidated the philosophy of Gita, emphasizing the ontological, epistemological, ethical and spiritual arguments of the text. In fact, the very nature of Gita is such that it is open to diverse interpretations. Here we only consider Gandhi's interpretation of Gita and not a general review of other interpretations. Gandhi's commentary on Gita is a discourse of persuasion that represents the value of action for spiritual attainment. The term action includes both its ordinary meaning and specific meaning in the spiritual sense. In fact, as earlier noted, Gandhi deconstructs the binary of ordinary and spiritual sense of action and sees no difference between ordinary and spiritual mundane or spiritual. For him, Gita is the blueprint for his activism.
2. Gandhi's active interest in Gita began in 1889 while he was a law student in London. He read the whole work on it for the first time in Sir Edwin Arnold's translation, *The Song Celestial*. During his prison term of 1922-24, he spent some part of his time preparing a Concordance (*Gita Padarth Koshas*) of the book. This was his first work on Gita. His second major work on Gita was *Gandhijinu Gita Shikshan* (English translation as Discourse on the Gita (CWMG:32:94-376). It is the commentary on 700 verses of the Gita given at Sabarmati Ashram to inmates. His third work on the Gita is Anasakti Yoga published on 12 March 1930. It was translated as The Gospel of Self-less Action or Gita According to Gandhi by Mahadeva Desai (CWMG: 41). The fourth and final work by Gandhi on Gita is 'Gita Bodh' which was written from Yervada prison between 1930-32. The English translation of this book is known as Letters on Gita (CWMG: 49: 111-49).
3. In Gandhi's expanded meaning, *yajna* means "any action performed with a view to the public good" (p. 155). And so the cherishing of the gods (Ch. III. 11) means that "we should serve the humblest human beings, even those whom we never see, with respect and honour and looking upon them as gods and not as our servants; we should, in other words, serve the whole world" (p. 156). (CWMG: 32: viii)
4. Why did Gandhi prefer Gita as a source of his inspiration is that the idea that *sannyasa* or renunciation was not the only way to *moksha* (spiritual liberation) appealed to Gandhi very much, as he himself endeavoured to be both an ardent seeker after truth and a *karmayogi*—a man of action. While remaining active in the world, one can perform all one's activities in the spirit of "*nishkama karma*", that is, without desire for the fruits of action; one can be like a "*sthitaprajna*"—a person well-established in wisdom—who is equipoised, detached, desire less, and dedicated to God.

5. It should be pointed out that Gandhi's interpretation of Gita is characteristically his own and it can be seen in the contrast of those of earlier commentators. Samkara saw the Gita as a work on the spiritual attainment of the *Sanyasi*. Ramanuja and Vallabha found it in the glorification of *Bhakti* and *sagunaupasana*. Tilak stressed *Karma-yoga* and Aurobindo the cultivation of divine consciousness.

   The new things that Gandhi says about the Gita is that; first, it is allegorical, second; Gita teaches non-violence because renunciation is impossible without observing *ahimsa*, and third the attitude of *Anasakti* (selfless action or the spirit of renunciation) is the basis of *karma*.
6. The idea of *karma-falatyaga* (karma: action; *fala*: fruit, and *tyaga*: renouncement) is also conveyed by another Sanskrit term: *nish-kama karma* (*nish*: non; *kama*: desire, and *karma*: action). This principle of renunciation of the desire for the fruits of action recurs like a refrain throughout the Gita; it is particularly emphasized in Sankhya Yoga (Ch. 2, v. 47): "*karmanyevadhikaraste ma phaleshukadachana:* your business is with the action only, never with its fruits;" in *Karma* Yoga (Ch. 3, v. 19): "tasmatasaktahasatatamkaryam karma samachar: therefore, perform action constantly without attachment"; in the Jnanavibhaga Yoga (Ch. 4, v. 20): "*tyaktvakarmaphalasangam*: abandon attachment to the fruit of action"; and in Bhakti Yoga (Ch. 12, v. 11): "*sarvakarma-phala-tyagamtatah kuru yatatmavan*: renounce therefore all fruit of action with self-control."
7. In fact, Gandhi extracted out of the Gita not only the message of non-violence, which is for him was an implicate of the whole conception of renunciation when thought through, but an *ethos of action*. *Gyan* is to be used to understand *situations* and gain insight into possibilities for action; *bhakti* speaks the law of love which enables us to respond to those in need; *karma* is the path not just of action but of *service*. It is through this service by which Constructive programme has to be carried out, not to maintain the stability of society- with all its injustice—but to transform it in accordance with the vision of new society Gandhi called it Ramrajya.
8. Thus there are three-fold factors that propel actions. These are *jñāna* (knowledge), *jñeya* (the object of knowledge), and *jñātā* (the knower). Together, the three are called the *jñānatripurī* (triad of knowledge). Or Knowledge, the object of knowledge, and the knower—these are the three factors that induce action. The instrument of action, the act itself, and the doer—these are the three constituents of action.
9. Monima Chadha gives five separate meanings for *karma*. *Karma* is firstly understood as an act, being physical, mental, intentional, unintentional, moral or amoral etc. *Karma* can further be understood in a more restricted sense as any form of mental activity in any state of consciousness, this is not the action itself, but the intention of the action. The third notion of *karma* is 'all acts that have the moral value'. In the fourth sense, karma is understood as an imperceptible force or law shaping the destiny of all living beings. This is the context in which *karma* is understood in Western culture.

Lastly, *karma* can be interpreted as the accumulated result (residue) of all acts during one's life. (see Monima Chadha. (1998). *Topics in Indian philosophy*. Churchill: Monash Philosophy)

The central premise of the law of *karma* is that the universe is essentially morally just and that good actions are rewarded and bad actions are punished. Good actions are those which are performed in accordance with *dharma*. There is no precise western equivalent by which to translate *dharma*. Austin Creel describes *dharma* as the pattern of ethical regulation and the justification of that pattern. Dharma refers to what one should do and why one should do so. (see Austin B Creel. (1972). '*Dharma* as an ethical category to freedom and responsibility'. (*Philosophy East and West* 22).

References

Austin B., Creel (1972). 'Dharma as an ethical category to freedom and responsibility', *Philosophy East and West* 22.

Chadha, Monima (1998). *Topics in Indian Philosophy*. Churchill: Monash Philosophy.

Gandhi, M.K. (2013). *An Autobiography or My experiments with Truth*, Ahmedabad: Navajivan.

Gandhi, M.K. (2014 a). *Ethical Religion*. Ahmedabad: Navajivan.

Gandhi, M.K. (2014). *From Yervada Mandir*. Ahmedabad: Navajivan.

Gandhi, M.K. (1945). *Gita the Mother (*ed. Jag Parvesh Chande). Karachi-Lahore Indian Printing Works.

Parel, Anthony (2006). *Gandhi's Philosophy and the Quest for Harmony*. New York: Cambridge University Press.

Sethi, J.D. (1994). *Gandhian Values in and 20th Century Challenges*. New Delhi: Publication Division.

Srimad Bhagvad Gita (1990). Mumbai: Bhaktivedant Book Trust.

The Collected Works of Mahatma Gandhi, (*CWMG*). Vol. 1-100, New Delhi: Publication Division, Government of India.
Retrieved from https://www.gandhiheritageportal.org.

5

Ethics of Gandhi's Action

Responsibility for One's Self

So far we have considered the metaphysical and epistemological basis of Gandhi's action. These discussions mainly dealt with the nature and basis of Gandhi's outward action, i.e. the action that is to be taken in response to the outward events and contexts. At the same time, we have also noted that Gandhi's all action, political, social or economic, is dedicated to his goal of self-realization[1]. Gandhi also argues that his self-realization is possible only through the service to the humanity in general and taking the action to uplift the poorest of people in particular. How his self-realization is related to the service of the people? The reason is that he believes in the 'unity of all existence' and 'God or Truth in all creation'. The precise understanding of 'unity of all existence' and viewing 'God or Truth in all creation' is not only a rational exercise, for Gandhi, but it also requires substantial and pragmatic actions that must be taken for oneself or for inward. Yet we must mention that for Gandhi inward action or outward action had no independent meaning as the life of individual form a coherent whole and it cannot be divided into compartments like inward or outward. However, for the purpose of analysis, one may assume 'inward' as space where something occurs to an individual and it is the individual who is responsible for that. This inward is not a fixed space but dynamic and evolving too. This inward is the self of the individual. Gandhi, like Vedantins, asserts that this self is not in clear or pure form because ignorance or *avidya* has covered it. Thus, he prescribes self-purification and it is here the call for action is aimed for inward in the form of methods for self-purification. This chapter strives to depict Gandhi's views on self and his proposed methods for 'self-purification' in the form of actions. Gandhi's methods for self-purification, as we will see, include traditional Hindu methods of self-purification but their new interpretation and practice by him in the given context of time and space.

Gandhi argues that self-purification is impossible without understanding one's own self. For this one has to go through the self-observation, self-examination, and self-correction. The first two naturally involves a psychological journey to understand one's own self. For instance, writing on his experiments, Gandhi notes in the preface of his *Autobiography,* "I have gone through a deep self-introspection, searched myself through and through, and examined and analyzed every psychological situation, (Gandhi, 2013: xiii). He further noted that "I claim to be a fairly accurate student of human nature and vivisect or of my own feelings" (Prabhu and Rao, 2002: 14).

Gandhi's view on the nature of human self is the complex one. It needs to be pointed out that the complexity of Gandhi's perception of self does not arise because he was not a trained philosopher but, in fact, the nature of self itself is a highly problematic issue in philosophy. The reason is that in different philosophical traditions—Indian and Western-self has been represented in very different ways.[2] Moreover, in contemporary philosophy self is considered more in term of its relation to the 'others' than 'oneself'. Gandhi seems to be challenging the notion of such a contemporary notion of self. In his paradigm, the major underlying premise is that one is responsible, first of all, for one's own self. In contrast to Gandhi's position on self, as we will see later on, in contemporary philosophical discourses responsibility to one's own self has been marginalized. The reason is probably the effect of post-modernism that gives the central place to 'subject', not to 'self'. They argue that there is no one 'fixed self' but 'many', as well as the self is 'fragmented' and it has no essence but 'images'. In such a situation a general question of the nature of self and how an individual perceives it becomes relevant and worth discussing.

This analysis also leads us to focus on a question as to how one's self and one's responsibility is related to each other. In general, responsibility is defined as a duty or obligation to satisfactorily perform or complete a task that one must fulfil. However, in philosophy, responsibility refers to a person's internal or external compulsion to carry out his or her moral duties. In philosophy, responsibility is also explicitly related to the consciousness and moral obligations of the individual. Thus, the concept of responsibility is both a *relational* and an *attributional* concept.[3]

As we may assume, the nature of responsibility towards one's self, here self as unified being as a source of an individual consciousness, depends upon one's ethical and its corresponding metaphysical position. In other words, it is one's metaphysical and its corresponding ethical criterion by which one feels compelled to carry out his internal responsibility or responsibility to one's self and external responsibility or responsibility towards 'others'. Yet it might be asked; is one's external responsibility has any relation to his/her internal responsibility? Gandhi's position is explicit in this regard. Gandhi did not only argue but also show in the practice that external responsibility must be guided by and should be in accordance with one's internal responsibility. In other words, internal responsibility is prior to external responsibility. This position seems more relevant in our time when individual views himself/herself fragmented from within and through this fragmented self he/she views the external world that seems to him/her chaotic, absurd and meaningless.

Before we examine Gandhi's position on self, it seems reasonable to discern how self has been viewed in philosophy—Indian and Western—and how responsibility to one's own self comes into the picture. Given the scope of the study, it is neither possible nor desirable to review all of the Indian and Western views on self, thus, only dominant views and related school of thought have been discussed here. It is also important in a sense that it may give us the substantial framework on the debate on self in philosophy in which Gandhi, if possible, can be placed to see how his views were influenced by other philosophical schools.

The Notion of Self in Indian Philosophical Tradition

In the earliest Vedic text, a non-duality of existence is imagined that carries the idea of a universe of non-duality—a creation that is completely unified with the creator, with no distinction. However, it is in the Upanishads, we note the supreme description of the Self. The first part of the Upanishads called *The Story of Creation* tells us about the creation of the universe and man. It narrates, in the beginning, this was Self alone, in the shape of a person (*Purusha*). He looked around and saw nothing but his Self. He first said, "This is 'I'; therefore he became I by name" (Max Müller, 1879: 85). Therefore, even now, if a man is asked, he first says, 'This is I,' and then pronounces the other name which he may have.

Thus, in the Upanishads, man's true nature is described as 'Brahman', meaning 'the Self', the same Self that is talked about when it is said, "In the beginning, this was Self alone". In describing the creation of Man, the Upanishads further states, "He (Brahman or the Self) entered thither, to the very tips of the finger-nails, as a razor might be fitted in a razor-case, or as fire in a fire-place. He cannot be seen, for, in part only, when breathing, he is breath by name; when speaking, speech by name; when seeing, eye by name; when hearing, ear by name; when thinking, mind by name. All these are but the names of his acts" (Max Müller, 1879: 86).

On the nature of self, the *Katha* and *Chandogya* Upanishads explains, "The light of the Atman, the spirit is invisible, concealed in all beings. It is seen by the seers of the subtle when their vision is keen and clear ... The Atman is beyond sound and form, without touch and taste and perfume. It is eternal, unchangeable, and without beginning or end: indeed above reasoning. An invisible and subtle essence is the Spirit of the whole universe. That is Reality. That is Truth. Thou art that" (Juan Mascoró, 1965: 61, 118). The Brahminical view on the nature of the Self as described in the Upanishads can be summarized as four major theses: the self exists; the self is immortal and without beginning or end; the self is essentially non-material and; the self is identical with Brahman, the highest reality.

Besides Upanishads, *Nyaya-Vaisesika* school of Indian philosophy also advances the concept of the self. They like Vedas agree that self is a substantial, persistent and non-material entity. They also agree with the *Vedantins* that the self cannot be perceived, but only inferred. However, the later *Nyaya* school rejected the idea that the self can only be known by inference and asserted that the existence of the self can be directly perceived. In fact, the *Nyaya* argument for the existence of the self comes from the notion of agency. Thus, "From the actions of the mind towards the contact of the sense-organ apprehending desirable objects, we infer the existence of the Self" (Chadha, 1998: 200). An analogy offered by the *Nyaya* is that from the action of regular breathing we infer the existence of the agent who would act like a blower of the wind-pipe. The *Nyaya* is clearly referring to intelligent actions and not mechanical actions.

There is another school of thought *Charvaka* that holds the totally different view of self. According to the *Charvaka* school, the body itself constitutes the Self (*dehaevaatma*). It means, the conscious body constitutes the Self. However, this immaterial element of consciousness in the body is considered an epiphenomenon of the material components of the body. The *Charvaka* school would establish the plausibility of the emergence of a property not contained in the elements by their coming together on the analogy of water, which possesses the quality of wetness, a property not possessed by the two gases of which it is composed.[4]

On the view of self, Buddhism also points out to no-existence of self. Gautama Buddha (563 B.C.-483 B.C.), in an attempt to construct a metaphysics that would side-step the Vedic revelation altogether, had taught a doctrine known as *anatta*, or no-self. According to Buddhism, the empirical reality which we experience about us consists of a never-ending, ever-fluctuating field of activity. This worldview can be summed up by the dual Buddhist doctrines of *anityata*, or the universal impermanence of all things, and *kshanikavada*, or the momentariness of all reality. There is, according to Buddhism, no continuity or permanence in anything that we experience or think. Therefore, neither is there any continuity of the soul. Kenneth Ch'en summarizes the Buddhist position in the following manner, "At any moment, according to him [Gautama Buddha], we are but a temporary composition of the five aggregates, and as these changes, every moment so does the composition. Therefore, all that we are is but a continuous living entity which does not remain the same for any two consecutive moments, but which come into being and disappears as soon as it arises" (Ch'en, 1968: 44). Thus, there is no self, according to Buddhism. Rather, our experience of self-hood is no more than a series of momentary semi-organic complexes of psychophysical elements continuously succeeding one another.

Later on, the Buddhist position on self was challenged by Shankara. Shankara and other Vedantic thinkers have pointed out, if there is no one, continuous, unitary entity who is craving, performing actions, and then experiencing the resultant suffering, then what is the meaning and purpose of the liberation of such a non-existent entity? Shankara's view on the nature of the self is based on his metaphysics which sets the criterion that the 'real' is that whose negation is impossible. From this criterion, it follows that the self is 'real' because no one will say "I am not". Sankara noted that "Just because it is the Self, it is impossible for us to entertain the idea even of its being capable of refutation" (Chadha, 1998: 200).

Shankara held the view that the very essence of the self is

Chaitanya or pure and unadulterated consciousness. Additionally, the self is unconditioned by such factors as space and time, being itself *Vibhu*, or all-pervasive. "It is neither atomic nor intermediary in size. If the self was atomic, it could not pervade all the parts of the body, and the quality of consciousness could not be perceived in the whole body" (Sinha, 1991: 170). The self, for Shankara, is one unitary entity. There is not a plurality of selves, but only one eternal, omniscient self, which simultaneously exists in all beings. Being undivided, and thus unchanging, it is devoid of qualities, agency and the ability to enjoy or suffer, all of which would entail a multiplicitous being.

As we noted above, various schools of philosophy point out to very dissimilar views on the nature of self. It ranges from the notion that there is no 'real' self as in the case of Buddhism and *Charvaka*, to the idea that the self is nothing less than the omnipotent, unlimited Absolute as in *Advaita*. Many other positions lay in between these two extremes. It is also important to note that even within the Brahminical view, the nature of self is different. Nevertheless, all philosophers and scholars agree that the Upanishads unquestionably confirm the eternal continuity, imperishability and coherent nature of the self.

The Notion of Self in Western Philosophical Tradition

The Western philosophical notion of self is radically different from the Indian Philosophers. Especially Descartes' view of self is central to the Western discourse. Descartes famous *Cogito ergo sum* signifies his idea of self or modern self (Hatfield, 2003: 5). Descartes stressed the autonomy of the first person. It means I can realize that I am existing regardless of what the world I live in is like. In other words, for Descartes, the cognitive foundation of one's own thinking is independent of its ecological relationships that mean factors such as gender, race, social status, upbringing are all irrelevant to capture the idea of the self. Besides Descartes, Kant's view of self is also worth mentioning. Kant viewed that each person is an autonomous being capable of envisaging courses of action that transcend any ecological relationship that is customs, upbringing, gender, race, social status, emotional situation.[5]

Another Western dominant view on self is the view of John Locke and his idea of *tabula rasa*. *Tabula rasa* refers to the epistemological idea that individuals are born without built-in mental content. Therefore, all knowledge comes from experience or perception. In Locke's philosophy, *tabula rasa* is the theory that at birth the (human) mind is a "blank slate" without rules for processing data, and that data is added and rules for processing are formed solely by one's sensory experiences.[6] Hume also contributed to the Western notion of self. He argued that we tend to think of ourselves as selves—stable entities that exist over time. But no matter how closely we examine our own experiences, we never observe anything beyond a series of transient feelings, sensations, and impressions. We cannot observe ourselves, or what we are, in a unified way. There is no impression of the 'self' that ties our particular impressions together. In other words, we can never be directly aware of ourselves, only of what we are experiencing at any given moment. Although the relations between our ideas, feelings, and so on, may be traced through time by memory, there is no real evidence of any core that connects them. This argument also applies to the concept of the soul. Hume suggests that the self is just a bundle of perceptions, like links in a chain. To look for a unifying self beyond those perceptions is like looking for a chain apart from the links that constitute it. Thus, Hume argues that our concept of the self is a result of our natural habit of attributing unified existence to any collection of associated parts. This belief is natural, but there is no logical support for it.[7]

On the other hand, Post-modernism posits a 'fragmented self' that has no essence, only images. Post-modernists advance their own argument in the favour of this fragmented self. They argue that in the everyday world, the [modern] idea of individuality was replaced long ago. Today, people have more than one way of being, and they have relationships and connections with one another. They are also made up of many, often conflicting parts. As they move in and out of different contexts, cultures, and sets of ideas (and/or between the different parts of themselves), they think differently and behave differently in relation to others. They know that there are different rules of conduct in different contexts, thus, they are constructed—and can construct themselves—differently in these different contexts.

It is on this basis, Jameson argues that the simple and indivisible ego-self that existed long ago, especially during the period of classical capitalism and the nuclear family, has come to an end in the postmodern era (Jameson, 1984: 56). The post-modern self is fragmented and de-centred with a kind of emotional flatness or depthlessness. According to Gergen, post-modern culture erases the category of self [modern]. The self is erased as the person is saturated with images from the media that "furnishes us with a multiplicity of incoherent and unrelated languages of the self" (Gergen, 1991: 6). In other words, the self is social or cultural construction and it has no metaphysical basis. Thus, in post-modern philosophy, the self is an effect of outside. As Goffinan argues, "The self is a dramatic effect arising diffusely from a scene that is presented" (Goffinan, 1959: 252-253). Goffinan further argues that a self awaits individuals in every situation and every situation is a multi-situated activity system.

In other words, the post-modern self is a 'hybrid self'. Self is not one and permanent self, but the person has many selves. one's self—and one's identity—is not 'fixed', but continually in 'process', as the boundaries between individual and others, and between the different parts of one's self are negotiated. Here it is significant to note the difference between self and subject which is often discussed in philosophy. Strinvorth suggests that what 'happens to us constitutes' only our 'subject' and not 'self' (Guru and Sarukkai, 2012: 63). He further adds that the self is what we are left with when we distance ourselves from anything that 'only happens to us'. In this view, as we may see, then the category of an individual is the 'sum' of the self and the subject.

As we may note, the idea of self in the history of mainstream Western thought is not one or homogeneous. Although Cartesian self has played an important role, there are other formulations of self as the Kantian self that is transcendentalist, the Humean self that does not believe in self at all like Buddhist tradition of Indian philosophy, the Lockean self which is identified with consciousness. Here it is also important to make another point in regard to the Western notion of self. As Steinvorth points out, 'the ideas of self in Western thought are closely interwoven with rationality' (qtd. in Guru and Sarukkai, 2012: 59). The sense of rationality associated with the self is emphasized through the capacity for judgment. This might be seen as a profound shift because judgment becomes a special capacity for human experience. The second important feature of Western notion of self is that there is an inherent sense of 'growth' of self. It means we acquire a self as we grow from a child to an adult and presumably as we move from premodern to modern. It also means it is the capacity of the self to judge and to act. Another point is that self was also viewed in two faces as Steinvorth informs us — a collectivist and authoritarian that precedes an individualist and fallible one. The latter self is a sign not of modernity but also of the Western self and such a self is in opposition to premodern societies or traditional societies. Furthermore, the western perspective of self and its relationship with the outer world as delineated represents a split that can be termed a broken totality.

Gandhi's View on Self and Individual's Responsibility to it

As Gandhi was not a systematic philosopher, thus, it will be unreasonable to see his ideas on self in the manner we notice in other philosophers. Yet in his voluminous and contextual writing, one may find his views on self and one's responsibility to one's self. Gandhi's view on self can be constructed on the basis of his views on the human being, human nature and his experiments with truth. As observed above, although theorized in a different way, the human being is generally understood as bipartite beings made up of the body and the mind or as tripartite beings made up additionally of the soul. But Gandhi saw "human beings as four-dimensional in nature" (Parekh, 1997: 54). These dimensions are—body, mind, soul, and *svabhav*. For Gandhi, as Parekh notes, the *body* has a twofold onto-logical significance (Parekh, 1997: 54). First, the body is *self-enclosed*, distinct, clearly *separated from others*, and capable of maintaining its integrity only by preserving its separateness. However, it does not mean the body is only self-contained and only externally related to others. The second feature of the body, in Gandhi's view, is that the body is also the seat of the senses, and thus of the wants and desires associated with them.

Gandhi had also different views on the mind. As Parekh argues, for Gandhi, "The mind includes *chetana* (stream of consciousness), which began at birth and ended with death. It includes *buddhi* (intelligence), which took many forms and operated at several levels, and gives rise to such capacities as discernment, analytical reason, insight, and intuition. Thus, for him, the *manas* was also the seat of passions, thoughts, memory, and moods" (Parekh, 1997: 54). Gandhi also saw the mind as primarily an instrument of knowledge and action. He also recognized that mind should be understood and control. Gandhi noted that although the mind is distinct from the body, they are closely tied. Gandhi also held the view that the human mind developed the notion of the ego or self which is the source of the human sense of agency and particularity. He argues that since the self desperately strives to preserve its temporal continuity, the mind becomes inherently restless and insecure. Thus, the mind becomes 'crowded' with thoughts and memories and it is 'weighed down' by the emotional baggage of the past. Consequently, it suffers from suppleness and the capacity for silence. Moreover in his view mind is always self-projecting, thus it becomes obsessed with the future.

For Gandhi, the *atman is* the third dimension of human beings. Although it is often translated as soul, and although Gandhi himself sometimes used that term, it is better translated as spirit (Parekh, 1997: 55). Gandhi believed that the cosmic spirit permeated or infused all living beings. The *atman* referred to the cosmic spirit as manifested in them, and represented the divine. The atman was not separate from but identical with the cosmic spirit. This meant that, for Gandhi, all living beings and not just the humans had the atman, that it was the same in all of them, and that it was not only a 'spark' or part of the cosmic spirit but one with and the same as the totality of the cosmic spirit. As Gandhi put it, 'we have but one soul' and are 'ultimately one'. Since he regarded the heart as the most appropriate metaphor for the soul, he often used the two terms interchangeably. Thus, we may note that Gandhi's thought was in harmony with the classical Indian traditions, especially the *Advaita* or monistic tradition.[8] Parekh further argues that following the Hindu philosophical tradition, Gandhi makes a distinction between self and *atman* (Parekh, 1989: 92). He notes, unlike the body and the *atman* which have no history, the self had nothing but history encompassing several life spans and largely beyond recall. Thus, the atman defines the destination, while the self only past. Finally, human beings had a distinct *swabhava*, or psychological and moral constitution made up of various tendencies and dispositions (Parekh, 1997: 56). For Gandhi, it was an obvious fact of life that, from their very birth onwards, human beings exhibited different temperaments and psychological and moral inclinations, were drawn to and repelled by different things, and developed according to their inner bent.

It is on this analysis of the nature of human being, Gandhi described the ultimate goal of human life what he termed as self-realization. In his words, "Life is an inspiration. Its mission is to strive for perfection, which is self-realization" (Prabhu and Rao, 2002: 46). Gandhi also believed that it is possible for every human being to attain the state of perfection which is a 'blessed and indescribable, sinless state' in which one feels 'within himself the presence of God to the exclusion of everything else' (Prabhu and Rao, 2002: 54). In the preface of his *Autobiography*, he noted, "What I want to achieve—what I have been striving and pining to achieve these thirty years- is self-realization, to see God face to face, to attain *Moksha* (Liberation). I live and move and have my being in pursuit of that goal. All that I do by way of speaking and writing, and all my ventures in the political field, are directed to this end" (Gandhi, 2013: xii).

Again, Gandhi writes in *Ethical religion*, "One ought to have a fixed aim in life. If we do not discover our life's purposes and keep steadily to the course, we shall be swept along like a rudderless ship on the high seas; we shall falter on the [moral] path. Man's highest duty in life is to serve mankind and take his share in bettering its condition. This is true worship—true prayer. He is a godly man who does God's work. Hypocrites and cheats going about invoking God's name are legions. Because a parrot utters the name of God, no one would call it godly. Contribution to an ideal order of human life is something everyone can aim at. With this aim in view the mother may legitimately rear her child, the lawyer may pursue his profession, the merchant may carry on his business or trade and the working man may labour. A person with that fixed aim would never deviate from the path of morality, for if he did, he could not fulfil his aim of uplifting mankind" (Gandhi, 2014: 30).

This may sound individualistic to the Western mind. But the self, Gandhi had in mind was not the ego or the "narrow" self (*jiva*) of egocentric interests. For him it is the supreme or universal Self—the *atman*—that is to be realized. It may also be noted that although Gandhi's idea on self seems close to Indian philosophical tradition, especially *Advait* tradition, however as we will see, his idea on the responsibility to oneself and method/technology to realize that self are quite innovative.

Action as the Responsibility to One's Self: Methods of Self-Purification/Self-Realization

Gandhi argues that the central purpose of life is to realize one's self or self-realization. For self-realization, one needs rigorous action in the proper direction. In his view, this has to be done through 'identification with everything'. As we may see, this view of Gandhi's makes one's responsibility to do self-purification. Developing the notion of self-purification he writes in his *Autobiography*, "Identification with everything that lives is impossible without self-purification; without self-purification, the observance of the law of *Ahimsa* must remain an empty dream; God can never be realized by one who is not pure of heart. Self-purification, therefore, must mean purification in all the walks of life. And purification being highly infectious, purification of oneself necessarily leads to the purification of one's surroundings" (Gandhi, 2013: 463).

Gandhi argues that the self-purification is not an easy task. He points out in the last chapter of his *Autobiography,* titled as 'Farewell', that the path of self-purification is 'hard and steep' and to attain 'perfect purity', one has to become absolutely passion-free in thought, speech, and action. One also needs to rise above the opposing currents of love and hatred, attachment, and repulsion for self-purification. He also accepts that he has not reached to the stage of self-purification what he terms as 'triple purity', in spite of constant ceaseless striving for it. He further argues that to conquer the subtle passions is more harder than the physical conquest of the world. He confesses his own experiences of the dormant passions lying hidden within him and accepts that the knowledge of them has made him 'humiliated though not defeated'. Gandhi further notes that the experiences and experiments have sustained him and given him the great joy, in this regard. Yet he recognizes that he has still to move through a difficult path. And for this, as he states, "I must reduce myself to zero. So long as a man does not of his own free will put himself last among his fellow creatures, there is no salvation for him" (Gandhi, 2013: 464).

But what methods do Gandhi propose for self-purification? Gandhi argues that self-purification is impossible without self-discipline and self-restraint. This notion of Gandhi is based on his view that the body is perishable while the Spirit is imperishable. Gandhi mentions that the body can be used as a playground of passions or it may be used as a temple of self-realization. It depends upon how we use it. In his view, one's spirit must curb flesh every moment to realize the self. In his words, "Who knows the perishable nature of flesh from the imperishable nature of the Spirit, instinctively knows that self-realization is impossible without self-discipline and self-restraint. The body may either be a playground of passion, or a temple of self-realization. If it is the latter, there is no room there for libertinism. The Spirit needs must curb the flesh every moment" (CWMG: 30:364-5).

Gandhi claims that one must advance towards the greater purity and the final stage is the 'perfect purity' of heart. Gandhi views heart as 'the *atman*' or 'the seat of the *atman*'. By way of examples, Gandhi makes a relation among the different aspects of self-purification of body, mind, heart, and *svabhav*... He writes, "If the heart is pure, the grosser impulses of the body will have no scope. But what do we mean by the heart? And when may we believe the heart to be pure? The heart is nothing else but the *Atman* or the seat of the *Atman*. To imagine that it is pure is to imply perfect realization of the *Atman* and, in the presence of such realization, the cravings, of the senses are inconceivable.... Perfect purity of heart, therefore, is the final stage. Before we have reached that stage, as we advance towards greater and greater purity, the cravings of the senses will subside in corresponding measure" (CWMG:12:376).

As a means of self-purification and self-discipline to realize one's self, Gandhi argues for taking vows. For Gandhi, a vow is a commitment to a principle of eternal Truth in order to confirm the body, mind, and soul, to that Truth.[9] For him, life without vows is like 'a ship without an anchor' or like 'an edifice that is built on sand instead of rock'. In his view, a vow is a 'deliberate commitment to a moral principle' or 'an unflinching determination'. Gandhi noted in his book *Ethical Religion,* "He alone can be called truly religious whose mind is not tainted with hatred or selfishness, and who leads a life of absolute purity and of disinterested service" (Gandhi, 2014: 30). In his view, without mental purity or purification of motive, external action cannot be performed in a selfless spirit.

Through the advocacy of vows, with its political and social implications, Gandhi makes his framework of ethics. As noted, a vow is a deliberate commitment to a moral principle, thus, he claims that a vow imparts stability, ballast, and firmness to one's character. In his view, the absolute value cannot be cherished or upheld in society or politics through action unless an increasing number of social and political workers accept the monastic ideal and introduce it into public life. This involves the taking of vows as the necessary means to self-purification and self-discipline. In Gandhi's view without the self-purification and self-discipline, purification of society and politics would be impossible.

Gandhi also argues that a vow is 'a promise made by one to oneself', and a life of vows is 'like a marriage, a sacrament'. In a letter to Kumarappa, he wrote, "You seem to think of vows publicly administered to audiences. This may not be good. The vow I am thinking of is a promise made by one to oneself. We have to deal with two dwellers within, Rama and Ravana. God and Satan, Ormuzd and Ahri-man. The one binds us to make us really free, and the other only appears to free us so as to bind us tight within his grips. A "vow" is a promise made to Rama to do or not to do a certain thing, which of good we want to do but have not the strength unless we are tied down, and which if bad we would avoid but have not the strength to avoid unless similarly tied down.... If you hold that I must speak and do the right thing at any cost, you grant my whole position and so you also do if you grant that at the peril of my life I should be faithful to my wife and friend. You can easily multiply such instances. For me, Jesus was pre-eminently a man of unshakable resolution, i.e. vows.... A life of vows is like a marriage, a sacrament" (CWMG: 44:264-5).

In another letter to Kumarappa, he noted that why vows should be taken. He mentioned that "God has a way of confounding us in our strength. Hence, the necessity of vows, i.e. invoking God's assistance to give us strength at the crucial moment" (CWMG: 44:264-5). Although for him, vows were important to keep oneself rooted in certain moral values and ideals, he also found the significance of vows in relation to others. He felt that our respect for each other in society must be based upon and can come only through the cultivation of firmness in adherence to carefully formulated and freely chosen ideals. In an atmosphere of moral flabbiness and general unreliability, there could be no real basis for mutual respect amid both disagreements and control. This aspect will be dealt with in detail in the next chapter.

As a method of self-purification, besides taking vows, Gandhi argues that silence is one of the tools that help people to purify oneself essential for the realization of truth. His views on silence seem to be influenced by the Christen monastery. Once he wrote, "It has often occurred to me that a seeker after truth has to be silent. I know the wonderful efficacy of silence. I visited a Trappist monastery in South Africa. A beautiful place it was. Most of the inmates of that place were under a vow of silence. I inquired of the Father the motive of it and he said the motive is apparent: 'We are frail human beings. We do not know very often what we say. If we want to listen to the still small Voice that is always speaking within us, it will not be heard if we continually speak.' I understood that precious lesson. I know the secret of silence" (CWMG:27:437).

Gandhi notes in his *Autobiography* that silence is 'the part of spiritual discipline' for a votary of truth. He argues that silence gives us time to think and stops us to exaggerate or suppress or modify the truth. It also provides us the opportunity to measure our words. In the Indian spiritual tradition, this is one of the methods that have been adopted by many seers also and Gandhi seems to follow them, although for a different purpose. On the virtue of silence and its usefulness for the realizing one's self, he writes; "Experience has taught me that silence is a part of the spiritual discipline of a votary of truth. Proneness to exaggerate, to suppress or modify the truth, wittingly or unwittingly, is a natural weakness of man, and silence is necessary in order to surmount it. A man of few words will rarely be thoughtless in his speech; he will measure every word" (Gandhi, 2013: 58).

Gandhi also notes that the modern world which has converted our life into din and noise, silence can play an important to understand one's own self. He argues that by observing silence in our everyday life, we may prepare our mind to listen to the 'Voice of the Great Silence'. Gandhi notes that 'the Divine Radio is always singing if we could only make ourselves ready to listen to it'. But, 'it is impossible to listen without silence'. He wrote it in his journal *Harijan* on 24-9-1938, "When one comes to think of it one cannot help feeling that nearly half the misery of the world would disappear if we, fretting mortals, knew the virtue of silence. Before modern civilization came upon us, at least six to eight hours of silence out of twenty-four were vouchsafed to us. Modern civilization has taught us to convert night into day and golden silence into brazen din and noise. What a great thing it would be if we in our busy lives could retire into ourselves each day for at least a couple of hours and prepare our minds to listen into the Voice of the Great Silence. The Divine Radio is always singing if we could only make ourselves ready to listen to it, but it is impossible to listen without silence" (Gandhi, 1955: 47).

Gandhi also shares his personal experiences of observing silence. He notes that initially, he observed silence only to relieve 'the sense of pressure', then to get 'time for writing', then he realized its 'spiritual value' and finally recognized it as 'a medium of communion with

God'. In his words, "It (silence) has now become both a physical and spiritual necessity for me. Originally, it was taken to relieve the sense of pressure. Then I wanted time for writing. After however, I had practiced it for some time, I saw the spiritual value of it. It suddenly flashed across my mind that that was the time when I could best hold communion with God. And now I feel as though I was naturally built for silence" (CWMG:68: 172).

In Gandhi's views, it is the attitude of silence where the soul finds the clear path. It is silence by which we understand what is elusive and deceptive. His argument is that if our life is a long quest after Truth, then sour requires restfulness and silence provides this opportunity. In his words placed in *Harijan* on 10-12-1938, "Silence is a great help to a seeker after truth like myself. In the attitude of silence the soul finds the path in a clearer light, and what is elusive and deceptive resolves itself into crystal clearness. Our life is a long and arduous quest after Truth, and the soul requires inward restfulness to attain its full height" (Gandhi, 1955: 48). However, for Gandhi silence should not be trusted upon oneself. He argues that the silence of the sewn-up lips is no silence. One may achieve the same result by chopping off one's tongue, but that too would not be silence. Thus, in his view, "He is truly silent, who, having the capacity to speak, utters no idle word." (CWMG:55:212).

Like silence, Gandhi also finds prayer as one of the methods to achieve self-realization/self-purification. Again for him, prayer is not an only a repetition of words but it requires 'living faith in God'. He also recognized prayer as 'the first and the last lesson in learning the noble and brave art or sacrificing self'. Making a relationship between prayer and self, he wrote, "Prayer is the first and the last lesson in learning the noble and brave art or sacrificing self in the various walks of life, culminating in the defensce of one's nation's liberty and honour. Undoubtedly, prayer requires a living faith in God" (CWMG: 83:372).

For Gandhi, prayer is not for selfish interest or 'temporal power' but 'to relieve the pain of those who are in pain'. It is worth mentioning that prayer was an integral part of his ashram life and he did prayer every morning and evening in the ashram. Further, his prayer was not sectarian in content but it was a remembrance of metaphysical power. Reciting prayer meant to remember that power which is beyond our senses and perceptions. On the recitation of morning prayer that comprised several hymns from different religious texts, he wrote,

"In another *shloka* which is recited during the morning prayer it is said, 'I do not ask for temporal power, not do I ask to go to heaven, nor even to attain *Nirwana*, What I ask for is that I may be able to relieve the pain of those who are in pain.' The pain might be physical, mental or spiritual. Spiritual pain due to slavery to one's passions is sometimes greater even than the physical" (CWMG: 84:11).

Gandhi writes that he is not a 'man of learning' but humbly claims 'to be a man of prayer'. He also shares his personal experience in regard to prayer and its relation with self. He claims that if he has never lost peace amidst of political despair this is only because of prayer. Gandhi mentions that the great teachers have shown us the path of prayer and 'it is safe to walk along the beaten tracks, trod by the ancient teachers'. He wrote, "In spite of despair staring me in the face on the political horizon, I have never lost my peace. In fact, I have found people who envy my peace. That peace, I tell you, comes from prayer; I am not a man of learning, but I humbly claim to be a man of prayer. I am indifferent as to the form. Everyone is a law into himself in that respect. But, there are some well-marked roads, and it is safe to walk along the beaten tracks, trod by the ancient teachers....I have given my personal testimony. Let everyone try and find that, as a result of daily prayer, he adds something new to his life, something with which nothing can be compared names on my lips, I will die cheerfully" (Prabhu and Rao, 2002: 85).

Gandhi observes that prayer is 'an unfailing means of cleansing the heart of passions' and it really needs no speech. Moreover, it is independent of any sensuous effort. On the nature of prayer as he pointed out, "Prayer needs no speech. It is in itself independent of any sensuous effort. I have not the slightest doubt that prayer is an unfailing means of cleansing the heart of passions. But, it must be combined with the utmost humility" (Gandhi, 2013: 67).

Gandhi's view of prayer, it should be noted, was actually quite specific. Gandhi had three conditions for prayer to be effective. These are: one needs to be deeply concentrated, the prayer must be selfless and there must be some recognition that the power to which one prays is within, not outside, of oneself. Thus, he argues that prayer should be a 'thing of the heart, not a thing of outward show', nevertheless it helps us to overcome our greatest fears and feelings of inadequacy. Moreover, Gandhi maintained that prayer honours our human capacity. In his merely the intellectual conception of the things of life is not enough, we must rely on the spiritual concept that eludes the intellect, and which alone can give one satisfaction. Prayer should be seen from this perspective.

Besides silence and prayer, one of the significant measures by which one can realize the self or for the spiritual pursuit Gandhi proposes *Naamsmaran* as the form of action. Gandhi had practiced *Ram-nama* and tasted the efficacy of this *naamsmaran*. He informs us that *Rama-nama* alone helped him pass through the struggles in the political, social, economic and religious spheres which he underwent. He also discovered that the Name was a remedy against physical ailments. Further, there is no limit on the number of times the Name is to be remembered or chanted.

Gandhi argues that chanting nama or Rama-naam had been identified by spiritual practitioners on the basis of their vision and experience, thus, its effect cannot be doubted. In his view, *naamsmaran* is therefore like algebraic formulae arrived at through research and experimentation, and verification of effect.

Gandhi argues that *naamsmaran* is not illogical and it came out of experience and understanding of spiritual teachers. He views *naam smaran* in terms of faith and purity of heart. In his view, its significance lies in the fact that it can open the door of purity even to those who are unlettered. He provides the experiential and psychological explanation of *naamsmaran* in his writings on many occasions. Writing the effect of *namajapa* (repetition of the name) he mentions, "*Namajapa* cleanses the heart thus a person who repeats the name with a pure heart does so with faith. He begins with the resolve that *namajapa* will purify his heart. What is on his lips will ultimately possess his heart and purify him. Such experience is universal and knows no exception. Psychologists are also of opinion that as a man thinks so he becomes. *Ramanama* conforms to this rule. I have firm faith in *namajapa.* Discovery of *namajapa was* born out of experience and understanding and is of utmost importance. The doors of purity should be open even to the unlettered, and *namajapa* will unlock them" (Gandhi, 1996: 198).

Gandhi had strong faith in *naamsmaran* and he argues that *namasmaran* is not superstition if it is done consciously not mechanically. He answered skeptics and said that he was speaking from experience—his own and that of others, "Repetitions when they are not mechanical produce marvelous results. Thus I do not regard the rosary as a superstition" (CWMG: 71: 386). Gandhi also argued that he was nor propagating a new variety of superstition through *naamsmaran*. In his view, "....God is not a person. He is the all-pervading, all-powerful spirit. Anyone who bears Him in his heart has accession of marvellous force of energy comparable in its results to physical forces like steam or electricity, but much more subtle" (CWMG:84:399). For Gandhi, *Ramanama* was not like 'black magic'.[10] It had to be taken with all that it symbolized. He likened it to a 'mathematical formula' which sums up in brief the results of endless research and experimentation. "Mere mechanical repetition of *Ramanama* could not give strength. For that, one had to understand and live up to the conditions attaching to its recitation. To take God's name one must live a Godly life" (CWMG: 84:399).

He argues that *naamsmaran* brings power and it come from the *sankalpa*. At a meeting of the Gandhi Seva Sangh, in 1939, Gandhi said: "There is no independent power in *Ramanama*. It is not a pill of quinine. Whether one believes in it (quinine) or not, it works equally, whether 'A' is afflicted with malaria or 'B' is afflicted. It destroys the bacteria of malaria, wherever it may be found. *Ramanama* does not have such independent power. A *mantra* acquires power from the power of *sankalpa* (imagination). For me Gayatri is a *mantra*. I have visualized it as the door to liberation. For the Muslim, his *Kalama* is the *mantra*. There is a difference between my reading the *Kalma* and a Muslim reading the *Kalma*. If the Muslim reads the *Kalma*, he evolves a different person because he has faith that that is the way to his liberation." (CWMG: 69:215). He also mentions that people repeat the name of God parrot-wise and expects fruit from so doing. But in his view, the true seeker must have that living faith which will not only dispel the untruth of parrot-wise repetition from within him, but also from the hearts of others.

Gandhi also finds fasting as a process of action for cleaning body mind and spirit—an essential requirement for self-realization. "A genuine fast cleanses the body, mind, and soul. It crucifies the flesh and, to that extent, sets the soul free.... What the eyes are for the outer world, fasts are for the inner. My religion teaches me that whenever there is distress which one cannot remove, one must fast and pray. Fasting will bring spiritual rebirth to those of you who cleanse and purify your bodies. The light of the world will illuminate within you when you fast and purify yourself. More caution and perhaps more restraint are necessary for breaking a fast than in keeping it" (CWMG:17: 110).

Moreover, he saw complete fast as denial of self. In his words, A complete fast is a complete and literal denial of self. It is the truest prayer. 'Take my life and let it be, always, only, all for Thee' is not, should not be, a mere lip or figurative expression. It has to be reckless and joyous giving without the least reservation. Abstention from food and even water is but the mere beginning, the least part of the surrender" (CWMG:54: 414). Again he pointed out, 'It is my own firm belief that the strength of the soul grows in proportion as you subdue the flesh' (CWMG:25:183). He also suggested the condition for fast. He asserted in his Journal *Harijan* on 15 June 1947, "I cannot fast at the dictation of anyone. Such fasts [unto death] cannot be lightly undertaken. They can conceivably be wholly undesirable. They cannot be undertaken out of anger. Anger is a short madness. I must, therefore, undertake the fast only when the still small voice within me calls for it."

As a method of action, another significant method, in regard to Gandhi's self-purification and self-realization is the confession. His childhood confession is famous by which he learned the cleansing capacity of confession. Letter on he mentioned that Confession of errors is like a broom which sweeps away the dirt and leaves the surface brighter and clearer.

Summing up

Gandhi's ethics begins with realizing oneself and it requires certain actions. We noted, Gandhi's action, first of all, invites one to take responsibility for one's self that further requires action for understanding self, self-discipline, self-restraint, and self-purification. For this, Gandhi developed some of his own methods and adopted some methods from the Western and Indian philosophical system. In this endeavour, body mind and *atman* work together. He reinterpreted vows in the form of powerful action and showed how they are important for us to realize one's self. Gandhi also argued that silence is one of the tools and form of action that help people to purify oneself essential for the realization of truth. Besides, prayer is also one of the techniques Gandhi employed for self-realization/self-purification. Taking nourishment from Indian Vaishnava tradition, he also adopted *Naamsmaran*. It is one of the techniques as an action that Gandhi employed in his spiritual pursuit. As we all know Gandhi had practiced *Ram-nama* and tasted the efficacy of this *naamsmaran*. As a form of action, Gandhi also finds fasting as the process of cleaning body mind and spirit – an essential requirement to self-realization. Another significant form of action, in regard to Gandhi's technology of self to purify it and to reach the stage of self-realization, is the confession.

Notes

1. Gandhi writes, "The whole of my activity, whether it may be called social, political, humanitarian or ethical, is directed to that end [Seeking Truth]". (Prabhu and Rao, 2002: 13)
2. Nietzsche points out in the preface of his work *On the Genealogy of Morality*, "We remain strange to ourselves out of necessity, we do not understand ourselves, we must confusedly mistake who we are, the motto, 'everyone is furthest from himself' applies to us forever—we are not 'knowers' when it comes to ourselves" [See Keith Ansell Pearson (ed.). (2006). pp. 3-4]. Nietzsche's concern about the strangeness of the 'self' is right as the strangeness of self is not only confined to our common understanding of the self but also philosophically it is very vague and complex.
3. This has been discussed in detail in the next chapter.
4. For more detail see Encyclopedia Britannica, Self in Indian philosophy. https://www.encyclopedia.com/humanities/encyclopedias.../self-indian-philosophy.
5. Brook A. (2004). *Kant's view of the mind and consciousness of self*. The Stanford Encyclopedia of Philosophy (Winter 2004 Edition), Edward N. Zalta ed.). Retrieved from http://plato.stanford.edu/archives/win2004/entries/kant-mind/.
6. Retrieved from www.britannica.com/topic/*tabula*-rasa.
7. *Op. cit.*, Brook. (2004).
8. Parekh argues that Gandhi gave it a new twist and argued that, since the cosmic spirit was manifested in all living, especially human, beings, identification with it consisted in identifying oneself with them in a spirit of universal love and service. By lending the idea of *moksha* such a humanist or worldly orientation and defining spirituality in moral terms, Gandhi gave the Indian traditions an activist turn for which he was both much admired and criticized by his countrymen. (See Parekh, 1997: 56).
9. Iyer has rightly pointed out that 'to understand Gandhi's position regarding vows, it is necessary to put it in the context of Indian tradition and especially of his active faith in the truth of the doctrine of rebirth'. (Iyer, 2007: 74).
10. Gandhi explains that the effect of *namajapa* is not like black magic. On another occasion, Gandhi explained that the effect of *Ramanama* or *namajapa* was not like that of chemical or medical formulae. To explain the difference, he gave the example of quinine. He pointed out that the effect of quinine would be the same on one who believes in its power, and also on one who did not. That was not the case with *Ramanama* or *namajapa*. In the case of *namajapa*, the power or effect came from faith and the power that faith generated in the mind.

References

Brook, A. (2004). *Kant's view of the mind and consciousness of self*, The Stanford Encyclopedia of Philosophy (Winter Edition), Edward N. Zalta (ed.). Retrieved from http://plato.stanford.edu/archives/win2004/entries/kant-mind.

Chadha, Monima (1998). *Topics in Indian philosophy*, Churchill: Monash Philosophy.

Ch'en, Kenneth K.S. (1968). *Buddhism: The Light of Asia*. New York: Barron's Educational Series, Inc.

Frank Morales. (1999). *The Ontology of Self in Three Systems of Indian Philosophy: A Comparative and Veridical Analysis*. Retrieved from indunet.org/home/dharma_and_philosophy/vvh/vvhself.html.

Gandhi, M.K. (1955). *Truth is God*, Ahmedabad: Navajivan. Retrieved from https://www.mkgandhi.org/ebks/truth_is_god.pdf.

Gandhi, M.K. (2014). *Ethical Religion*. Ahmedabad: Navajivan.

Gandhi, M.K. (2013). *An Autobiography or My Experiments with Truth*, Ahmedabad: Navajivan Publication.

Gandhi, M.K. (2008). *Hind Swaraj*. Ahmedabad: Navajivan

Gergen, Kenneth J. (1991). *The Saturated Self*. New York: Basic Books.

Goffinan, Erving (1951). "Symbols of Class Status", *British Journal of Sociology*, 11(4): 294-304.

Guru, Gopal and Sunder Sarukkai. (2012). *The Cracked Mirror*. New Delhi: Oxford University Press.

Hatfield, G. (2003). *Routledge Philosophy Guidebook to Descartes and the Meditations*, Routledge.

Iyer, Raghvan. (2007). *The Moral and Political Thought of Mahatma Gandhi*. New Delhi: Oxford University Press.

Jameson, Fredric (1984). "Postmodernism, or The Cultural Logic of Late Capitalism." *New Left Review*, Number 146: 51- 92.

Mohanty, Jitendra N. (1997). "Indian philosophy", in *Macropedia*, Volume 21, 15th edition Encyclopedia Britannica, Chicago.

Juan Mascoró (1965). *The Upanishads*. Delhi: Penguin Books.

Keith Ansell Pearson (ed.) (2006). *Nietzsche Reader*. U.K: Blackwell Publishing Limited.

Max Müller (1879). *The Upanishads*, Part 2 (SBE15), see sacred-texts.com.

Parekh, Bhikhu (1989). *Gandhi's Political Philosophy*. London: Macmillan.

Parekh, Bhikhu (1997). *Gandhi: A Very Short Introduction*. Oxford: Oxford University Press.

Prabhu, R.K and U.R. Rao (2002). *The Mind of Mahatma*. Ahmedabad: Navajivan.

Sinha, K.P. (1991). *The Self in Indian Philosophy*, Calcutta: Punthi Pustak.

The Collected Works of Mahatma Gandhi (*CWMG*), Vo. 1-100. New Delhi: Publication. Division Government of India.
Retrieved from https://www.gandhiheritageportal.org.

6

Gandhi's Action

Self and its Responsibility to Other

In the previous chapter, we have considered how Gandhi's action is a duty and responsibility to oneself. It engages one in the process of self-purification through self-observation, self-examination, and self-correction. However, this self-purification, aimed to realize the God, is not to occur in isolation or 'going into the cave' or 'Himalaya', but as mentioned earlier it has to be made through the active engagement with the world or given context. We have earlier also noted that this engagement has to be made through 'selfless service' to humankind or other. Gandhi argues that if a man seeks *moksha* and still believes that he is, he will utterly fail in his aspiration. Thus, one who seeks *moksha* must be society's servant. In other words, for Gandhi *moksha* does not lie outside the realm of other. In this sense, *moksha* or self-realization becomes a constant process that critically engages one's to the society/others also. But what is the nature of such an engagement? As *moksha* is to be attained through serving others, the service is not here a passive act but an active one, that involves a deeper responsibility towards others. Although, in Gandhi's worldview self and other as well related responsibility attached with them cannot be divided into separate entities, however, for the sake of analysis, this chapter intends to focus on how Gandhi's action implies responsibility towards others and it will be demonstrated through interpretation of his writings on this subject.

In Gandhi's writings, action as responsibility towards others emerges specifically when he writes about Satyagraha, Swaraj, Sarvodaya, and Swadeshi. In these discussions, there also emerges Gandhi's response to the critical question of the relation between self and others.

For instance, Gandhi's engagement with other in relation to self can be seen in his argument for Satyagraha, what he called passive Resistance, in his seminal text *Hind Swaraj*. He writes, "It involves sacrifice of the self. Everybody admits that sacrifice of self is infinitely superior to sacrifice of others. Moreover, if this kind of force is used in a cause that is unjust, only the person using it suffers. He does not make others suffer for his mistakes" (Gandhi, 2008: 54).

Thus, for Gandhi, then otherness is a relation; one that entails a sacrifice of the self in order to uphold its own otherness. Further, it renders the "others" the same kind of response, of course through the means of non-violence. Here we notice that both the self and the others are tied to a relationship of responsibility. This responsibility belongs to the recognition of each other's free will to experiment in the field of ethical realm directed to the truth. This relationship is a non-violent relationship, for which one undergoes for personal suffering. But this cannot be made either by any domination from outside by others or through violence from within the self. It's a demand for self from both sides which makes it possible in the Gandhian conception to begin an ethical relationship, based on justice. As we may infer, Gandhi's notion of this ethical relationship throws a tremendous responsibility upon the individual.[1]

Similarly, Gandhi's idea of Swaraj evokes action that involves responsibility for one's own self as well as towards others. For example, in the last paragraph of *Hind Swaraj,* Gandhi notes "Let each do his duty, If I do my duty, that is, serve myself, I shall be able to serve others." He further noted in the same paragraph that the 'Real Swaraj is self-rule or self-control' and the way to achieve it is '*satyagraha* that is soul force or love force'. He also mentioned that 'in order to exert this force, Swadeshi in every sense is necessary'.

In this paragraph, we may note that connections are explicitly drawn among his key ideas of Swaraj, duty, satyagraha, and swadeshi. We may analyze these concepts in term of self and other to unpack Gandhi's views on its relationship.

In fact, Gandhi's Swaraj refers to practices of contemplation that engages self with others in a very crucial way. This is a kind of relationship that relates the individual to the phenomenal world or *samsara*. The medium of engagements by which individual relates to *samsara* or other is the chain of human actions or *karma* and a normative order or *dharma*. From this perspective, as we may argue, swaraj engages one to feel a deeper responsibility to one's own self and *samsara* or others. Moreover, Gandhi's writings on swaraj point to a deeper, self-generated change within the individual as well as the corresponding transformation of other. In short, it evokes radical reanimation of self and other simultaneously. Thus, Swaraj means essentially 'being open to others', but at the same time, it means building a character for oneself by living one's life as a moral project. For Gandhi, Swaraj could come only through acceptance of considerable personal, moral and political responsibility that involved enormous self-sacrifice and social service. This is Gandhi's philosophical position on Swaraj that he also demonstrated in his analysis concerning the face of others.[2]

In the same way, Gandhi's concept of *Sarvodaya*, i.e. welfare of all and its related social action also shows a close relationship between the one's moral responsibility towards other in the view of universal welfare.[3] He categorically rejected the 'utilitarian' idea in which some are left. He argued that a votary of *ahimsa* cannot subscribe to the utilitarian formula of the greatest good of the greatest number and he would strive for the greatest good of all and die in the attempt to realize the idea. In his words, "He will, therefore, be willing to die, so that the others may live. He will serve himself with the rest, by himself dying. The greatest good of all inevitably includes the good of the greatest number, and therefore, he and the utilitarian will converge in many points in their career, but there does come a time when they must part company, and even work in opposite directions. The utilitarian to be logical will never sacrifice himself. The absolutist will even sacrifice himself" (CWMG: 32:402).

Thus, Gandhi's notion of *Sarvodaya* does not exclude 'others'. It is not satisfied with the greatest good for the greatest number. Moreover, his *Sarvodaya* project also envokes a moral responsibility on the individual to an extent that one should be ready to die or willing to die so that 'others' may live.

In praxis, the concept of *Sarvodaya* evokes the *Antyodaya* that means the welfare of the last person. Inspired by the ideal of *Antyodaya*, we may recall talisman of Gandhi, which states, "Whenever you are in doubt or when the self becomes too much with you, apply the following test. Recall the face of the poorest and the weakest man whom you may have seen and ask yourself if the step you contemplate is going to be of any use to him. Will he gain anything by it? Will it restore him to a control over his own life and destiny? In other words, will it lead to Swaraj for the hungry and spiritually starving millions?' then you will find your doubts and yourself melting away" (CWMG:96:311).

This is a fine illustration and working method by which one sees how one has the responsibility towards others and also in which way self is related to others. Related to *Sarvodaya*, one may also remind here Gandhi's idea of Swadeshi. By definition, for Gandhi, "Swadeshi is that spirit in us which restricts us to the use and service of our immediate surroundings to the exclusion of the more remote' (Prabhu and Rao, 2002: 410). He also notes that 'Swadeshi is the law of laws enjoined by the present age" (Gandhi, 2014: 42). This is 'self-acting' and 'ingrained in the basic nature of man'. For Gandhi, 'its votary will, as a first duty, dedicate himself to the service of immediate neighbours'. Gandhi categorically states that it does not imply national selfishness and the exclusion of the 'other'. Although "This involves exclusion or even sacrifice of the interests of the rest, but the exclusion or the sacrifice would be only in appearance" (*ibid.*, p. 42). He argues, "Pure service of our neighbours can never, from its nature, result in the disservice to those who are far away, but rather the contrary" (*ibid.*, p. 42). Swadeshi is, in fact, a moral responsibility to our immediate neighbours which also shows the limitations of an individual to serve remote and all. Here we may note that for Gandhi Swadeshi simply implies that in the case of face to face with other, moral responsibility for the neighbours has priority over other geographical units.

Having discussed the key concepts of Gandhi in term of self and other and its relation, now let us explore the basis on which self is related to other in Gandhi's worldview.

I

To explore the basis of the relation between self and other in Gandhi's worldview, first of all, we may recall Gandhi's concept of *moksha.* Gandhi had argued that the main aim of the individual is to attain *moksha*. We have noted that Gandhi's notion of *moksha* is both philosophical and pragmatic in nature. In fact, being a man of action, Gandhi had a more profound and practical understanding of *moksha*. His life also explains that he was neither an escapist nor a pessimist. His interpretation of the *Gita,* as noted earlier, points out that man cannot attain complete self-realization in the sense of being one with God in *this* life, but it does not mean that man should voluntarily renounce activity or sit at home quietly or commit suicide. Instead,

Gandhi defines his concept of *moksha* in very active and practical terms. Gandhi writes in his commentary on the *Gita*, that if we agree that man cannot attain *moksha* in this life, as mentioned above, we need not spend much thought or indulge in intellectual exercises over this problem. He observes that we should rather concentrate on the means. If means are right, the end is as good as attained. What we note is that through this Gandhi shifts the attention from the end (*moksha*) to the means. Through such shifting, Gandhi offers a practical idea of *moksha* through action or active life in this world. According to Gandhi, this is the only possible way in which humans can achieve *moksha* and it must be ceaselessly pursued here and now by engaging with others.[4] The active life must be, in his view, developed and tested through the power of self-discipline and self-control. Thus for Gandhi, if attaining *moksha* is the chief aim of life, then, considering 'others' is part and parcel of achieving *moksha*. One cannot ignore 'others' as *moksha* is not something outside the realm of other.[5]

Second, the basis of the relation between self and other in Gandhi's paradigm can also be explored in his analysis of human nature and individual's place and his/her role in this universe. For Gandhi, the human being is a trinity of animality, humanity, and divinity. He argues that human behaviour is regulated by many factors such as moral standards, the sense of shame, conscience, and duty. For him, the basic manifestations of the ethical life are the sense of social and personal responsibility and the awareness that he/she is part of the whole and linked with others. As noted earlier, the basis of this idea is 'unity of existence' and an 'underlying moral harmony' in the universe.[6] As Gandhi believed in the 'essential unity of God and man and for that matter of all lives', it was natural for him to take the next step and claim a universal responsibility that binds us all through our common transcendence. Gandhi also insisted, 'if one gains, all gain, if one falls, all fall; we can't stand by and watch' the suffering of our fellow humans as we are all involved in realizing our oneness through mutual service and uplift. Thus, humanity's moral solidarity and its corresponding responsibility is an ever-present fact for Gandhi.

Third, the basis of the relation between self and others in Gandhi's worldview can also be explored in his view on *purushartha.*[7] Gandhi does not accept the view that an individual is essentially helpless in the face of the forces that influence him from within and outside.

Invoking *purushartha,* he argues that the responsibility one feels is not merely an illusion. It is real and the choice one determines through consciousness is substantial and profound.

We may argue that the idea of *purushartha,* which Gandhi evokes, implies that human being owes a responsibility which is not only moral but also psychological and socio-political one. Yet, it might be asked; what is the defining feature of responsibility in Gandhi's worldview? Gandhi seems to argue that responsibility is a state of conscious feeling of duty towards oneself and other/society. Further, for him, responsibility is not only a theoretical construct for philosophizing the role of the individual in this living world but it also involves an active awareness of the purpose of the actions performed and their corresponding consequences. Moreover, Gandhi's notion of responsibility deconstructs the binary of responsibility to oneself and responsibility to other as the individual is not separate from others. He is the same as others. In his worldview, there are no others, there is only the self, or versions thereof. In fact, Gandhi's belief in our 'oneness with others', as noted above, was fundamentally based on his perception of the divinity of humanity, as he claimed that individual is 'part and parcel of the whole' and 'cannot find [God] apart from the rest of humanity'. This intersubjective definition of the ground of being is the foundation of Gandhi's notion of responsibility.[8]

But, what is the meaning of being responsible, in a practical sense, in Gandhi's worldview? In Gandhi's sense, to say that a person is responsible means that he/she is capable of correctly understanding the question of what is true/right in the political and social filed or other aspects of social life and to act accordingly. This correct understanding of true/right and to act accordingly forms the relative truth of Gandhi. In Gandhi's worldview, it must be pointed out that only knowing the responsibility is not enough but also *to act* accordingly. Further, any responsibility, in Gandhi's framework, is based on 'knowledge' and 'will to act' which are to be in the direction of Absolute truth.

Gandhi's writings clearly point out that every human being has his own responsibility to both himself and to others or society. He argued that even a person who has left this society for his own spiritual attainments like a mendicant or an anchorite or a monk or a *sanyasi* cannot escape from his social and moral responsibility. The reason is that such persons also owe a debt to his heritage and society and they must repay the debt. In Gandhi's view, this can be done only through discharging social responsibility by them. In fact, in Gandhi's view, the spiritual aspirants have *more and greater* responsibility towards the society than the others as they have overcome the ego and self-interest and fear. Thus they can, and should, set an example in the society. Once addressing Buddhist monks in Burma, he said: "I do not for one moment grant that a *sanyasi* needs to be a recluse caring not for the world. A *sanyasi* is one who cares not for himself but cares all the time for others. He has renounced all selfishness. But he is full of selfless activity. *Swaraj* (self-rule) does not merely stand for National independence, but for the self-rule of the individual. A *sanyasi,* having attained Swaraj in his own person, is the fittest to show us the way..." (qtd. in Varma, 2001: 46).

Thus in Gandhi's worldview self and other is related to each other with the notion of responsibility.[9] In other words, Gandhi's notion of responsibility towards others emerges out of his views on the relationship between self and other. Now discuss the nature of responsibility in Gandhi's worldview and the question as to how to act responsibly.

II

For this purpose, i.e. Gandhi's views on responsibility and its nature, we may concentrate on his writings related to question in hand. In this regard, his small booklet *Ethical Religion* helps us to find out his views on individual's duty or responsibility in relation to others. In the last chapter titled as 'Personal Morality' of *Ethical Religion*, Gandhi observes, 'I am responsible for this,' or 'This is my duty': this is a moving and wonderful thought. A mysterious, resounding voice seems to say, "To thee, individually, O man, is given this task. Whether defeat or victory, both belong to thee. Thou art what no one else in the world is, for nowhere has nature created two similar objects. Thou hast a duty which no one else in the world can do, and if thou does not do it that loss will stand debited to thee in the world's balance-sheet" (Gandhi, 2014 a: 28-29).

"What is that duty I owe to myself?" Gandhi puts this question and in response to it, he quotes a verse; *Call not man God for man is not God/Yet man is not distinct from God's glory* (Gandhi, 2014a: 28-29). Thus he points out that, "My duty is to rest secure in the belief that I am a ray of God's light" (*ibid*., p. 29). However, Gandhi presents other visions also on this issue. He points out, "Another may answer that the duty is to have sympathy and fraternal regard *for others*." He further notes, A third may answer that it [duty] is to revere parents, care for one's wife and children, and acquit oneself well with brother, sister or friend" (*ibid.*, p. 29). Gandhi argues that duty is not only limited to respect other but it is also about respecting oneself. "Alongside of all these virtues, it is also a part of my duty to respect myself even as I respect others". His argument is that 'as long as I do not understand myself, how shall I understand others?' and 'how shall I respect one whom I do not know?' (*ibid.*, p. 29). On the other hand, he also ponders over the other side of this issue. "Many holds the view that the obligation of proper conduct arises [only] in relation to others and that, in the absence of contact with others, one may do just as one pleases." Gandhi finds such a view hopeless. He notes, "He who holds this views does not know what he says. In this world, none can, with impunity, act as he pleases."

Gandhi then goes on to describe the meaning of duty in detail. He begins with the 'duty to ourselves' and consider the 'private habits which are unknown to all but ourselves'. Gandhi observes, "We are responsible for them since they affect our character." But, this is not all and argues that "We are responsible for them also because they affect others." In other words, personal habits are not personal but it has public implications also. On this grounding, he provides a code of conduct and mentions, "Every person ought to control his own impulses, and keep his soul as well as body clean." He further mentions that our private habits also make our future. In his view, "Worldly success never comes to him who does not abstain from sensual pleasures and does not thus save his body, mind, intellect, and soul."

He extends the detail of code of conduct by which duty can be conducted in a proper manner. Thus, he mentions that 'one ought to have a fixed aim in life'. Otherwise, "If we do not discover our life's purposes, and keep steadily to the course, we shall be swept along like a rudderless ship on the high seas; we shall falter on the [moral] path." But what should be the aim of life and the highest duty of men? He argues, "Man's highest duty in life is *to serve mankind* and take his share in bettering its condition." In Gandhi's view, the common aim of every individual should be 'an ideal order of human life'. All acts, of whatever of the kind, should be performed keeping this view in mind. Such thing is, as he argues, is 'true worship—true prayer'. In his words,

> "Contribution to an ideal order of human life is something everyone can aim at. With this aim in view the mother may legitimately rear her child, the lawyer may pursue his profession, the merchant may carry on his business or trade and the working man may labour. A person with that fixed aim would never deviate from the path of morality, for if he did, he could not fulfil his aim of uplifting mankind. This is true worship-true prayer" (*ibid.*, p. 30)

But for Gandhi only fixing the aim of life is not enough. He feels that an individual should constantly examine whether his/her way of life 'tends to improve human life or to worsen it'. This is the criteria by which Gandhi wants to show how the individual is responsible for his actions in relation to others. Through examples he makes his point clear, "Thus the merchant should ask himself whether, in transacting a business, he is cheating himself or another. The lawyer and the physician, acting according to this standard, will give more thought to their client or patient than to their fees. The mother in rearing her child would proceed very cautiously lest she should spoil the child out of misguided by these considerations and do his duty. The result of all this would be that, if the worker fulfils his function in conformity with the moral ideal, he would be deemed better and higher than the wealthy merchant, physician or lawyer who lives without any discipline. The worker would be the true coin and those selfish men, even though more intelligent or wealthy, would be counterfeit. This further shows that any man, whatever his place in life, has the power to fulfil this aim" (*ibid.*, p. 30).

Gandhi also argues that a man's value depends upon his way of life, not upon his status. Further, the way of life does not mean the outward action but the inner learnings. In his words, 'one's way of life is not to be judged by one's visible outward actions, but by one's inner leanings'. Again he provides a wonderful example to illustrate it, "For instance, if of two men, one gives a dollar to a poor person to rid himself of his presence and the other half a dollar but with love and out of compassion for the man, obviously, the one who gave half a dollar is truly moral, while the other who gave a dollar, the sinner."

Summarizing his arguments in this booklet *Ethical Religion*, he notes, "... he alone is religious, he alone is happy and he alone is wealthy, who is sincere in himself, bears no malice, exploit no one and always acts with a pure mind. Such men alone can serve mankind.

How can a damp matchstick kindle a log of wood? How can a man who does not practice morality teach it to another? How can a sinking man save another from drowning? The man who lives a moral life never raises the question as to how to serve the world, for he is never in doubt" (*ibid.*, p. 31). At many places, Gandhi has mentioned that individual action and goodness is not one's own concern; it is the concern of the whole community, of the whole world or the other.[10]

III

We have seen in the first section, in Gandhi's worldview, the self is related to others through responsibility. The second section elaborated on Gandhi's notion of responsibility, its different dimensions and their relation to human actions. Let us examine on *what ground* Gandhi fixes the responsibility of self towards others. This will also show the philosophical basis on which responsibility is fixed by Gandhi, although with the risk of slight repetitions of the arguments earlier mentioned.

Although, we do not find any systematic writings by Gandhi on this subject, yet we may trace some philosophical concepts in his writings that provide us sufficient clue to reconstruct the basis of responsibility of self to others in his worldview.

In this context, one may refer to his notion of 'mutual love' in his writings by which he seems to argue that every human being is responsible to others. His argument is that not only our own social life but even nature cannot survive without the mutual love. He accepts that there exists a force of repulsion in nature as well as in our own social life but finally it is the force of love that prevails. This is the reason the humanity is progressing otherwise it would have been collapsed long before. In this sense, mutual love or force of attraction is the fact of life and nature whether human being knows it or not. Gandhi's writings also suggest that one must consciously understand the dynamics of mutual love and feel the responsibility to others to avoid his own destruction as well as the progression of humanity. He argues that we have to extend the field of mutual love from our own family to the nation which is 'larger family'. To quote him, "Though there is repulsion enough in Nature, she lives by attraction. Mutual love enables Nature to persist. Man does not live by destruction. Self-love compels regard for others. Nations cohere because there is mutual regard among individuals composing them. Someday we must extend the national law to the universe, even as we have extended the family law to form nations —a larger family" (Gandhi, 1969: 118).

Similarly, in Gandhi writings, one may note his repeated notion that humanity is 'undividable whole'. This 'undividable' humanity is the philosophical basis on which Gandhi fixes the individual responsibility. To recognize Gandhi's notion of 'undividable whole', we may take help of a metaphor that Gandhi has used to describe the paradigm of 'undividable whole'. The metaphor is about the relation between the 'drop of water and the ocean'. He wrote, "The ocean is composed of drops of water; each drop is an entity and yet it is a part of the whole; 'the one and the many'. In this ocean of life, we are little drops. My doctrine means that I must identify myself with life.... that I must share the majesty of life in the presence of God" (qtd. in Roy, 1985: 103). He further noted, "Individuality is and is not even as each drop in the ocean is an individual and is not. It is not because apart from the ocean it has no existence. It is because the ocean has no existence if the drop has not, i.e. has no individuality. They are beautifully interdependent. And if this is true of the physical law, how much more so of the spiritual world!" (qtd. in Roy, 1985: 88).

Another metaphor is about the 'chain and the link'. He mentioned, "And one discovery I have made is that, really speaking, there is no distinction between individual growth (read self) and corporate growth (other), the corporate growth is therefore entirely dependent upon individual growth and hence that beautiful proverb in the English language that a chain is no stronger than the weakest link" (CWMG:34:505).

There are certain points that need to be considered here. First, Gandhi seems to argue that individual growth (self) is more important and it is an essential condition of corporate growth (other). However, it does not mean the supremacy of individual (self) over society since the individual cannot become a person if society is subordinated to the needs of the individual. As a matter of fact, as we saw earlier, in Gandhi's view one of the important traits of the individual (self) is the person's willingness to sacrifice himself for the sake of society. Thus what we note is that when a person is defined in terms of seeking authentic self-hood, the very conception of self incorporates other or society.

Second, as may infer Gandhi seems to argue that since human beings and other beings are linked in the manner of the chain, one has to realize that the strength of the chain depends on the health of what may be the weakest link. Thus, the conscious concern for the weakest link or other links is demanded of the human being because unlike other animals the human being is capable of visualizing alternatives and acting in a manner that ignores or infringes the unalterable law of nature. It is only this concern that can ensure his long-range interest.

Both these paradigms and perceptions lead to the similar conclusion and throw significant light on how self and other are related to one another and why one should be responsible towards others. The necessary corollary of this idea is that no man can degrade, or brutalize another without also degrading and brutalizing himself. Again no man can inflict psychic and moral damage on others without inflicting it on himself as well. In this regard, Parekh argues that this was so in at least three ways (Parekh, 1989: 89). First, to degrade others was to imply that a human being may be so treated, and to lower the expected level of the moral minimum due to every human being from which all alike suffered. 'To slight a single human being is to harm not only that human being but with him the whole world'. Second, to degrade and dehumanize others was to damage their pride, self-respect, and potential for good, and thus both to deny oneself and the world the benefits of their possible contributions and add to the collective moral, psychological and financial cost of repairing the damage they were likely to do themselves. Third, as a being endowed with moral sense and capacity for reflection, no men could degrade or maltreat others without hardening himself against their suffering and cries for help, building up an elaborate and distorted system of self-justification and coercive apparatus to put down disconnect, and thus both coarsening his moral sensibility and lowering his own and collective level of humanity. As Gandhi put it, "no man takes another down a pit without descending into it himself and sinning into the bargain. Since humanity was indivisible and vital human interests were identical, every man was responsible to an for others and should be deeply concerned about how they lived" (qtd. in Parekh, 1989: 89-90).

Similar to the notion of undividable humanity, one may find the repeated expressions of 'oneness of mankind' in Gandhi's writings. Although this notion has been explained by him in different contexts, it can be interpreted in the sense that why one should be responsible to others. He wrote, "Mankind is one, seeing that all are equally subject to the moral law. All men are equal in God's eyes. There are, of course, differences of race and status and the like, but the higher the status of a man, the greater is his responsibility" (Gandhi, 1969: 118). Thus, Gandhi accepts the different kind of differences among human beings but in spite of that differences, in his view, there is an underlying unity because they all are subject to the same moral law. Further, as noted in his view the higher status of men has greater responsibility.

Related to it, one often finds the idea of 'brotherhood and identity with all forms of life' in his writings by which it can be argued that how he viewed one's responsibility to others. He wrote, "I want to realize brotherhood or identity not merely with the beings called human, but I want to realize identity with all life, even with such things as crawl upon earth. I want, if I don't give you a shock, to realize identity with even the crawling things upon the earth, because we claim descent from the same *God,* and that being so, all life in whatever form it appears must be essentially one" (Gandhi, 1969: 119). Here we note that Gandhi extends the individual's responsibility not only to the human being but to all forms of life arguing that they are essentially one. Similarly, Gandhi describes the idea of 'kinship with all' in his writings. This 'kinship with all' extends not only to human beings but the animals too. He notes that his kinship extends to 'horse and sheep, the lion and leopard, the snake and the scorpion" (Prabhu and Rao, 2002: 424). The logic of 'brotherhood and identity with all forms of life' and 'kinship with all' is that, as Gandhi notes, 'every man and woman has unilateral obligation' as 'man is made in the image of God' (Prabhu and Rao, 2002: 424).

Further, one may deduce the basis of responsibility of self to other, in Gandhi's worldview, by tracing out his notion of interdependence. In fact, the extension of self as a basis for 'identification with others' implies interdependence. Thus, he does not see that duty to self is separate from the other spheres of the society. The reason is, as mentioned, the interdependence of individual with the different spheres of the society. He notes, "Duties [responsibility] to self, to the family, to the country and to the world are not independent of one another. One cannot do good to the country by injuring himself or his family. Similarly, one cannot serve the country injuring the world at large" (Gandhi, 1969: 120). He focuses on this interdependence in a more philosophical way in one of his writings. He wrote,

> "Interdependence is and ought to be as much the ideal of man as self-sufficiency. Man is a social being. Without interrelation with society, he cannot realize his oneness with

> the universe or suppress his egotism. His social interdependence enables him to test his faith and to prove himself *on* the touchstone of reality. If man were so placed or could so place himself as to be absolutely above all dependence *on* his fellow-beings he would become so proud and arrogant as to be a veritable burden and nuisance to the world. Dependence *on* society teaches him the lesson of humanity. That a man ought to be able to satisfy most of his essential needs himself is obvious, but it is *no* less obvious to me that when self-sufficiency is carried to the length of isolating oneself from society it almost amounts to sin. A man cannot become self-sufficient even in respect of all the various operations from the growing of cotton to the spinning of the yarn. He has at some stage or other to take the aid of the members of his family. And if one may take help from one's own family, why not from one's neighbours? Or otherwise what is the significance of the great saying, 'The world is my family'?" (Gandhi, 1969: 119-20)

Again in Gandhi's writings, we note the 'idea of self-sacrifice' by which we may deduce the basis of responsibility of self to others. Earlier, we have noted that how the self is engaged with other, especially in his argument for Satyagraha. As a 'practical idealist' Gandhi knew that an individual can take some action, unknowingly or unwillingly, in relation to other in such a way that may harm others. He also argues that if a person gets engaged in an unjust cause by mistake, he cannot escape from the responsibility. To safeguard it, Gandhi argues that one must be ready to sacrifice oneself rather than sacrificing others. In his words, 'sacrifice of self is infinitely superior to sacrifice of others'. For this Gandhi presents the idea of soul force and claims, "... 'if this kind of force is used in a cause that is unjust, only the person using it suffers. He does not make others suffer for his mistakes. Men have before now done many things which were subsequently found to have been wrong. No man can claim that he is absolutely in the right or that a particular thing is wrong because he thinks so, but it is wrong for him so long as that is his deliberate judgment. It is, therefore, meet that he should not do that which he knows to be wrong, and suffer the consequence whatever it may be. This is the key to the use of soul-force [satyagraha]" (Gandhi, 2008: 54).

Related to the notion of sacrifice, there is an idea of 'dialogical empathy' in Gandhi's worldview that reminds responsibility. This is two-sided. One side is the classical meaning of empathy; perceiving another person's experience through the person's eyes and appreciating that person emotions under the condition of conflict. Dialogical empathy calls for understanding what is going on in the minds of your opponents and recognizing their human side, including their fears and insecurities. It is very opposite of demonizing one's enemy. On the other side, dialogical empathy means trying to look at one's behaviours through the other's eyes, recognizing critically one's moments of distrust, fear, and anger. Thus dialogical empathy has two components—first emphasizing with the other, i.e. appreciating the others perception and second, comprehending the other's perception of one's own role in engagement. This, as we may note, is a move forward to the question of responsibility. In fact, a degree of responsibility, as a moral experience, is involved in this process of dialogical empathy, no matter how individuals transform themselves as they move from a passive role in society to non-violent engagement with others.

IV

It might be argued, if self feels a responsibility towards others then what about individual freedom? This invites us to think Gandhi's idea of freedom and its relation to responsibility.[11]

Gandhi does not view freedom in an absolute way but locates it in the context of other or society. He is not against the individual freedom but wants to adjust it to the requirements of social progress. However, for Gandhi, to value human freedom only as the freedom to pursue one's self-interest lacks moral and spiritual depth and creates a life devoid of meaning and truth. On the other hand, he criticized the unrestricted individualism and called it 'the law of the beast of the jungle'. In fact, he wanted that we must learn to strike the mean between individual freedom and social restraint.[12] In his view, such a willing submission to social restraint for the sake of the well-being of the 'other' or society enriches both the individual and the society of which one is a member.

Thus, freedom for Gandhi was not merely a right but was a responsibility and duty. True freedom is not merely the freedom to do what one desires, but also the ability to ensure that what one chooses is the result of a sense of duty and self-knowledge. For Gandhi, this choice is not exercised as 'freedom from restraints' but as 'freedom through restraints'. [13]

It is on this grounding, Gandhi equates freedom with his notion of Swaraj or self-rule or self-constraint. In this regard, as Iyer observes "Gandhi equated freedom with self-rule because he wished to build into the concept of freedom the notion of obligation to others as well as to oneself while retaining the element of voluntariness that is the very basis of freedom. The notion of self-rule implies the voluntary internalization of our obligation to others which will be obstructed by our placing ourselves at the mercy of our selfish desires" (Iyer, 1973: 349). This states precisely what Gandhi intended and achieved. [14]

For Gandhi, Swaraj could come only through acceptance of considerable personal and political responsibility that involved enormous self-sacrifice and social service. No nationalist before Gandhi had embraced the responsibility of the colonized so unequivocally. As he wrote in Hind Swaraj, "To blame the English is useless," Gandhi's "Editor" (speaking in the author's voice) declared to the Reader, "they will either go or change their nature only when we reform ourselves. We shall become free only through suffering" (Gandhi, 2008: 63-4). Indians must recognize this duty because "Swaraj has to be experienced, by each one for himself" (Gandhi, 2008: 39). It can be achieved only through commitment to the cause of freedom, so "it is our duty to say exactly what we think and face the consequences" (Gandhi, 2008: 64).

Gandhi uses this theory of *dharma* to shape his idea of rights: "Having a right surely does not mean that I should exercise that right in utter disregard of my sense of proportion. The exercise of right depends on one's sense of duty. It is my duty to follow *dharma*. I do what I consider my duty" (CWMG: 69:208). This follows from what he had written in Hind Swaraj, where he argued that "real rights are a result of the performance of duty" and criticized "in England the farce of everybody wanting and insisting on his rights, nobody thinking of his duty" (CWMG: 10:44).

For him, freedom is not only freedom from coercion and domination, it is also self-regulation through self-restraint. Thus, freedom or swaraj was understood by Gandhi both in the sense of personal and political responsibility.

Summing up

Gandhi argues that human action is not isolated and it is both self -

and other-regarding. The reason, he gives, is that mankind is constituted an organic whole and men are necessarily interdependent. On this basis, Gandhi concludes that directly or indirectly, visible or invisible, human action affects the quality of the prevailing pattern of human relationship. He also observes that we cannot recognize it as we are nearsighted but it remains an inescapable law of our interdependent world. Gandhi also argues that since the paradigm of interdependence is unalterable and governs our existence and achievements, there can be no irreconcilability in the basic interests of human beings who constitute a society. Thus, whatever one does affect all others and whatever others do similarly affect one. Again, since the human being is a conscious part of the 'whole', he has to understand and be mindful of what is necessary to protect and preserve the whole of which he is a part, the whole without which he cannot survive. It means the welfare of one is dependent on the welfare of all. No one can, therefore, seek or attain his well-being at the cost of others. Since human beings and other beings are linked as a chain, one has to realize that the strength of the chain depends on the health of what may be the weakest link. Thus, conscious concern for the weakest link or other links is demanded of the human being because unlike other animals the human being is capable of visualizing alternatives and acting in a manner that ignores or infringes the unalterable law of nature. It is only this concern that can ensure his long-range interest. Finally, since there is much in common in all sentient beings, particularly in beings that belong to the same species, it is easy for one to understand the feelings of another, and the working of another's mind, by watching one's own reactions, how feelings rise within one and take control of one, how these feelings weaken and even disappear, or transform themselves; how the mind arrives at or adopts views, whether it is always preceded by an evaluation of evidence or pros and cons or often times a view that flashes to the surface of the mind, and then gets entrenched through inertia, prejudices, perceptions of self-interest, intransigence and the egoistic reluctance (resistance) to change a position one has taken.

Thus Gandhi seems to propose that selfhood is impossible without sociality, without the self-extending itself to cover the other and making the other very important for its own development. In his perspective, the self and society or other are not separate entities. The separation between self and society or other dissolves is the self is considered an extension of its physical existence to the embodiment of the universe as a whole. Self and other, therefore, are not two static concepts denoting two irreconcilable entities but are two mutually dependent aspects of the same process.

Notes

1. This ethical relationship, indeed, presupposes non-violent fearlessness which Gandhi sought to cultivate in the Indian. This fearlessness is essentially another perspective on how one can respond to the feeling of infinite responsibility. Gandhi sought to instill in Indian a resolute sense of courage and fearlessness in the pursuit of truth and justice. He repeatedly lamented that Indians were in the habit of saying 'yes' to everything and needed to develop the courage in order to say 'no' to evil, injustice, untruth, and violence. Gandhi' also shown how an active life in the face of infinite responsibility must accept self-suffering as the path to infinite courage.
2. We may note that in *Hind Swaraj* (1909), Gandhi had insisted that Indians must accept moral responsibility for colonization. His argument is that Indians had allowed colonialism to happen and they could end it if they resolved to do so. In the same way, in the face of tragedies like the Great Calcutta Killing, he demanded that people accept responsibility for what had happened. In fact, for Gandhi, the moral claim to rule was non-sensical, even reckless, without a practical demonstration of Swaraj.

   Further, when Gandhi's non-cooperation movement was in full swing in 1921-22, a group of non-violent protesters was beaten up by some policemen in the small town of Chauri Chaura in Northern India. In retaliation, the crowd then set fire to the police station, killing 22 policemen. Gandhi, without even consulting with the Congress Working Committee, called off the national civil disobedience movement. He took personal responsibility for the atrocity. After he had withdrawn the movement, the British Government ordered his arrest. In the trial Gandhi stated,

   "...I wish to endorse all the blame that the learned Advocate-General has thrown on my shoulders in connection with the Bombay occurrences, Madras occurrences, and the Chauri Chuara occurrences. Thinking about these things deeply and sleeping over them night after night, it is impossible for me to dissociate myself from the diabolical crimes of Chauri Chaura or the mad outrages of Bombay. He is quite right when he says, that as a man of responsibility, a man having received a fair share of education, having had a fair share of experience of this world, I should have known the consequences of everyone of my acts. I know them. I knew that I was playing with fire. I ran the risk and if I was set free I would still do the same. I have felt it this morning that I would have failed in my duty if I did not say what I said here just now." Retrieved from bombayhighcourt.nic.in/.../historicalcases/.../TRIAL_OF__MAHATMA_GANDHI-19.

3. Gandhi received the idea of Sarvodaya from Ruskin. Gandhi received a copy of Ruskin's *Unto This Last* from a British friend, Mr. Henry Polak while working as a lawyer in South Africa in 1904. In his *Autobiography*, Gandhi remembers the twenty-four-hour train ride to Durban (from when he first read the book, being so in the grip of Ruskin's ideas that he could not sleep at all. He notes in his *Autobiography*, "I determined to change my life in accordance with the ideals of the book" (Gandhi, 2013: 275). Gandhi advances the concept of Sarvodaya, which were the based on three basic principles:
   (a) That the good of the individual is contained in the good of all.
   (b) That a lawyer's work has the same value as the barber's in as much as all have the same right of earning their livelihood from their work.
   (c) That is a life of labour, i.e. the life of the tiller of the soil and the handicraftsman is the life worth living.

   Gandhi mentions in his *Autobiography*, the first of these I knew. "The second I had dimly realized. The third has never occurred to me. *Unto This Last* made it clear as daylight for me that the second and third were contained in the first. I arose with the dawn, ready to reduce these principals to practice" (Gandhi, 2013: 275).
4. Gandhi seems to be relating 'Advaita' with Gita's *karma yoga*. The reason is: a belief in the divine unity of all existence clearly lends itself to a certain interpretation of a life of service. Thus, it is not surprising to see that Gandhi found a life of truth as actively following an imperative to be engaged in the world.
5. In regard to the relation between self and Other from the point of view of Gandhi's notion of *Moksha*, Parekh observes, "Since self and Other were interdependent polarities, each creating and being in turn created by the other, *moksha* involved the complementary processes of dissolving the 'Other' by attaining total identification with all creation. Hindu religious tradition had stressed the former and Gandhi did not add much to it. The way he defined the latter and related the two contained novel insights and represented his great contribution" (Parekh, 1989: 95).
6. As pointed out earlier, Gandhi's insistence on 'the unity of existence' is derived from the metaphysical presuppositions of Satya in the Advaita school of Hindu philosophy. Further, Gandhi's belief in Satya leads to the belief in an underlying moral harmony. The moral bond connecting all life implies an inescapable moral obligation to all our fellow human beings.
7. In his recent book on Gandhi, Anthony Parel focuses precisely on the doctrine of "*purusharthas*" and Gandhi's worldview. In the Indian tradition, "*purusharthas*" are four in number: comprising pleasure (*kama*), economic and political achievement (*artha*), ethical virtue (*dharma*), and salvation (*moksha*). Parel's book seeks to highlight, above all, is the balanced, or sattva, quality of Gandhi's character and how his entire life, including his politics, was essentially a "quest for harmony" among the goals of life. Parel also argues that relying on classical Indian scriptures and especially the theory of

the four *purusharthas*, Gandhi aimed to establish a "working harmony" between the political, economic, ethical, aesthetic, and spiritual pursuits and thereby to remedy the "malaise of modern secularism." (see Parel, 2006).

8. Thus, at the same time, for him, responsibility is both personal and social. Personal responsibility includes exploring one's own self through self-observation, and self-correction. Besides, the individual has also responsibility towards others because he is not separate from others.
9. This might be seen as the crux of Gandhi's notion of self-realization. For Gandhi self-realization means 'to see the universal and all-pervading spirit of Truth face to face one must be able to love the meanest of creation as oneself. And the man who aspires after that cannot afford to keep out of any field of life'.... (Gandhi, 2013: 463) In other words, one's own internal responsibility is always related to others (meanest creation).
10. In his words, "Whether an individual is good or bad is not merely his own concern, but really the concern of the whole community, nay, of the whole world." His argument is that "There is not a single virtue which aims at, or is content with, the welfare of the individual alone. Conversely, there is n*ot a single moral* offense which does not, directly or indirectly, affect many others besides the actual offender." (Prabhu and Rao, 2002: 439).
11. On this issue Ramin argues, "Responsibility for Gandhi precedes freedom because it leads us towards a just treatment to other, the ideal presented by freedom should, in turn, reinform one's neighbourliness towards the individual other. Moreover, the process of facilitating contact between opponents and overcoming evil requires an appreciation of each other's self-experience and experience of others" (Ramin, 2013: 85).
12. He wrote, "I value individual freedom, but you must not forget that man is essentially a social being. He has risen to his present status by learning to adjust his individualism to the requirements of social progress. Unrestricted individualism is the law of the beast of the jungle. We have to learn to strike the mean between individual freedom and social restraint. Willing submission to social restraint for the sake of the well-being of the whole society enriches both the individual and the society of which one is a member" (Prabhu and Rao, 2002: 312).
13. There is an ontological difference between these two formulations. In the first formulation, restraint refers to a situation imposed by an 'other', for example, colonialism. In the second formulation, restraint refers to a self-imposed situation, Gandhian Swaraj.
14. In fact, Gandhi deliberately disassociated Swaraj from the mere transfer of power and political independence in the literal sense. To Gandhi, the moral claim to rule was nonsensical, even reckless, without a practical demonstration of Swaraj.

References

Gandhi, M.K. (1969). *All Men are Bothers*. Switzerland: Unesco. unesdoc.unesco.org/images/0007/000710/071082eo.pdf

Gandhi, M.K. (2008). *Hind Swaraj*. Ahmedabad: Navajivan.

Gandhi, M.K. (2013). *An Autobiography or My Experiments With Truth*. Ahmedabad: Navajivan.

Gandhi, M.K. (2014). *From Yervada Mandir*. Ahmedabad: Navajivan.

Gandhi, M.K. (2014 a). *Ethical Religion*. Ahmedabad: Navajivan.

Iyer, R. (1973). *The Moral and Political Thought of Mahatma Gandhi*. New York: Oxford University Press.

Parel, Anthony J. (2006). *Gandhi's Philosophy and the Quest for Harmony*. Cambridge: Cambridge University Press.

Parekh, B. (1989). *Gandhi's Political Philosophy*. London: Macmillan Press.

Prabhu, R.K. and U.R. Rao. (2002). *The Mind of Mahatma*. Ahmedabad: Navajivan.

Ramin Jahanbegloo. (2013). *The Gandhian Moment*. London: Harvard University Press.

Roy, Ramashray. (1985). *Self and Society: A study in Gandhian Thought*. New Delhi: Sage.

Varma, Ravindra. (2001). *The Spiritual Basis of Satyagraha*. Ahmedabad: Navajivan.

The Collected Works of Mahatma Gandhi (*CWMG*) Vols. 1-100. New Delhi: Publication Division. Retrieved from https://www.gandhiheritageportal.org/

7

Esthetics of Gandhi's Action

Unison of Universal Love, Responsibility and Detachment

The core of Gandhi's philosophy of action can be summarized in three words—universal love, responsibility, and detachment. In Gandhi's worldview, while universal love is motive and intention of action, responsibility—both to oneself and others—, is a dynamic process by which action takes a shape and detachment shows the attitude towards the result of the action. Moreover, Gandhi extends and attaches special meaning to these terms. For him, *Universal love* means placing oneself at the service of all living beings and devoting all one's energies to 'wiping every tear from every eye'. *Responsibility*, at the personal level, implies; controlling one's actions, to combine word and deed, and to be able to use one's freedom rationally in the public sphere. By *detachment*, he meant that one must not worry whether the desired result follows from one's action or not if the motive is pure. These three terms/notions as a coherent whole are the essence of the Gandhi's philosophy of action. Let us discuss it in a more focused form.

I

We have noted that Gandhi's action springs from his metaphysics of Truth and non-violence. In his writings, Gandhi repeatedly argues that 'force of truth' is the same as the 'force of love'.[1] His argument is that "... when you want to find Truth as God the only inevitable means is Love, i.e. non-violence, and since I believe that ultimately the means and ends are convertible terms, I should not hesitate to say that God is Love" (Gandhi, 1955 a: 15). He also mentions the nature of this force of love which is 'cohesive' and it works whether we know it or not (unconsciously). He equates 'force of love' to the 'force of gravitation', and argues that what the force of gravitation is to inanimate objects, love is to the human being and the human species (Prabhu and Rao, 2002: 416). He also claims that love is the greatest creative force in the Universe as well as 'the strongest force the world possesses' (CWMG:28:30). Further, in his view, love is the 'source of harmony' in the individual, family, and society.

In his writings on this subject, besides viewing love as a force, Gandhi also claims that there exists a law in human species that should be termed as 'law of love'. He provides the proof of the 'law of love' in human species pointing out that 'if love was not the law of life, life would not have persisted in the midst of death' and destruction (Prabhu and Rao, 2002: 417). He further argues, "If love or non-violence be not the law of our being,... there is no escape from a periodical recrudescence of war, each succeeding one outdoing the preceding one in ferocity" (Prabhu and Rao, 2002: 417). He also views the law of love as 'the sovereign rule' which 'makes no distinction' (Prabhu and Rao, 2002: 419).

It might be asked: why does Gandhi argue that the law of love is the law of the human species especially? The reason is that since the human being is capable of encompassing the whole animate and inanimate world in the canvass of love, outside the compulsions and inhibitions of the instinctual framework to which animals are confined, Gandhi believed that the law of love is the law of the human species.

Although Gandhi observed that there exists the 'law of love' but he did not use this term extensively in his speeches and writings. He provided the reason for it in his one of the speeches given at Lausanne in 1931. In that speech he noted that although 'the nearest approach to Truth is through love', but "... love has many meanings, in the English language at least, and human love in the sense of passion becomes a degrading thing also".[2] Thus, instead of love Gandhi used the term *Ahimsa* or non-violence that, in his views, refers to the first step that has to be taken by anyone who wants to extend this love to "all that exists". Thus, to him, non-violence is a positive and active force that arises from Truth and Love. Gandhi sees non-violence also as 'universal love' and points out, "Non-violence means universal love; it implies compassion for all living beings and the resultant strength to sacrifice oneself" (CWMG:38:22).

Gandhi's philosophy of love needs more examination in regard to his whole philosophy of action. Gandhi's notion of love suggests that he does not confine love to the ordinary meaning of it. The 'love' that Gandhi refers to is not love based on passion or desire or instinct. Further, for him, love is also not an emotional stage of mind, as generally perceived. He does not view love as emotion based on the attraction for what is ephemeral or momentary or unreal. Again for him, love does not refer to 'possession' also. In fact, he noted that perfect love means perfect non-possession. In his words, "Love and exclusive possession can never go together. Theoretically, when there is perfect love, there must be perfect non-possession" (Prabhu and Rao, 2002: 191).

Further, in his worldview, love is not selective or restrictive but it is 'universal' in its nature. He also affirmed the faith that the human being can love all beings and claimed that one can identify oneself with others only through love. In his view, love also changes one's attitude. Thus, he argues that a human being can use love to transform their attitudes as well as to nourish other beings. We may note, his notion of love takes love to a spiritual height and he argues that the human heart is capable of infinite love, love which may be unilateral and universal.

To strengthen his position on love, Gandhi argues that the human being depends on love at every point in his life. In his view, it is love that sustains the earth. He also argues that 'there only is the life where there is love and life without love is death' (Prabhu and Rao, 2002: 417). It may be argued; why does Gandhi view love in such exalted terms?

As noted, in his view, the feeling of love changes oneself and others also. He argues that without love it is impossible to overcome anger, hatred, indifference, selfishness and the ego. In his view, love is the antidote for anger (Rao and Prabhu, 2002: 420*)*. He notes that true love enables one to overcome all these divisive and destructive emotions and to bring about transformation in the most hard-hearted and intransigent persons. It is on this basis Gandhi's Satyagrahi and Constructive worker come into action.[3]

Love, thus, is a spiritual force in Gandhi's worldview, and a supremely active and constructive force. True love, for him, does not arise from the body or the mind, but from the heart which is the seat of comprehension through compassion, or feeling. Thus for Gandhi, love is based on *compassion* and *identification*. In other words, it enables one to see the similarity between one and others, to see one in others, and others in oneself. From his perspective, love is, therefore, a force that transforms, liberates, and frees one from attachment to whatever is harmful, momentary, transient and unreal. It is also a force that unites one with all others.

It must be reminded that although Gandhi equated love with *ahimsa* or non-violence but his *ahimsa* or non-violence, as noted earlier, is not restricted to desisting from violence or *himsa*. Love, to Gandhi, is more than desisting from violence. It is a positive attitude of the mind and heart, and action flowing from this kind of attitude. Further, for him, this attitude does not arise from a moral code laid down by a prophet, or a code that bases itself on the promise of rewards and the threat of retribution.

If we analyze Gandhi's view on universal love, we find that his notions of love are the outcome of his paradigm of 'essential unity of all that exists' and its related paradigm of 'interdependence'. We have noted that Gandhi believed in the oneness of all that exists (*advaita).* This *advaita* philosophy has three essential components. First unity of men, second, the unity of all livings and third unity of creation. If all that exists is one, then, there is only one attitude that is consistent with the belief in the oneness of all, which is universal love. Further, when one's existence and achievements are conditioned by interdependence, one has to have positive concern for all others human beings, other life and the environment on whom or on which one depends, with whom one's life is interwoven. This concern is universal love and can only be expressed through universal love. Logically, it can neither be expressed through hatred nor indifference. The reason is that hatred or indifference is based on a sense of separateness. Love, on the other hand, enables one to overcome the sense of separateness and hostility. Thus to realize the oneness of all creation, or one who wants to identify himself with all 'creation, discovers that the means of identification lie in love. Universal Love is, therefore, the *sine qua non* of human existence in Gandhi's worldviews.[4]

It should also be reminded that Gandhi's perception of love does not permit him to condone or countenance the wrongs of those whom he loves. His love is not a counsel of indulgence or helpless acquiescence in the demands or acts of the one whom he loves. On the other hand, he believed that his love compelled him to dissociate from or cooperate with, and even resist, the wrong acts of those whom he loved. As he noted, "My goal is friendship with the whole world, and I can combine the greatest love with the greatest opposition to wrongs." (Gandhi, 1955: 79). Further, "Civil Disobedience is sometimes a peremptory demand of love" (Gandhi, 2001: 221). Thus for him, the resistance of unjust acts was a duty imposed on the Satyagrahi both by his love of Truth, and his love, for all those who were suffering as a result of injustice or evil acts and attitudes. It is only when a fight is motivated by love, and carried on by weapons that are consistent with love, that it becomes Satyagraha. [5]

It is his notion of love by which he distinguishes between 'evil' and 'evil doer'. If one is to love all human beings, one has to distinguish between the evil and evil-doer. The logic is: while one resists and fights evil, one can still love the evil-doer who is a human being and a victim of a mental attitude that has made him mistake what is evil for what is good or just. In fact, the process of correction or transformation in attitudes, that Gandhi emphasizes in his philosophy, can begin only when one distinguishes between the evil and the evil-doer. If one does not distinguish between the two, one acts on the assumption that eliminating the evil-doer is eliminating the evil. This is the assumption generally causes violence in the society.

Yet it must be submitted, universal love is not a theoretical abstraction on which Gandhi pondered. For Gandhi, universal love is a positive concept that can be experienced through active service of humankind. Service, in his view, is a positive love, 'love in action' or 'active love'. It is on this ground Gandhi argued that Universal love meant placing oneself at the service of all living beings and devoting all one's energies to 'wiping every tear from every eye'. He noted, "We may not know God. But we know His creation. Service of His creation is the service of God" (CWMG:63:233). Thus, we see that in Gandhi's perception, love is the way to Truth as well as the way to identify oneself with the Law.

Thus, Gandhi's notion of universal love is not logically empty in practice. But how it can be experienced in practice? In his view, 'the first step for cultivating universal love' is to overcome the anger and ill-will and patient endeavour.[6] In his writings, there appear different facets of universal love that indicates how universal love can be put into the practice in our own context of time and space. He seems to be fixed the criteria of how to realize it. In his view, in so far as *ahimsa* means universal love it can have direct application in our serving the creatures that are nearest us.

Gandhi also shows how this universal love can be applied to politics, society, and economics. He argued that we must first love those who are most needy. For example, in the context of using *Khadi* for the betterment of immediate neighbours, he argued that "Instead of talking of universal love, it would be enough if we give up the calico made in the mills of Ahmadabad, Japan or England and win instead the simple love of the poor by wearing cloth spun and woven by our own brothers and sisters" (CWMG:26: 324).

Gandhi argues that national action or national service is not contradictory to universal love. Rather national action or national service is an important facet of universal love. In his words, "The *dharma* of national service means all-embracing love. It is not universal love, but it is an important facet of it" (CWMG:27:303). Moreover, national action or service lifts one to the highest peak of universal love. He wrote, "Love of one's country is not opposed to the love of mankind, but it is a concrete instance of it. It ultimately lifts one to the highest peak of universal love" (CWMG:27:304).

Again Gandhi finds that abolishing the untouchability is one of the facets of universal love. Referring to Swami Shraddhanand, in one of his condolence messages, he noted, "A great hero and patriot Swami Shraddhanandji died for the sake of the untouchables. He loved them as dearly as his own life. He regarded them as his own children, and, if it was in his power, he would have banished untouchability from the shores of India. And what does that banishment mean? It means universal love" (CWMG:32:510).

Gandhi also equates universal love with his philosophy of non-violence, although with a new interpretation of the latter that also includes active compassion. He clearly mentioned, "Non-violence means universal love; it implies compassion for all living beings and the resultant strength to sacrifice oneself. Since many mistakes may be made while this love expresses itself we cannot give up the quest for the whole of this *dharma*. Even the mistakes committed while seeking the pure path take us a step forward in the quest" (CWMG:38:22).

To sum up, Gandhi's philosophy of love is closely linked with his paradigm of 'essential unity of all that exists' and its related notion of 'interdependence'. In his worldview, love is the only way of identifying oneself with other living beings. It means opening up oneself to their presence, relieving them of their otherness and making them part of oneself. His logic is as love deepens, the distance between the two decreases, and at its highest love culminates in total identification. Thus for him, universal love is the only way to attain identification with all living beings. It involves infinite openness, breaking down all the barriers between self and others, letting them flow into one's being and suffuse one's thought and feelings with the deepest concern for their well-being. As we may deduce from above, his notion of love logically puts the bigger responsibility on individuals. Thus his notion of love inherently involves the notion of responsibility.

II

We have noted in the previous chapter that for Gandhi there are two inseparable and interrelated responsibilities that human being owes. These are the responsibility to oneself and responsibility to others. In other words, in Gandhi's worldview, responsibility is not only limited to the personal level but it goes beyond oneself and encompasses other or the public sphere also. In fact, responsibility for the other is the essential, primary, and the fundamental ingredient in Gandhi's worldview. This responsibility, as discussed earlier, emerges from his metaphysical and ethical standpoint that view everything that exists coming out of one source and interdependent to each other. This constructs a paradigm of an ethical relation among the individuals. It needs to be pointed out that this ethical relation to the Other is not built around a plain notion of responsibility or a rational choice of being responsible for what the modern paradigm suggests. In carrying out such responsibility, Gandhi argues, one must feel universal love or dialogical empathy for others which is the metaphysical essence of his paradigm.

It must be stressed that Gandhi's notion/embodiment of responsibility is different from working out an *a priori* plan of ameliorating the suffering of others. Gandhi's engagement with others was always and at the same time turned towards an inner journey and it was more an exploration of his own being than removing the suffering of others with a set political-social agenda. It was never only limited to the working out of the pre-established method to the welfare of others. This inner journey also engaged him with constant questioning of himself. It is this process of constant questioning of himself which puts his action apart from the other self-sanctifying 'social service' based on representation. In a sense, every decision and action of Gandhi was a process by which he opened to himself. Thus, in Gandhi's worldview appropriate response to other requires appropriate preparation for one's own self.

Gandhi's notion of responsibility is logically related to his theory of life/truth/love. Gandhi saw a life of truth/love as actively following an imperative to be engaged in the world, both in the term of reconstruction and resistance. As Gandhi believed in the 'essential unity of God and man and for that matter of all lives', it was logical for him to claim a universal responsibility that binds us all through our common transcendence. We have already noted that Gandhi's belief in our oneness with others was fundamentally based on his perception of the divinity of humanity, as he claimed that he was 'part and parcel of the whole' and he 'cannot find [God] apart from the rest of humanity'. He also claimed, 'if one gains, all gain, if one falls, all fall'; thus one can't stand by and watch the suffering of other fellow humans as we are all involved in realizing our oneness. In fact, the underlying structure of Gandhi's thought that we are all responsible for each other compels one to the vision of moral commitment that is fundamentally rooted in protecting the sanctity and value of human life. For Gandhi, the dignity of the self-arises in and through a feeling of unfulfillable moral responsibility to the other person, which eventually leads to a demand for justice for all humanity. Thus, in his worldview, responsibility is placed exclusively in a way that one cannot refuse without relinquishing a part of his/her own self; since the self becomes the sole measure of responsibility. In short, for him, an individual's responsibility is an ever-present metaphysical and ethical fact rather than simply a formulated political social ideal. In other words, Gandhi's notion of responsibility is moral and ethical in nature.

Gandhi's notion of responsibility is radical and infinite in nature. But how it can be argued that for Gandhi responsibility is infinite? There are two reasons for it. First, for Gandhi, responsibility for the other is infinite not because there is an infinite amount of suffering in the world, and not because there are infinite numbers of people for whom one is responsible, but because infinite responsibility is the core constitutive element of individuation. In so far as being an individual means being able to respond, one can become an individual only by responding his/her social-political reality or surroundings.

The second reason is that, for Gandhi, ethical responsibility is fundamentally non-reciprocal. We have noted Gandhi views responsibility in terms of selfless service or *anasakti*. For him, to be in selfless service to others is to be responsible for the other's suffering and death irrespective of her being right or wrong, good or evil. In other words, *the moment* of responsibility cuts across these dualities. It needs to be pointed out that in Gandhi's worldview, responsibility is not an interested investment and it goes beyond the discourse of modernity which primarily views responsibility as a contractual, reciprocal exchange of limited obligation and commitment to one another. Further, Gandhi's notion of responsibility does not mean a return to selfless service as advocated by traditional discourses such as Christianity.[7] Thus, Gandhi's articulation of responsibility stands outside of reciprocity and modernity and at the same time it differs from charity, benevolence, pity and/or assimilating the other into the same. In his view, one is responsible not because one has a mission to spread the truth, and not because one is impelled to act by a sense of charity, but because other is suffering and that other is not separate from me.

Although for Gandhi, responsibility is infinite in nature, it does not mean that it is 'unrestricted'. In Gandhi's worldview, there is a notion of 'proximity' that plays a central role in his notion of responsibility. It also shows the practicality of Gandhi's notion of responsibility. Gandhi repeatedly used the term 'neighbour' to signify the structure of one's relationship to the other in the form of responsibility. For Gandhi, responsibility arises in the immediacy of the face to face relationship with the concrete other before its concealment in a universal idea of thought. For him, proximity is the ontic relation between self and other; people literally live and breathe in one another's proximity. It is on this ontic relation Gandhi offers his idea of *swadeshi.*

Gandhi's idea of responsibility also offers the critique of modern and prevalent response to human suffering. His writings suggest that he was not satisfied with the contemporary response to different forms of human suffering like exploitation, tyranny, and political-economic violence. Gandhi, in fact, found that the prevalent responses were ineffective and insufficient. These responses take a multitude of forms: private or public charity that eventually exists its own costs; a blind and violent reaction that is unaware of its own injustice; the investment of hope in a state's impersonal and bureaucratic machinery; or. even worse, pervasive indifference to the others' suffering. Gandhi's worldview amounts to a radical objection to both the violence that is launched in the name of liberation and anaesthetization of the political in the name of reason.

Gandhi also views responsibility as courage in his worldview which he terms as *abhay* or fearlessness. His whole philosophy of action in the form of resistance or Satyagraha and reconstruction or Constructive Programme is grounded in it. His mode of resistance as Satyagraha can be viewed as a non-violent *response to infinite responsibility* but it is more than a response in the practical sense.

In fact, his notion of Satyagraha is not only a response but an individual's moral responsibilities in the face of other. It is a response in the form of responsibility. What is important to note is that for Gandhi feeling of responsibility for the other is not a rational choice but a metaphysical compulsion and ethical call or obligation. The ethical call is; serve the other and to suffer from his suffering, an imperative that precedes all other consideration. Satyagraha as a moral responsibility to fight against injustice is based on resolute fearlessness which accepts self-suffering and non-violence as sources of strength.[8] Like Satyagraha, his notion of *Sarvodaya* has its metaphysical underpinnings in *Satya*, which leads to a further interpretation that speaks much more closely to the issue of moral responsibility in the notion of universal welfare. Gandhi's belief in *Satya* leads to the belief in an underlying moral harmony. As noted, the moral bond connecting all life implies an inescapable moral responsibility to all our fellow human beings. As the culmination of these beliefs, *Sarvodaya* is fundamentally concerned with embodying and implementing the practical aspects of moral harmony.

But, it can be argued that what methods Gandhi propose as a method of action to remain engaged in this world or responsibility can be born out?

From the philosophical point of view, out of his metaphysical reflections and acts of service, he came to conclude that *ahimsa* (non-violence) and *tapasya* (self-suffering) and *Abhay (fearlessness)* were indispensable methods and modes of action for remaining engaged with the world. Most importantly, Gandhi redefined these three traditional Hindu concepts in order to develop an entire framework of action. Again, this inherently includes his efforts in redefining the idea of courage. This notion of courage accepts suffering and sacrifice as essential for developing an infinite fearlessness, which Gandhi saw as the truest and most powerful way to remain active in the world in the face of infinite responsibility. Again, like other notions, in articulating the idea of courage Gandhi's reading and his interpretation of the *Gita* played a significant role.[9]

On this basis of his understanding of the *Gita*, Gandhi shows the practical path by which one can bear out responsibility. It is the path of voluntary service of others. As a believer in *karma yoga*, Gandhi believed that selfless service to the other was essential. But what is real service? On the basis of *Gita*, he responds, "In order to obtain the right answer to this question, restraint of the senses is essential, as it gives us a clearer and clearer vision of the God of truth. Service rendered with selfish motives ceases to be sacrifice. Hence the urgent need for the spirit of detachment" (Gandhi, 1930: 15). He further argues that where service is rendered for service's sake, there should be no room for attachment, likes and dislikes. For him, life is given to us for service and not for enjoyment. Gandhi also notes that service must be rooted in love and it should be only through bread labour. He wrote, "Service is not possible unless it is rooted in love or *Ahimsa*. True love is boundless like the ocean and rising and swelling within one spreads itself out and crossing all boundaries and frontiers envelops the whole world. This service is again impossible without bread labour, otherwise described in the *Gita* as *Yajna*. It is only when a man or woman has done bodily labour for the sake of service that he or she has the right to live (Gandhi, 1947: 56).

He epitomizes his notion of service in the following way: "Voluntary service of others demands the best of which one is capable, and must take precedence over service of self. In fact, the pure devotee consecrates himself to the service of humanity without any reservation whatever" (Prabhu and Rao, 2002: 231). We may view that for Gandhi service must be voluntary and to the best of one's capability. Moreover, he puts the service of other first than the service of oneself. And the service does not exclude anyone as it is 'without any reservation' and this should be taken as service of humanity.

Arguing that taking responsibilities into all that matter and an endless responsibility for justice Gandhi seems to absolutize the individual's responsibility to society. The reason for such an absolutism is the belief that every person is responsible for everything that happens in the world. Gandhi seems to argue that every individual is responsible for everything because this "everything" is the conscious production of his/her will and its related agencies. Yet, it does not mean the passive submission of the individual before the happening of the world but Gandhi envokes the idea of *purushartha* in his notion of responsibility which is based on the premise that the individual will is independent of the flow of historical events.

One may note here Gandhi's subjective idealism. Like Sartre, who maintained that man is condemned to freedom, Gandhi also seems to assume that the weight of the whole world is on his shoulders and he is responsible for the world and for himself. He also argues that there is no point in complaining because nothing external has determined what we feel, how we live or what we are. Here law of *karma* may come into the picture in which Gandhi believed but the law of *karma* is not determinism. Even there is the law of *karma* that undoubtedly exists, Gandhi argues one must do *purushartha*. Thus the absolute responsibility, which Gandhi favours, is not mere submission but simply the logically necessary condition for awareness of individual freedom.

At this point, there emerges a significant question of the relationship between the individual and society. Gandhi does not view the relationship between individual and society in contradictory form. For him, responsibility expresses society's specific demand on the individual in the form of duty. Although there are certain social standards, yet, there is also freedom of choice which also includes the possibility of violating these standards or courage to say 'no'. Gandhi views this freedom of choice from the perspective of moral consideration. He further argues that individual responsibility to society shows a tendency that shows how a human being is heading towards the moral and social progress. It is on this ground, he indicates that how in contemporary society the importance of every individual's civil, political and moral responsibility to society has increased that is also determinantal for the fate of nations and of all humanity.

Gandhi's notion of responsibility is not confined only to structural analysis and intervention, but equally, it offers a philosophy of self-transformation. Thus, for him, the individual's task is to make a sincere attempt to live according to the principles of truth and non-violence. Its fundamental tenets are, therefore, personal and moral, but Gandhi cuts the binary of personal and public morality as well as responsibility and offers a whole set of responsibilities that include: resisting injustice, developing a spirit of service, selflessness and sacrifice, emphasizing one's responsibilities rather than rights, self-discipline, simplicity of lifestyle, and attempting to maintain truthful and nonviolent relations with others. Thus, Gandhi's notion of responsibilities embodies a multi-dimensional responsibility with multiple others-especially the sufferers, violated and marginalized in a non-hegemonic way.

An important form of responsibility is responsible for the future, both near and distant. The immediate and near aspect of responsibility might again be noticed in his notion of Satyagraha. For him, in the given Indian colonial context the near or immediate response was that an individual was to resist injustice, untruth, in conjunction with others or alone. He argues that such resistance should be non-violent if at all possible, yet he does not exclude the use of violent means in certain circumstances. For example, preferring violence before the injustice instead of cowardice and to remain a helpless witness, he stated categorically, "Where there is only a choice between cowardice and violence I would advise violence…" (Prabhu and Rao, 2002: 142).

On the other hand, for distant responsibility, that has to be borne out by the individual and take appropriate methods and steps, he presents the vision of Ramrajya, i.e. *Kingdom of God.* His vision of Ramrajya which means 'perfect nonviolent society' is based on the 'sovereignty of the people based on pure moral authority (Prabhu and Rao, 2002: 326). On the nature and possibility of Ramrajya, he once wrote, "I do not know it will be like in Heaven. I have no desire to know the distant scene. If the present is attractive enough, the future cannot be very unlike (Prabhu and Rao, 2002: 326).

As we may deduce, his argument for responsibility carries a heavy burden on human beings. From his perspective, 'we are not responsible for what we do but also *what we tolerate'* (Tercheak, 1998: 194). This Gandhian responsibility 'implicates us in the actions of the institutions around us whether or not we derive some benefit from them' (Tercheak, 1998: 195). From his perspective anyone who tolerates injustice nourishes and exonerates it. Moreover, he/she is escaping from his responsibility. For Gandhi modern complexities confuses the issue of responsibility by assigning it to impersonal institutions where no one seems accountable or masking power and domination with the imperatives of efficiency or productivity. However, complexities, Gandhi claims, can never repeal personal responsibilities, at least if we want to continue to govern ourselves.

III

The third significant aspect of Gandhi's philosophy of action is Detachment. We have already noted that how Gandhi's theory of action is directly linked with his notion of detachment. By *detachment,* he meant that one must not worry whether the desired result follows from one's action or not if the motive is pure. In his words, "By detachment I mean that you must not worry whether the desired result follows from your action or not, so long as your motive is pure, your means correct. Really, it means that things will come right in the end if you take of the means and leave the rest to Him" (Prabhu and Rao, 2002: 463).

Gandhi's idea of detachment comes out of his reading of the *Gita*. But most significantly it was one of the *mantras* of *Ishopanishad*, and it is in the light of this *mantra* Gandhi read *Gita*. As he notes, "I read the *mantra* in the light of the *Gita* or the *Gita* in the light of the *mantra* I find that the *Gita* is a commentary on this *mantra*" (Gandhi, 1996: 20). The mantra states,

> Isha vasyam idam sarvam, yatkimcha jagatyam jagat.
> Ten tyakten bhunjitha, ma gridhah kasya swid dhanam.

It means, "This whole circle of nature is fully pervaded by God whatever is in the universe is under existence and control of almighty God. Renounce all that is injustice and enjoy all that is pure delight."

Gandhi offers a passionate description of this *mantra* in one of his writings.[10] He writes, "... this *mantra* divides itself into four parts. The first part is *Isha vasyam idam sarvam*. It means as I would translate, "All this that we see in this great universe is pervaded by Gods.' Then come the second and third parts which read together, as I read them: *Ten tyakten bhunjitha*. I divide these into two and translate them thus: 'Renounce it and enjoy it.' There is another rendering which means the same thing, though: 'Enjoy what He gives you.' Even so you can divide it into two parts. Then follows the final and most important *part ma gridhah kasya swid dhanam* which means: 'Do not covet anybody's wealth or possession" (Gandhi, 1996: 20).

We have noted that Gandhi formally interpreted the *Gita* and produced his own interpretation, published under the title of *Anasakti Yoga*. *Anasakti yoga* means yoga of freedom from attachment. Gandhi had already prescribed the disciplines of restraint and detachment for his Satyagraha action and movement, but with daily talks on the *Gita*, which he delivered to his followers as a *kathakar*, he crystallized his thinking in order to grasp its real meaning. His interpretation informs us that he understood *anasakti* to be central to the *Gita*.

Moreover, he defined *anasakti* both in terms of positive and negative connotations. He wrote, "*Anaskati* certainly means freedom from attachment to anything concerning oneself and one's relation, but also such deep attachment to Truth, to God" (CWMG:56:43). Thus non-attachment was not simply to disconnect from worldly attachments, but a means to connect to Truth.

Thus in Gandhi's view detachment is not a negative notion or disconnection but it also inherently implies the connection or deep attachment to Truth.

But how one should practice detachment? Gandhi responds as he mentioned in *Discourse on Gita*, "Rather than indulge in such senseless inactivity, is it not better that a man should control the senses, overcome his likes and dislikes, and engage himself in some activity or other without fuss and in a spirit of detachment? Do your allotted duty, restraining the organs of sense, for that is better than inaction. An idler will only meet his end the sooner for his idleness. But while acting, remember that action leads to bondage unless it is performed in a spirit of sacrifice. Sacrifice *(yajna)* means exerting oneself for the benefit of others, in a word, service. And where service is rendered for service's sake, there is no room for attachment, likes and dislikes. Perform such a sacrifice; render such service" (Gandhi, 1930: 12).

Gandhi argues that renunciation is not an intellectual exercise but it is a matter of constant heart-churn. He mentions, "But desirelessness or renunciation does not come for the mere talking about it. It is not attained by an intellectual feat. It is attainable only by a constant heart-churn. Right knowledge is necessary for attaining renunciation. Learned men possess a knowledge of a kind" (Gandhi, 1930: 141). He also argued that renunciation is a kind of test of the right kind of knowledge and devotion also. He mentioned, 'knowledge and devotion, to be true, have to stand the test of renunciation of fruits of action' (Gandhi, 1930: 141). Gandhi argues that one must perform their daily action or duty in the spirit of detachment. "Therefore do your duty from day to day without entertaining likes and dislikes and in a spirit of detachment" (Gandhi, 1930: 141).

He also noted that duty or action is based on attitude and it is the attitude of detachment that matters in performing. He wrote, "But there is a difference between My attitude and the attitude of the common man. I act in the spirit of perfect detachment while he harbours attachment and works in his own interest" (Gandhi, 1930: 13).

Thus he argues that detachment should govern our action with the mere presence of detachment is not enough and one must have patience in his/her efforts. "When detachment governs our actions, even the weapon raised in order to strike an enemy down falls out of our hand. But a mere presence of detachment serves no useful purpose. If only we persevere in our effort, detachment may come to us, perhaps the very first day, or maybe only after a thousand years. We must not worry over the time this takes, for the effort carries within itself the seeds of success. We must, however, be on our guard and make sure that it is a genuine effort, and that there is no self-deception. And this is certainly possible for us all" (Gandhi, 1930: 16).

It is through detachment Gandhi argues that one can purify himself/herself and enter into real peace. Such efforts are the nature of a true *yogi*. In his words, "Therefore a *yogi* (man of selfless action), performing action with the body, mind and understanding in a spirit of detachment and without egotism, purifies himself and enters into peace" (Gandhi, 1930: 21). In his view, the man attached to the world seeks happiness from outside himself. On the other hand, he who acts in a spirit of selfless detachment discovers the spring of eternal peace in himself having withdrawn his mind from external objects.

It is through this kind of attitude and mindset if one performs action one becomes an instrument in the hands of God. Gandhi writes that he who acts in a spirit of detachment, having destroyed his egotism and renounced the fruit of action, becomes a mere machine moving at the will and pleasure of Master Mechanic or an instrument in the hands of God.

We have seen above that, in Gandhi's worldview, right action is service to humankind. He further argues that real service, which is the path to realize God, is possible only through the spirit of detachment. "But what is real service? In order to obtain the right answer to this question, restraint of the senses is essential, as it gives us a clearer and clearer vision of the God of truth. Service rendered with selfish motives ceases to be sacrifice. Hence the urgent need for the spirit of detachment" (Gandhi, 1930: 15). He also argues that even while serving others, a man should act in a spirit of detachment. Otherwise, his activity is likely to be mixed up with evil.

Here we must remind that for Gandhi detachment is not indifference. It is the prerequisite for effective involvement with other. Often what one thinks is best for others is distorted by one's attachments to his/her opinions. One wants others to be happy in the way one thinks one should be happy. It is only when one wants nothing for oneself that one becomes able to see clearly into others needs and understand how to serve them.

Thus for Gandhi detachment does not mean a passive disinterest or cold indifference. Instead, he is pointing to an active state of conscious awareness of the unity of life. One can only glimpse this unity of life when one works to weed out private, selfish attachment and the tiresome obsession about the results of one's actions. In other words, one is detached from *oneself*. When one thinks, how does this benefit me? Then we are not detached. When one thinks, how does this benefit others? Then, we do have some measure of detachment from ourselves, and our ability to use non-violence more effectively comes into its own. Gandhi argues that when we couple that sense of selfless detachment with a burning passion, the apparent paradox becomes a brilliant power.[11] As he writes, "A burning passion coupled with absolute detachment is the key to all success" (CWMG: 85: 370).

However, Gandhi's views on detachment in his overall philosophy present two apparent and significant contradictions/questions. Detachment or *anasakti* is *nivriti marg* and on the other hand, Gandhi favours active life or *karma yoga*, then, how does Gandhi reconcile the tension between active life and *anaskati*? Or how does Gandhi reconcile asceticism and activism? Second, how does Gandhi's idea of universal love, which means psychological attachment, is compatible with his ideal of detachment? How these two are philosophically coherent in Gandhi's worldview? The following section will deal with these issues.

Let us consider the first problematic. The active engagement with this world and *sannyasa* or *nivriti* are often seen conflicting to each other. Gandhi's writing suggests that he disagreed with this kind of argument as, in his views, this type of argument is based on three false assumptions. First, in such an argument God is understood as separate from the world. Second, such argument proposes that only personal salvation is every men's highest concern and third, personal salvation might be in conflict with and be hampered by worldly involvement.

But we have noted that for Gandhi God is not separate from but identical with the totality of human beings. Further, as all beings are manifestations of the cosmic spirit thus personal salvation is indivisible. Thus, the concept of personal salvation is, therefore, philosophically incoherent in Gandhi's worldview. Third, Gandhi seems to argue that far from being hindrance to spirituality, the life of worldly involvement was its necessary training and testing ground. In his view, it was only in the course of a life of action that men learned to discipline themselves, resist temptations, cultivates willpower and cooperative impulses. Further only in the life in world men learn to subordinate his personal to social interests. Moreover, in Gandhi's view, it was only in the realm of action that men are fully tested and stretched and discovered themselves. Gandhi repeatedly argued, as pointed out earlier, that sitting in a forest or a monastery for *sadhna* or personal salvation is no guarantee that one has overcome anger or other *shadripu*. In his view, a *Sannyasi* is one who cares for others and he has renounced all selfishness, but he is full of sleepless and selfless activity. In his view, only in active engagement with the world one can meet the challenges of *shadripu* and find whether he has succeeded in overcoming of those or not. As we note this is Gandhi's redefinition of *nivriti* that reconciles active life and *sannyas* at the same time.

In fact, Gandhi's reconciliation of *nivriti* and *pravirti* or activism and asceticism is based on his critique of two aspects of Hinduism namely philosophical Hinduism and historical Hinduism which had taken the form of popular Hinduism.[12] Gandhi's writings offer the critique of philosophical Hinduism, i.e. Vedantic metaphysics or the Hindu tradition of *nivriti marg* or otherworldly. Although Gandhi was largely inspired be Vedantic idea especially its vision of the unity of all existence and moral harmony in this universe, yet he for many reasons he was not happy with the way it presented itself in due course of time. For Gandhi Philosophical Hinduism defined salvation in personal terms and encouraged selfishness. Second, it lacked social conscience and showed indifference to worldly suffering on the ground that material suffering was spiritually inconsequential. He also found that Vedantic ideas have become 'negative' and 'passive' and had created a horror of *karma* or action. Although Gandhi appreciated the view that active life tends to strengthen the individuality and led to worldly attachments, yet he thought that the *Gita* had already shown how to act in a spiritually blameless manner or *nishkaam bhava*. On the other hand, he also argued that the life of action promote and test the powers of selfdiscipline, and self-control and had profound significance.

Besides, Gandhi also observed that philosophical Hinduism failed to develop an adequate theory of morality. Thus in Gandhi's view, philosophical Hinduism has become unworldly and had restricted itself only to the inner life.

On the other hand, Gandhi also found historical Hinduism or popular Hinduism also problematic in the modern context. In his view, this had become intensely worldly and was mainly interested in the external side of the life. Further, it had more or less reduced religion to *karmkanda*, rituals, rites and ceremonies, pilgrimages to holy places and other rituals with the hope that they would bring religious merit. Moreover, he also found that it had also reduced morality to an uncritical observance of caste duties and social customs.

On the basis of the above critique, Gandhi concluded that both popular and philosophical Hinduism needed to radically reform. The philosophical Hinduism stressed the Brahama and ignored the world while popular Hinduism stressed the worldly affairs and ignore the Absolute. Since neither grasped the fundamental fact of their identity, they ended up misunderstanding both. Thus in his redefining exercise, Gandhi reoriented Philosophical Hinduism to be worldly while popular Hinduism towards the inner life and morality of human order.

Now let us consider the second question raised above. The concept of love was relatively new to Indian philosophical tradition that Gandhi used in his discourse on the action. In fact, the *advaita* tradition of Hindu religion had been deeply suspicious of it. The reason was that love is understood as an emotion that compromised the agent's autonomy. Moreover, it is taken as addictive in nature that also creates desires that finally build up attachments to the person or things loved. On the other hand, detachment means lack of desire and the question before him was to show how his proposed universal love is compatible with the notion of detachment. Gandhi was fully aware of it and he attempted to resolve the tension by redefining both love and detachment. We have noted that for Gandhi love is not an emotion but an objective concern for others well-being. Love for him was also not a subjective feeling but a sentiment of goodwill.

In the same way, he tried to redefine the notion of detachment. We have noted that for Gandhi detachment did not mean indifference but the absence of attachment, not lack of interest but self-interest. By redefining both love and detachment Gandhi tried to show that love and detachment are not only compatible but interdependent. Thus to love one's fellow men was to be guided by consideration for their well-being, not by any reference to one's own interests and desires. To help others because one could not bear to see them suffer because helping them had become a powerful craving or desire was not an expression of love but a form of self-assertion, even of self-indulgence.

Gandhi argued that true love must be totally selfless, not only in an ordinary sense of being unselfish but in the profound sense of not involving the self in any form at all and being wholly non self-referential. It, thus, required dissolution of the self and total detachment. Gandhi argues that God's love for the World was of this kind; deep and warm yet non-emotional, serene and detached.

Summing up

The core of Gandhi's philosophy of action can be summarized in three words—universal love, responsibility, and detachment. For him, *Universal love* means placing oneself at the service of all living beings and devoting all one's energies to 'wiping every tear from every eye'. *Responsibility*, at the personal level, implies; controlling one's actions, to combine word and deed, and to be able to use one's freedom rationally in the public sphere. By *detachment*, he meant that one must not worry whether the desired result follows from one's action or not if the motive is pure.

Gandhi's philosophy of Love is closely linked with his paradigm of 'essential unity of all that exists' and its related notion of 'interdependence'. In his worldview, love is the only way of identifying oneself with other living beings. It means opening up oneself to their presence, relieving them of their otherness and making them part of oneself. His logic is as love deepens, the distance between the two decreases, and at its highest love culminates in total identification. Thus for him, universal love is the only way to attain identification with all living beings. It involves infinite openness, breaking down all the barriers between self and others, letting them flow into one's being and suffuse one's thought and feelings with the deepest concern for their well-being. As we may deduce from above, his notion of love logically puts the bigger responsibility on individuals. Thus his notion of love inherently involves the notion of responsibility.

In Gandhi's worldview, responsibility is not only limited to the personal level but it goes beyond oneself and encompasses other or the public sphere also. Gandhi's notion/embodiment of responsibility is different from working out an *a priori* plan of ameliorating the suffering of others. His notion of responsibility is logically related to his theory of life/truth/love. In his worldview, responsibility is placed exclusively in a way that one cannot refuse without relinquishing a part of his/her own self; since the self-becomes the sole measure of responsibility. His notion of responsibility is radical and infinite in nature. However, it does not mean that it is 'unrestricted'. His notion of responsibility is not confined only to structural analysis and intervention, but equally, it offers a philosophy of self-transformation.

Besides the notion of universal love and responsibility, the notion of detachment is a crucial component of Gandhi's philosophy of action. His idea of detachment comes out of his reading of the *Gita*. In Gandhi's view detachment is not a negative notion or disconnection but it also inherently implies the connection or deep attachment to Truth. He noted that duty or action is based on attitude and it is the attitude of detachment that matters in performing any action. For Gandhi detachment does not mean a passive disinterest or cold indifference. Instead, he argues that detachment is an active state of conscious awareness of the unity of life.

Although love and detachment seem contradictory but Gandhi resolved it by redefining both love and detachment. He tried to show that love and detachment are not only compatible but interdependent. Through such redefinition, he tried to reconcile the *nivriti marg* and the *pravirti marg* of the Hinduism or activism and asceticism.

Notes

1. In his words, "The force of love is the same as the force of soul or truth". (Prabhu and Rao, 2002: 416). Both Truth and love — which Gandhi has described as two sides of the same coin are manifestations of the force of the spirit. "To me God is Truth and Love. He is a personal God to those who need His touch." (CWMG:26:224). He further noted, "One of the axioms of religion *(dharma)* is, there is no religion other than truth. Another is, religion *(dharma)* is love. And as there can be only one religion *(dharma)*, it follows that truth is love and love is the truth. We shall find too, on further reflection, that conduct based on truth is impossible without love. Truth-force then is love force" (CWMG:15:248).
2. Giving a speech at Lausanne on 8 December, 1931, he mentioned, "I found that the nearest approach to Truth is through love. But I found also that love has many meanings, in the English language at least, and human love

in the sense of passion becomes a degrading thing also. I found too that love in the sense of *ahimsa* an non-violence has only limited number of votaries in the world. (CWMG:48: 404). Ravindra Varma offers insightful discussion on it. He notes, "Some readers may point out that the word Gandhi has used more often is 'Ahimsa' or 'Non-Violence', and not 'Love'. One is not sure whether this contention is borne out in Gandhi's writings. However, three observations may be offered. Firstly, as Gandhi himself explained in his speech at Lausanne (1931), the word 'Love' is capable of being used with different meanings, particularly in the English Language. Secondly, non-violence or Ahimsa refers to the first step that has to be taken by anyone who wants to extend his love to "all that exists" *(sarvabhuta),* i.e. to desist from doing harm. Thirdly, it is easier to see what one should desist from if one wants to desist from doing harm than to see what can and should be done for the positive expression of the plenitude of 'Love' " (Varma, 2001: 52).

3. Gandhi argues that Satyagraha proceeds on the active principle of love. It is this power that the Satyagrahi employs in disarming and transforming the person who is ranged against him. Love is a means of transformation. Hatred and violence are means of annihilation. He noted, "It is my firm belief that it is love that sustains the earth. There only is the life where there is love. Life without love is death. Love is the reverse of the coin of which the obverse is truth. It is my firm faith, and it is my experience of forty years that we can conquer the world by truth and love" (CWMG:15:*237*).
4. For him, universal love cannot be possessive and suppressive of individuality. It has to be based on human dignity and the needs of existence, growth, and fulfilment.
5. The Satyagrahi earns the right to non-co-operate and disobey through his love, and through establishing the bonafides of his love, through establishing that his Satyagrah is meant to heal, and not to hurt. Gandhi was perhaps the first person to emphasize the view that love may compel one to resist the beloved, through non-cooperation and disobedience, in order to harmonize and reconcile, not to dominate. The Satyagrahi is motivated by love, and this love includes love for the 'opponent' since what he wants to eliminate is the evil and not the evil-doer (see CWMG:15:*237*).
6. For example, on the question of killing snakes he replied, "Let him not worry if he cannot avoid killing them [snake], but try for all he is worth to overcome the anger and ill-will of men by his patient endeavour as a first step toward cultivating universal love" (CWMG:37:225-6).
7. Gandhi's rejection of the solution offered by Christian missionaries to the problem of untouchables exemplifies this approach.
8. We have earlier noted, satyagraha, Gandhi's method of non-violent resistance, reflects a lifetime of deep reflection on the unity of life and the striving for Truth. One could not stand by, either idly or inefficiently, if one accepted this idea of an inherent trust and responsibility to care for others

and resist evil. Here this responsibility comes again from his understanding of *Advaita* philosophy. In this regard, it is important to relate Gandhi's *Advaita* with his insistence on following *Gita*'s *karma yoga*, since a belief in the divine unity of all existence clearly lends itself to a certain interpretation of a life of service.

9. In this regard, as mentioned, the *Bhagavad Gita*, a central Hindu religious text, was his most important guide for developing this notion of service and the associated necessity of self-suffering. This latter concept is the basis for Gandhi's reconstructed notion of courage along Hindu rather than traditional Western lines. His ideals of fearlessness and self-suffering lead us to a sense of infinite courage that enables us to fulfil the humanist demand amidst the challenge of infinite responsibility.
   Gandhi's notion of courage is essentially another perspective on how to respond to the feeling of infinite responsibility. Gandhi seeks to instill in us a resolute sense of courage and fearlessness in our pursuit of truth and justice. He once complained that Indians were in the habit of saying 'Yes' to everything and needed to develop the courage in order to say 'No' to evil, injustice, untruth, and violence.
10. "....I have fixed upon one *mantra* that I am going to recite to you, as containing the whole essence of Hinduism. Many of you, I think, know the *Ishopanishad*. I read it years ago, with translation and commentary. I learnt it by heart in Yeravda Jail. But it did not then captivate me, as it has done during the past few months, and I have now come to the final conclusion that if all the Upanishads and all the other scriptures happened all of a sudden to be reduced to ashes, and if only the first verse in the Ishopanishad were left intact in the memory of Hindus, Hinduism would live for ever" (Gandhi, 1996: 20).
11. Although Gandhi says that burning passion coupled with absolute detachment is 'key' to all success. At a deeper level, there are many things else at work; our capacity for empathy, joyful determination, and selflessness.
12. He noted, "... a Hindu as one who believed in the Vedas and Upanishads, recited the Gayatri and subscribed to the doctrine of rebirth and transmigration etc., I added that so far as the popular notion of Hinduism was concerned, its distinguishing feature was the belief in cow-protection and reverence for the cow" (Gandhi, 1996: 29). Gandhi also used the term popular Hinduism in one of his writings. He mentioned, "There are two aspects of Hinduism. There is, on the one hand, the historical Hinduism with its untouchability, superstitious worship of stocks and stones, animal sacrifice and so on. On the other, we have the Hinduism of the *Gita*, the Upanishads and Patanjali's *Yogasutras* which is the acme of *Ahimsa* and oneness of all creation, pure worship of one imminent, formless, imperishable God" (Gandhi, 1996: 4).

References

Gandhi, M.K. (1930). *Discourse on Gita*. Ahmedabad: Navajivan. Retrieved from https://www.gandhiashramsevagram.org/pdf-books/discourses-on-gita.pdf.

Gandhi, M.K. (1947). *India of My Dream*. Ahmedabad: Navajivan. Retrieved from https://www.idc-america.org/wp-content/uploads/2015/09/india_dreams.pdf.

Gandhi, M.K. (1955). *My Religion*. Ahmedabad: Navajivan. https://www.mkgandhi.org/ebks/my_religion.pdf

Gandhi, M.K. (1955 a). *Truth is God*. Ahmedabad: Navajivan. https://www.mkgandhi.org/ebks/truth_is_god.pdf.

Gandhi, M.K. (1969). *All Men are bothers*. Switzerland: Unesco. unesdoc.unesco.org/images/0007/000710/071082eo.

Gandhi, M.K. (1996). *The Essence of Hinduism*. Ahmedabad: Navajivan.

Gandhi, M.K. (2001). *Nonviolent Resistance*. New York: Dover Publication.

Prabhu, R.K and U.R. Rao. (2002). *The Mind of Mahatma*. Ahmedabad: Navajivan.

Varma, Ravindra. (2001). *The Spiritual Basis of Satyagraha*. Ahmedabad: Navajivan.

Tercheak, R.J. (1998). *Gandhi Struggling for Autonomy*. New Delhi: Vistaar Publication.

The Collected Works of Mahatma Gandhi (CWMG). Vol: 1-100. New Delhi: Publication Division Government of India. Retrieved from https://www.gandhiheritageportal.org/.

8

Gandhi and Indian Philosophy of Action (Karma)

We have earlier noted that Gandhi's action is profoundly influenced by the notion of *karma* explained in Indian philosophy and especially in *Gita*. In Indian philosophy, the term action has been conceptualized by the notion of *karma*, which is also commonly known as the law of *karma*. This chapter first briefly introduces the views on *karma* illustrated in different Indian schools of philosophy and then traces out how Gandhi views and interprets the Indian philosophy of *karma* in general and the Hindu philosophy of *karma* in particular. It also attempts to show that what Gandhi contributes to the Indian philosophy of *karma*.

I

The law of *karma* is the basic foundation of the entire ancient philosophical and religious thought, right from the Vedas to the modern Vedanta of Sankara. If this presupposition is negated then, all Indian philosophical systems and religious systems become redundant. The law of *karma* is not only the foundation of India's philosophy and its related religion or sect but it also guides all social actions of the most of the Indians. In fact, Indian religion has a moral base and morality is related to practice. The Indian moral ideals have evolved from the Vedic traditions and law of *karma* is one of the central principles of which Vedic philosophy rests. Thus, the law of *karma* has greatly influenced the different schools of thought of Indian philosophical system as well as the life and actions of the people of India.

Karma is the Sanskrit term with root *Kri* that means 'to do', 'to perform', 'to act'. *karma*, then, is action, but more properly speaking, appropriate action. It is noteworthy that the term *karma* has a wider meaning in Indian philosophy and it is not only limited to ordinary human action.[1] It is related to the notion of rebirth, destiny, and liberation of human beings also. The term *karma* in classical Indian philosophies refers to multiple meanings in multiple contexts. The reason for such variation in meaning is that various schools of thought disagree over the nature of the karmic agent and the process of rebirth. Besides, they also differ on the significance of human acts and decisions and the relationship between knowledge and action and the possibility and method of achieving liberation or transcending the cycle of rebirth. Thus, we find multiple meaning of *karma* and interpretation of the law of *karma* even within one school of Indian philosophy.

In spite of the disagreements in meaning and interpretations, the doctrine of *karma* is accepted by all Indian philosophical systems i.e. six orthodox schools as well as the Jainas and the Bauddhas. Broadly, within the Indian philosophical tradition, the Hindu concepts of *karma* differ in important ways from the corresponding ideas found in Buddhism and Jainism. The reason is that most schools of Hinduism place God in the position of administrator, supervisor, and even mitigator of *karma*, while Jainism and Buddhism regard *karma* as an impersonal force or law operating independently of God. With this preliminary note, let us first briefly examine the commonalities on the doctrine of *karma* among Indian philosophical system and then notice the differences among them.

Commonalities among Indian Schools of Philosophy in Regard to the Doctrine of *Karma*

In spite of both major and minor differences, all schools of Indian philosophy agree on certain vital assumptions related to the doctrine of *karma*. In fact, it is these assumptions on which the law of *karma* rests. First such assumption of the law of the *karma* is that the world is linked together in the chain of cause and effect. All Indian philosophical schools agree on this assumption. In fact, this profound assumption serves as a bedrock to the law of *karma* for all Indian philosophical schools. It means everything or event has a definite cause behind it. It is regarded that the law of cause and effect is the most universal law of all laws. Moreover, it is the only law which governs all phenomenon. In this law, every event is accepted as the effect of some invisible force. Further, at the same time, one event can be both a cause and an effect. It is also claimed that under the law of *karma* there is no room left for chance or accident. They view chance or accident as the product of some unknown but definitive causes. Thus, everything is governed by the law of causation.

The second assumption of the law of the *karma* on which all Indian philosophical schools agree is that there exists 'an eternal moral order in the universe'. The law of *karma* in its different aspects is regarded as the law of the conservation of moral values, merits, and demerits of actions in regard to human beings and their actions. "This law of conservation means that there is no loss of the effect of work done and that there is no happening of events to a person except as the result of his own work" (Chatterjee and Datta, 2015: 14-15).

Third, all schools of Indian philosophy schools agree that the law of *karma* implies all actions, good or bad, produce their proper consequences in the life of the individual who acts, provided they are performed with a desire for the fruits of thereof. Thus in a more broad sense, according to the law of *karma*, a person's individual and collective actions determine the nature of his or her future existence in the present life or in a future life. Thus, *karma* is not punishment or retribution, but simply an extended expression of natural acts. In fact, in Indian philosophy, the doctrine of *karma* and *samsara*, i.e. the realm of rebirth and karmic retribution provides causal explanations for the phenomena of life, serves as a foundation for ethical and religious understanding, and rationalizes the commitment to seek liberation from the painful and unsatisfactory worldly existence.

Fourth, all Indian schools of philosophy agree that *karma* is associated with earthly existence as well as with future. It implies that every soul embodied in a human being has the will to make decisions and choose what actions to take. Those decisions and actions generate *karma*, which determines the future circumstances of that human soul's earthly existences.[2] Further, *karma* may determine the circumstances into which a person is born, the various experiences to which he or she is subjected, and the person's natural predispositions, but it does not determine how the person will act in those circumstances. It is argued that human beings can choose to act in such a way that may diminish negative *karma*, such as the practice of asceticism, which denies the physical body and lessens its attachment to the material world. Similarly, human beings can choose to act in such a way that may generate positive *karma*, such as devotion to God, the performance of religious rites, and the fulfilment of filial duties.

Fifth, all Indian schools of philosophy agree that the law of *karma* is not limited only to human beings; it is also extended to the order and arrangement of the physical world. Thus in Indian philosophical schools, the word '*karma*' means both this law in nature and also the force generated by an action by the human being and having the potency of bearing fruit. It is noteworthy that the principle of '*karma*' is not a mechanical one, but a 'spiritual necessity' in Indian philosophy (Radhakrishnan, 1960: 73). In some of the schools of Hindu philosophy, *karma* is also seen as 'the embodiment of the will and mind of God'. Thus, the God is also called '*karmadhyasha*' or the supervisor of our actions.[3]

Sixth, all Indian schools of philosophy agree that law of *karma* does not mean fatality or determinism from which there is no escape. As we may infer, the law of *karma* indeed encourages the individual to see that it is never too late to change his/her perception of life. It does not shut the gates of hope against despair, guilt, and suffering. It engages one in doing the right action. In fact, the significant dimension of the philosophy of *karma* is *dharma*. Here '*Dharma*' is taken as 'duty' or 'right action'. The term *dharma* has special meaning in Indian philosophy and it not institutionalized religion. The *dharma* is formed from the root *dhr* (to hold) which means that which holds a thing and remains its being. Thus every form of life has its *Dharma*, which is the law of its being. It is also seen as conformity with the truthof things. Professor Radhakrishnan has expounded the 'principle of *Dharma*' in the day to day life and its relation to *karma* or human actions. He notes, "Desires constitute the springs of human action. The life of man centres in certain basic cravings, each distinct from the other in its object, and each stimulating men to a particular mode of activity in order to satisfy it. If the several desires were independent of one another and never crossed or modified one another, then their different expressions would be separate and uncoordinated. Family life will have little to do with economic pursuits. Industrial relations will be ethically colourless. Religious activities may be indifferent to the secular sides of life. But man is a whole, and so, all his activities have an overarching unity. Each individual has in him the sex and the parental instincts, love of power and wealth, desire for the common good and a hunger for communion with the Unseen. These different activities react upon and modify one another. They function in interdependence in man's life. If life is one, then there is one master science of life which recognizes the *four supreme ends of Dharma* or righteousness, *Artha* or wealth, *karma* or artistic and cultural life, and *Moksha* or spiritual freedom. The Hindu code of practice links up the realm of desires with the perspective of the eternal. It binds together the kingdom of earth and Heaven" (qtd. in Bharati, 1998: 70).

Thus *karma* or the human action is closely related with observing the *dharma* in Hindu philosophy. One more point needs to be discussed here. From a philosophical perspective, there is a lengthy debate between free-will and *karma*. If one is acting inappropriately now, one can justify this as a consequence of one's past only if *karma* exists. However, along with the theory of *karma*, one is bestowed with volition and one can act according to one's conscience. So while reaping the fruits of one's past *karma*, good or bad, one is accumulating new *karma* as well as acting on one's free-will. This also gives one an opportunity to act in such a way that one may liberate oneself.

Though all scholars declare the unique significance of the Doctrine of *karma*, they are not sure when and where it originated. Further, the concept of *karma* has been differently interpreted by each school of Indian thought. The reason is the metaphysical basis of each philosophical school. In fact, the law of karmain each school is based upon their metaphysical standpoint. Here I would like to illustrate the different views on the law of *karma*, very briefly, that is upheld in different Indian schools of philosophy.

Differences among Indian Philosophical Schools in Regard to the Doctrine of *karma*

The historical origins of the doctrine of *karma* cannot be clearly determined. In the Vedic Philosophy, the law of *karma* has been recognized in the form of the 'Doctrine of *Rta*'. Literally '*Rta*' means 'the course of all things'. It also stands for law and justice. Everything that is ordered in the universe has '*Rta*' as its principle. It is the 'Law of morality and righteousness'. *Rta* is the law, which pervades the whole world, which must be obeyed by all (Radhiakrishnan, 1983: 58). The term *karma* (action) can also be traced back to the early Upnishadas. Early Hindu texts, the Vedas, the *Brahmanas,* and the *Upanishads* prior to 500 B.C., contain some suggestions of the doctrine, but do not indicate a clear and definitive understanding of it. In Hindu philosophy, the theory of *karma* is more dominant in the Vedanta School.

The Samkhya school views the *karma* through its metaphysical outlook.[4] In this school, the law of *karma* is assumed as a valid principle of life. They hold that our life, its character, and everything is determined by it. They argue that though we do not remember our past lives, we can infer particulars about them from the tendencies of the present. These tendencies, according to them, will cease to exist on the disappearance of their cause (*hetu*), motive (*phala*) and substratum (*ashrya*) and object (*alambana*). The root cause is avidya, though we may have other proximate causes. The motive refers to the purpose with reference to which any conation becomes operative in the present. *Chitta* is the substratum of the residual potencies, and the object is that which excites the potencies. Samkhya theory of *Satkaryavada* also points out the admissibility of the law of *karma.* According to it, the effect of subsists in latent form in the cause. They argue for the same reason that the non-existent cannot be existent. In the same way, our present is an outcome of our past lives and on the same logic, the future will be the result of our present lives. Thus, the Samkhya system like other systems believes in *karma* and transmigration. What transmigrates, however, is not the self, but the subtle body, called the *linga Sharir* which consists of eleven organs of sense together with *Buddhi, Ahankaar* and five rudimentary elements (*tanmatras*). This is a permanent annex. Death and birth are the mere change of the gross body and not the subtle. In the subtle, all our vasnas are stored up along with past thought and action (Swami, 1995: 51-60).

Similarly, Nyaya Vaisesika School also views the law of *karma* from its metaphysical position that observes the world as a combination ofmultiple factors. Elements like earth, water, fire, space, time, mind, and *Atman* or self-combine together to make a man or a thing. God is responsible for bringing them together and then separating them. Therefore, the ultimate creation or destruction is the work of God. Every action creates potency and that potency, according to *Nyaya* system, is known as a 'blind force'. They call it *Adrasta* 'The unseen'. It is an unseen force that is generated by all actions and this force is guided by the God. So it is God who is the link in connecting the good act with reward and bad act with punishment in the form of good or bad rebirth (Mittal, 1990: 14)

Thus, Nyaya-Vaisesika believes that the law of *karma* is under the guidance and control of God the Supreme Being who creates the world in accordance with the law. It is here held that the *adrasta* or the stock of merits and demerits of *karmas* held of the individual souls, cannot by itself lead to their proper effects because it is an unintelligent and unconscious principle. It is God who controls our *adrashta* and dispenses al the joys and sorrows of our life in accordance with *karma* (Chatterjee and Datta, 2015: 16).

Mimamsa school attempt to prove the Doctrine of *karma* with the help of its metaphysical doctrine of *apurva.* They say that our acts are enjoyed with a view to their fruits. There is a necessary connection between the act and its result. An act performed today is not bound to produce its results the same day. It may produce its results in the future also. But an act performed today cannot produce its result at some future date unless it produces before exhausting itself to some unseen force. Jaimini terms it as *apurva,* i.e. something new, not known before, so '*apurva*' is the metaphysical link between work and its result (Mittal, 1990: 14). According to them, man enjoys the hits of actions performed in the present life with the help of *apurva.* This is the substance of the Law of *karma* explained by Mimamsa philosophy.

The Vedantic thinker Shankara views the doctrine of *karma* from his famous view of *Brahma* and *Maya*. For *Sankara*, individuality is due to *karma,* which is a product of *avidya.* For him, the world we live in is just the return of the work of the doer. The metaphysical point of *Vedantic* perspective is that they uphold ultimately on reality, called *Brahman.* On the other hand, 'all manifestation is a mysterious appearance. They use the term *Maya* for that. *karma* under this perspective is that activity which appears to be a definite activity, appearing to be initiated by a definite activity and leading again to a definite one but is an expression of that being which is beyond activity and non-activity and can issue into any activity or inactivity whatsoever. The individual for them is a working machinery intended to produce its effects in the form of suffering and happiness. The moral life is always active and is never exhausted. It takes endless forms, owing to the variety of the demands of the conditions of human life. This process goes on for ever unless perfect knowledge is attained." Perfect knowledge consumes the seed of *karma* and makes rebirth impossible. Freedom from the subjection of the Law of *karma* is the end of human life. Even those tendencies with which we are bound can be overcome by the strength of will. Man is not a sum total of his impulses. There is the infinite in him. He possesses freedom with him. He can act according to his own choice. Thus the history of man is a creative evolution (Dasgupta, 1975: 2-6).

Now let us discuss the Hindu philosophical tradition in detail to grasp Gandhi's view on *karma*. Within the Hindu philosophical traditions, most of them agree on three types of *karma*: *prarabdha*, *sanchita*, and *kriyamaka* which mean *karma* to be experienced in this lifetime, latent *karma* which we have not yet reaped, and *karma* that will result in our future lives, respectively (Tilak, 1995: 374-7).

Related to this there is the notion of liberation or *Mukti*. Some argue that liberation is possible within this birth or body while others argue that liberation is not possible unless we are not free from this body. Thus there is a concept of *jîvanmukta* or a living individual who is actually liberated and thus does not accumulate *karma* anymore. In later Hindu traditions which are primarily theistic, the grace of God plays an important role in overriding the karmic implications or completely relieving one and thus leading to *moksha*. Hindu texts such as the Mahabharata illustrate a fully developed and generalized understanding of the doctrine of *karma* and rebirth. It was adopted and interpreted in various ways by most schools of Hindu philosophical and religious thought.

However, the Saivite interpretation is different. The Saivite interpretation of the law of *karma* is that *karma* does not operate autonomously, but depends on the will of God, who acts as an agent and administrator of *karma*. According to the Upnishadik Texts, *jivas* (souls) are without beginning and exist eternally. However, the *jivas* can never enjoy the highest form of liberation without pure knowledge, which cannot be attained without going through the experiences of earthly existence. God is the agent who associates souls with earthly bodies and arranges the circumstances in which each individual *jiva* can work out the *karma* generated by its past actions. Good and bad deeds are qualities of the mind of a person. Each person performs good or bad actions according to his or her inclinations, which were acquired in previous existences, and those deeds determine God's creation of future circumstances in which the law of *karma* can be fulfilled. When a person's deeds are finally exhausted through enjoyment and suffering, self-knowledge arises which leads to the supreme bliss of liberation.[5]

Ramanuja attributes all evil and suffering to the accumulation over time of evil *karma* associated with the *jivas*, or human souls, and maintains that God is a *mala*, without any stain of evil. While Madhava, the founder of the Dvaita School, believed that even if *karma* is accepted as without beginning and as the cause of evil, there must be an initial cause for the variations in *karma*. The fact that the *jivas* have many different kinds of *karma*, both good and bad, must mean that all must not have started with the same type of *karma* from the beginning of time. Thus, Madhva concludes that the *jivas* are not God's creation, but are rather entities co-existent with Vishnu, although under His absolute control. The souls (*jivas*) are dependent on Him in their pristine nature and in all transformation that they may undergo. According to Madhva, although God has control, He does not interfere with humanity's free will, and although He is omnipotent, He does not engage in extraordinary feats. Rather, God must enforce a rule of law and give the *jivas* (souls) full freedom to follow their own natures and experience the consequences of their own actions. Thus, God is the sanctioner or divine accountant, and the *jivas* act freely according to their innate natures and accumulate *karma*. The ultimate power of existence comes only from God; the *jivas* utilize that power for good or evil according to their innate natures. Madhva's doctrine that the *jivas* (souls) were not all equal at their inception led to a concept of eternal damnation which differs significantly from traditional Hindu beliefs. He divided *jivas* (souls) into three classes: *Mukti-yogas*, which qualify for liberation; *Nitya-saṃsarins*, who are subject to eternal rebirth or eternal transmigration due to *Samsara*; and *Tamo-yogas*, who is eventually condemned to eternal hell (*andhatamas*). No other Hindu philosopher or group of Hinduism holds such beliefs; most Hindus believe in universal salvation, the concept that all souls will eventually obtain *moksha,* even if it occurs after millions of rebirths.[6] Thus we find that within the Hindu tradition there are several interpretations of the law of *karma*. Now we discuss how Buddhism and Jainism view *karma* and law of *karma*.

The Notion of *Karma* in Buddhism

Buddhism does not accept God as well as soul (*anatmvaad*). It argues that everything is in a sort of changing process that has been termed as *anityatata.* There is no discontinuity or *Kshanbhangurvaad.* Law of *karma,* according to Buddhism, is a dynamic doctrine and it explains the continuity of appearances in terms of the Law of *karma*. It argues that human beings are trapped in a vicious circle where every action generates further action. This vicious circle is known in Buddhism as *samsara,* the round of birth-and-death, and it is driven by *karma,* the never-ending chain of cause and effect. Thus a proper understanding of *karma* and its causality means that we are free, that we are not bound by *karma* by nature and we can get rid of it is the essence of Buddhism (Mittal, 1990: 9).

In Buddhism, the unresolved *karmas* manifest into a new form composed of five *skandhas* (constituent elements of a being) in one of the six realms of *samsara*. The eventual *nirvana* (salvation) comes through the annihilation of residual *karma* which means the ceasing of the alleged existence of being. The actions with the intention (*cetana*) carried out by the mind, body and speech and which are driven by ignorance, desire and hatred lead to implications that tie one down in *samsara*. Following the eightfold path—the set of eight righteous ways of thinking and acting suggested by Buddha—one can attain *nirvana*. Buddhist teachings appear to have contributed to a strong sense of moral responsibility and its consequences.

Thus, in brief, Buddhism also regards *karma* as a causal principle, which contributes to the continual cycle of rebirth. The term *karma* in Buddhism is usually associated with the action that is 'tainted' with ignorance; ignorance and *karma* continue to determine each other and ensure that the agent remains trapped in an everlasting cycle of *samsara*. Thus the individual's present actions are the result of impressions (predispositions) of the *karmas* of past lives, and they in turn shape predispositions that will affect future lives. Only intentional actions are karmic 'acts of will'. An individual can generate liberating *karma* that will allow him to break the cycle of rebirth which always leads to suffering. In this situation, the individual will leave the *samsara* and permanently enter into the stage of *Nirvana*. This is possible by developing proper insight into the (un) reality of *samsara*. This can be accomplished in a number of ways, including the practice of ethical self-discipline, asceticism and various forms of meditations.

The Notion of *Karma* in Jainism

For Jainism, *karma* does not mean merely a 'deed' or 'work' or a mystical invisible force. In Jainism *karma* is conceived as a subtle matter, atomic particles, pervading the entire Universe in form of particles (Chatterjee and Datta, 2015: 95). They argue that these extremely subtle particles cling to the soul obscuring its intrinsic pristine form. It is sometimes described as the contamination that infiltrates the soul and taints it with various colours. Thus *karma* is the link which ties the soul to the body, and the cause of bondage and sorrow. Every action that a person performs, good or evil, opens up channels of the senses (sight, hearing, touch, taste, and smell), through which *karma* filters in and adheres to the *jiva*. According to Jainism, ignorance of truth and four passions of anger, greed, pride, and delusion attract the flow of karmic matter which obscures the radiance of the soul.

Jainism argues that the way to deliverance from this bondage is through the three jewels of right faith (belief in real existence), right knowledge (knowledge of real nature without doubt or error) and right conduct (the practice of the five virtues) (Chatterjee and Datta, 2015: 98). Through them, the flow of *karma* into the soul is stopped, and existing *karma* is discharged. When the last particle of *karma* has been exhausted, 'the partnership between soul and matter is dissolved', and the soul achieves infinite faith, knowledge, bliss, and power. In such a stage, it then transcends the cycle of earthly existence (*samsara*) and goes to a place or state called Siddhashila, where the *jiva,* identical with all other pure *jivas,* experiences its own true nature in eternal stillness, isolation, and non-involvement and dwells in eternal bliss. Jains believe that this highest and most exalted state, the permanent release of the *jiva* from all involvement in worldly existence, can only be achieved by individuals through their own efforts without the assistance of any god or spirit.

Having discussed the views on the law of *karma* in different schools of thought in Indian philosophy, now examine Gandhi's writings on this subject.

II

Gandhi's writings show that like the traditional Indian philosophical thinkers, he believes in the existence of the law of *karma*. His belief in the law of *karma* is based on his extreme respect for Hindu beliefs and traditions and especially on his reading of *Gita*. Although Gandhi did not write systematically on the law of *karma*, his writings indicate that his views on the law of *karma* serve as bedrock in his entire philosophy of action.

Before we deal with Gandhi's view on *karma*, it is important to point out how he views the soul in men as the law of *karma* presupposes the existence of Soul. According to Gandhi, man is not a mere bundle of flesh and bone but rather constituted with a more vital force 'Soul' (*atman*). Being influenced by the metaphysical belief of Hinduism that every living being has an 'imperishable soul', Gandhi accepts that every person possesses a soul and the soul is the manifestation of the divine.[7] He writes "....though men are not of the same age, the same height, the same skin, and the same intellect, these inequalities are temporary and artificial, the soul that is hidden beneath this earthly crust, is one and the same for all men and women belonging to all times" (Prabhu and Rao, 2002: 419).

Thus Gandhi believes that although we have different bodies but the soul which resides within us is one and the same. He writes, 'What though we have many bodies? We have one soul' and to make his point clear, he makes an analogy of the sun and rays in this regard and mentions, "The rays of the sun are many through refraction. But they have the same source" (Prabhu and Rao, 2002: 8).

He also argues that human body, the material objects and all other empirical things must exist within time and space, but soul transcends time and space and is unborn, eternal, indivisible, all-pervading and self-conscious. This is, as we have noticed, is a distinctive Vedantic view. This Vedantic view has significant implications in Gandhi's philosophy of action that we have discussed in the earlier chapter. In fact, it is on this ground Gandhi claimed that the spiritual gain of one means the spiritual gain of all and one's fall means the fall of the whole of humanity. Here again, Gandhi shares the Vedantic belief in the identity of man within his innermost being with transcendent reality.

In other words, 'other' and 'self' are chained in the same ring. Names and forms are not real but transitory. Because of *avidya* or ignorance, one sees many but when *avidya* or ignorance is removed there is unity of all lives. Thus, for Gandhi, the relation between the individual self and universal Self, so long as one thinks oneself as a distinct entity and so long as one cannot destroy this stale of ignorance, there is a barrier between the two; but when one exterminates one's egotism and selfishness and swims into the ocean of humanity, one can realize the oneness with God and other fellow beings. Thus, as we may deduce, Gandhi believes in the notion of soul and its immortality that play the significant role in the spiritual development of the individual which is the core of his philosophy of action.

Now we see how does Gandhi define *karma*? For Gandhi, *karma* is the 'process of creation', i.e. 'the process through which all beings come into existence'. As he notes "*karma* is the process through which all beings come into existence, or in other words, the process of creation" (Gandhi, 1930: 28). He also related *karma* to God and mentions that God is a 'sum total of *karma*' that 'impels men to do good things'. In his words, "The sum total of *karma* is God. That which impels man to do the right is God. The sum total of all that lives is God. That which makes man the mere plaything of fate is God. That which sustained Bradlaugh throughout all his trials was God. He is the Denial of the atheist" (CWMG: 26: 571). It is important to note that for Gandhi the law of *karma* is also 'inexorable' and 'impossible of evasion'. Moreover, he finds this law 'independent' even to God although God laid down the law. He noted, "The law of *karma* is inexorable and impossible of evasion. There is thus hardly any need for God to interfere. He laid down the law and, as it were, retired" (Gandhi, 2013: 223).

As noted, Gandhi's idea of *karma* was influenced by the *Gita* which was his 'spiritual reference book'. There are ample writings on this issue by Gandhi that inform us that Gandhi candidly accepted the Hindu notion of the law of *karma*. He repeatedly notes that he is a firm believer in the 'inexorable law of *karma*'. For example, he mentions, "I am a devotee of the *Gita* and a firm believer in the inexorable law of *karma*. Even the least little tripping or stumbling is not without its cause and I have wondered why one who has tried to follow the *Gita* in thought, word and deed should have any ailment.... The fact that any event or incident should disturb my mental equilibrium, in spite of my serious efforts, means not that the *Gita* ideal is defective but that my devotion to it is defective" (Gandhi, 1996: 177).

Gandhi also affirms that aspect of Indian philosophical notion of the law of *karma* which means 'everything that happens is the effect of *karma*'. Besides, he also recognizes that *karma* is 'an unfathomable mystery'. As he wrote, "It is perfect logic to say that everything that happens is the effect of *karma*. But the true nature of *karma* is an unfathomable mystery. We, mortals, are so utterly ignorant that we cannot know all the *karmas* which are the cause of even the most ordinary event. It is, therefore, true to say that everything happens through the grace of God. Really speaking, that is the perfect truth" (CWMG: 49:32).

On the basis of his reading of *Gita*, Gandhi also considers how *karma* arises. He locates his idea in his discussion on God, and His *maya* and how *vikaras* born out of *maya* and give rise to various *karmas*. He mentioned, "God and His *maya* (nature) are both without beginning. Modifications (*vikaras*) are born of *maya* and these give rise to various kinds of action (*karma)*. On account of *maya,* the soul experiences pleasure and pain and the fruit of merit (*punya*) and demerit (*papa)*. He who, having realized this, does his duty in a spirit of detachment is not born again in spite of his activity, for he beholds the face of God in all faces, and seeing that not a leaf moves but by the divine will he is free from egotism, understands that he is separate from the body and that the soul, though living in the body, remains by means of knowledge unaffected like the omnipresent ether.' (Gandhi, 1930: 39). Thus we note that he views *punya* and *papa* in terms of pleasure and pain and locates them in the context of God and *Maya*. Besides these direct writings on the law of *karma*, there are many other indirect writings by Gandhi that informs us that Gandhi strongly believed in the law of *karma*. Most significant of them is his *belief in rebirth*. In fact, the law of *karma* and rebirth assumes prime importance in the philosophy of Gandhi's action. Although he did not systematize this idea in a philosophical form, nevertheless it forms a coherent theological whole in his entire writings. Let us examine it.

We have earlier noted that the law of *karma* presupposes the existence of Soul and the concept of rebirth.[8] As seen, Gandhi believed in the philosophical notion of the soul which logically comes into the picture while discussing *karma*. Gandhi employs a traditional Hindu term *Samskars* to elaborate his views on *karma* and rebirth. He wrote, "We take birth according to the *samskaras* of our previous births. New *samskaras* modify them to some extent. There is humility and conservation of strength in allowing ourselves to be known as we are born" (CWMG: 32:66). He further observed, "But it is not easy for all, at least for me, to efface past *Samskaras*. But the delay has not in the least dismayed me. For I have a mental picture of the perfect state. But even if I depart from this body before the hope is fulfilled, I would not think that I had failed. I believe in rebirth as much as I believe in the existence of my present body. I, therefore, know that even a little effort is not wasted (Prbhu and Rao, 2002: 478).

In other words, our action is responsible for other births. Not only this, he also noted that all our relationships are the result of our past *samskaras* or *karmas*. He writes, "I am believer in previous births and rebirths. All relationships are the result of the *Samskaras* we carry from previous births. God's laws are inscrutable and are the subject of endless search. No one will fathom them" (Prabhu and Rao, 2002: 488).

Gandhi candidly believed in the further life and in the continuity of *karma* through successive births. To quote him, "I believe in future life and in the continuity of *karma* through successive births. What we sow here, we must reap here and elsewhere—there is no escape. But, if one repents, even on one's death-bed the repentance will burn sin and sterilize it of consequences" (Gandhi, 1996: 159). He believed in re-birth so forcefully that once he mentioned that, "I believe in re-birth as much I believe in the existence of my present body. I, therefore, know that even *a little effort is not wasted*" (Prbhu and Rao, 2002: 478). Here we may note the optimistic tone of his conviction on the law of *karma* that informs us that no good effort is wasted, but has its reward: it enables one to realize oneself in life in a fuller way and it leads to self-fulfilment.

Gandhi candidly upheld the traditional metaphysical perspective of *karma* that birth and rebirth in various bodies are due to past *karma*. It is *karma* that creates tendencies which determine our subsequent bodies and tendencies. From the moral perspective, for Gandhi, 'what one is', is the result of 'what one has been'. If one suffers 'now' one deserves it due to one's past *karma*. He also sustains the traditional Hindu view that *karma* is cause and effect at the same time. He noted that every individual is unique because of his physical and mental constitution and the individual is the product of his *karmas*. As he points out, ".... What an individual now is, is the effect of his own actions, his habits of thinking, feeling, speaking, and acting in the past. Man makes himself through all these diverse activities, internal and external. They appear to be insignificant separately, but, taken together, they create the tremendous forces that shape his health, character and his entire destiny" (qtd. in Dutta, 1953: 77). From these discussions, it is clear that Gandhi was an adherent follower of the law of *karma*, although, he emphasized more on the moral, pragmatic and ethical side of this belief.

Gandhi's view on *karma* can be also found out in his views on *the incarnation*. It needs to be pointed out that reincarnation of the soul is recognized as a corollary to the doctrine of the law of *karma*.[9] There are ample writings of Gandhi that indicates that he believed in the incarnation, although his interpretation of the incarnation is radically different from the traditional Hindu views on the incarnation.

In common parlance, in traditional Hindu philosophy, incarnation means the descent of God to human flesh and blood for the salvation of human beings. But Gandhi does not view incarnation in this sense. He rejects the traditional idea that God incarnates himself as a human being. In his view, God is already in each and everybody. Thus, he noted that 'àll embodied life is, in reality, an incarnation of God' (Gandhi, 1996: 139). In some persons, the spirit of God remains in the dormant state, while it, in others, is developed. In Krishna, Rama, Buddha, Jesus etc., the spirit was fully awake. Thus, to quote him, "God is not a person. To affirm that He descends to earth every now and again in the form of a human being is a partial truth which merely signifies that such a person lives near to God. Inasmuch as God is omnipresent, He dwells within every human being and all may, therefore, be said to be incarnations of Him. But this leads us nowhere, Rama, Krishna etc. are called incarnations of God because we attribute divine qualities to them. In truth they are creations of man's imagination" (Gandhi, 1996: 52). For Gandhi the belief in incarnation is not 'idle superstition' but it is productive because it is 'testimony of man's lofty spiritual ambition' and thrust to satisfy 'an inmost spiritual want' (Gandhi, 1996: 139). The reason is, "Man is not at peace with himself till he has become like unto God" (Gandhi, 1996: 139).

Again Gandhi's view on the law of *karma* can be viewed in his views on Death. Gandhi views death as 'only a big change in life, and nothing more' and for him, death 'should be welcome whenever it arrives' (Prabhu and Rao, 2002: 461). He notes that 'life and death are phases of the same thing, the reverse and obverse of the same coin' (Prabhu and Rao, 2002: 461). Moreover, he recognized death as 'companion' and as a 'friend'. But why death should be considered a friend? He notes that death is the friend because it brings 'deliverance from the suffering'. He further argues that 'life becomes livable only to the extent that death is treated as the friend, never an enemy' (Prabhu and Rao, 2002: 462).

In a letter titled as 'Death as a welcome friend', Gandhi recognized death as 'wise plan in the economy of nature' and in the same writing, he noted death should be seen as 'unchangeable Law of *karma*. He wrote, "What a comforting thought it is to think of death, whenever it comes, as a wise plan in the economy of Nature! If we could realize this law of our being and be prepared for death as a welcome friend and deliverer, we should cease to engage in the frantic struggle for life. We shall cease to want to live at the cost of other lives and in contempt of all considerations of humanity. But to philosophize is one thing; to realize at the required moment the truth of the philosophy is totally another. Such realization is impossible without a due conception of the definite and grave limitations of the body and an abiding faith in God and His unchangeable Law of *karma*" (Gandhi, 1961: 435).

Further, Gandhi's conviction on the law of *karma* can also be found out in his views on 'fate' and 'destiny' In his view, fate is 'fruition of *karma*'. But he is not deterministic; he argues that human being may act in a way that he could get rid of adverse fate or reduce its impact. He states, "Fate is the fruition of *karma*. Fate may be good or it may be bad. The human effort consists in overcoming adverse fate or reducing its impact. There is a continuous struggle between fate and human effort. Who can say which of the two really wins? Let us, therefore, continue effort and leave the result to God" (CWMG: 79:258).

He strongly argues that one must act at any cost and should not leave everything on destiny. "Between destiny and human endeavour, there is an incessant struggle. Let us continue to endeavour and leave the result to God. Let us not leave everything to destiny, nor be vain about our endeavour. Destiny will take its own course. We should only see where we can intervene or where it is our duty to do so, whatever be the result" (CWMG: 79:433). As a true *karmayogi* he laments that "The pity is that even while knowing what our duty is, we fail to perform it! For this, let every man answer to himself" (CWMG:79:433). He further notes what we are today is the result of our *prarabdha karma*, yet we cannot/should not give up action. He mentions, "What we call *prarabdha* is nothing but the fruit of deeds in our previous births. Human efforts mean our attempts to make desirable changes therein. Sometimes one acts in opposition to the other, while at other times they run together harmoniously. Hence it cannot be said that one is always stronger than the other. We cannot disregard *prarabdha*; we cannot give up human effort. This explains the importance attributed to effort free from attachments." (CWMG:32:66).

Here the karmic theory seems fatalistic in that everything seems pre-determined which might leave one bereft of freedom. But as mentioned, the karmic law and freedom are not antithetic in Gandhi's view. It implies freedom that man can be creative and active and even alter his destiny, though previous *karmas* can influence and limit the freedom. Thus, Gandhi says: "the free will we enjoy is less than that of a passenger on a crowded deck" (Prabhu and Rao, 2002: 71). Here it is implicit that a human being shapes his own destiny. He is the creator of his own future. Once a person comes to this realization he will also try to be a responsible person. In spite of this Gandhi also recognizes the limit of human endevour. He notes, "Man is supposed to be the maker of his own destiny. It is partly true. He can make his destiny only in so far as he is allowed by the Great Power who overrides all our intentions, all our plans and carries out His own plans" (Prabhu and Rao, 2002: 463).

Let us examine this quote in more detail that opens up Gandhi's notion of relation between free will and the law of *karma*. Gandhi's view emphasizes that there is no antithesis between the law of *karma* and the freedom of will. In fact, the law of *karma* implies freedom, for it lays down that the man is the architect of his own destiny. He argues, "Although I know that my freedom is less than that of a passenger, I appreciate that freedom, as I have imbibed through and through the central teaching of the *Gita* that man is the maker of his own destiny in the sense that he has freedom of choice as to the manner in which he uses that freedom. But he is no controller of results. The moment he thinks he is, he comes to grief" (Prabhu and Rao, 2002: 71).

Thus, Gandhi's belief in the law of *karma* does not imply that he considers man's life and activities to be completely determined. In fact, freedom of will is considered by Gandhi as a necessary postulate of morality. The real question is not whether the behaviour is free or not for it is obvious that every behaviour being a response to some given stimulus, must be in some sense determined. The question is how it is determined; whether it is determined from within or from without the self? When we say that behaviour is 'free', what we really mean is, not that it is undetermined, but that the self-acts as a whole, making the action of its own, taking full responsibility. Such self-determined action is to be contrasted with the action at the instinctive level, where the action is determined in a manner. In the first type of action, we recognize personal volition; in the other, we see a creature of impulse. Mere mechanical action, performed under the influence of blind impulse or custom, cannot, therefore, be moral. Gandhi argues that no action which is not voluntary can be called moral. So long as we act like machines, there is no question of morality. If we want to call an action moral, it should have been done consciously and as a matter of duty (Gandhi, 2014: 8). We have discussed this in detail in the previous chapter.

Gandhi's belief in the law of *karma* can also be found in his writings on the correlation between means and end. In fact, his notion of means/end convertibility is the corollary of his conviction on Law of *karma*. All the Indian philosophical schools try to find out what would be the means in order to achieve the end, i.e. freedom from all kinds of suffering. In Indian philosophy, *moksa*—the ultimate end is regarded as *paramapurusartha*. For this, it is necessary to obey and perform the ethical principles in order to get this ultimate end. Thus naturally they give more importance to the means. Like the traditional view, Gandhi, too, gives more importance to means rather than the end. But the basis of this emphasis comes from his belief in the law of *karma*. The reason is it is *karma* which is both cause and effect at the same time. Iyer makes it clear, observing that "He [Gandhi] thought that both the concepts of end and means are the derivatives of the law of *karma* and *karma*yoga of *Gita*" (Iyer, 1967: 324). It is on the same basis of the law of *karma* Gandhi claimed that Truth and non-violence are same.

Indeed here Gandhi was led by his metaphysical belief in the law of *karma*. We have noted that the law of ethical causation or moral retribution links all the acts of interdependent individuals. This makes the relationship between means and ends in the form of organic unity. Thus the moral quality of the individual is causally dependent upon the acts he/she performs. Further, it is also on this grounding Gandhi claimed that "For me it is enough to know the means. Means and ends are convertible terms in my philosophy of life." (Prabhu and Rao, 2002: 226). This statement rejects the notion that in our actual conduct we can make a firm and decisive distinction between means and ends.[10] Gandhi's notion of purity of means is also the corollary of the law of *karma*. He noted, "I feel that our progress towards the goal will be in exact proportion to the purity of our means" (Prabhu and Rao, 2002: 226). Gandhi this statement again expresses the metaphysical belief in the moral law of *karma*, under which there is an exact causal connection between the extent of the moral "purity" (detachment and disinterestedness or the degree of moral awareness) of an act and the measure of individual effectiveness in promoting or pursuing and securing a morally worthy end, over a period of time.

Clearly, this metaphysical belief cannot be conclusively verified or falsified by evidence. Further in his views, "They say 'means are after all means'. I would say 'means are after all everything'. As the means so the end" (Prabhu and Rao, 2002: 226). The statement is a practical recommendation that we must be primarily or even wholly concerned with the immediate adoption of what we regard as a morally worthy (i.e. intrinsically justifiable) means.

Thus, we see that how his views on means-end relationship are deeply based on his belief in the law of *karma*. As Iyer emphasizes that Gandhi's reason for believing this to be wholly and always true was his metaphysical conviction that the whole world is governed by the law of *karma*, that there is a moral order (*rta*) at the heart of the cosmos (Iyer, 1967: 331). Those who do not share this conviction, which is common to all the great religions and is especially prevalent in peasant societies, may well think that a lesser evil could lead to a greater good. Gandhi also accepted that aspect of the law of *karma* according to which, human actions are responsible not only for individual virtues and vices but also for the physical calamities. He argues that that man becomes the victim of physical calamities only because of his own sins (bad *karma*).[11] Referring to the Bihar Earthquake of 1934, He wrote, "I share the belief with the whole world—civilized and uncivilized—that calamities such as the Bihar one [earthquake] come to mankind as the chastisement for their sins. When that conviction comes from the heart, people pray, repent and purify themselves...." (Prabhu and Rao, 2002: 77).

Although it sounded superstition and unscientific and Gandhi was criticised for such a statement but on 25 January, 1934, speaking at Tuticorin, Gandhi clearly mentioned his same position, "I want you to be 'superstitious' enough with me to believe that the earthquake is a divine chastisement for the great sin we have committed and are still committing against those whom we describe as untouchables" (CWMG: 57: 46).

By sin, Gandhi was referring to the practice of untouchability committed by the so-called upper-class Hindus. Gandhi also tried to posit a *connection* between the 'Act of God' and the man-made 'calamity' of untouchability. He letter on wrote, "For me there is a vital connection between the Bihar calamity and the untouchability campaign. The Bihar calamity is a sudden and accidental reminder of what we are and what God is, but untouchability is a calamity handed down to us from century to century. It is a curse brought upon ourselves by our own neglect of a portion of Hindu humanity. Whilst this calamity in Bihar damages the body, the calamity brought about by untouchability corrodes the very soul. Therefore, let this Bihar calamity be a reminder to us that, whilst we have still a few more breaths left, we should purify ourselves of the taint of untouchability and approach our Maker with clean hearts" (CWMG: 57:45-46).

Gandhi argues that although he has limited knowledge of God's purpose but 'Such calamities are not a mere caprice of the deity or Nature'. In his view, "They obey fixed laws as surely as the planets move in obedience to laws governing their movements. Only we do not know the laws governing these events and, therefore, call them calamities or disturbances" (Prabhu and Rao, 2002: 77). He further argues that 'There is a divine purpose behind every physical calamity'. His solution is that "let us get rid of the distinctions of high and low, purify our hearts and be ready to face our Maker when an earthquake or some natural calamity or death in the ordinary course overtakes us" (Prabhu and Rao, 2002: 78).

However, Gandhi cleared that one cannot be certain about a particular calamity to a particular human action, yet what is desirable in the face of such a calamity is introspection, repentance, and self-purification. He mentioned, "This is not to say that we can with certainty attribute a particular calamity to a particular human action.... All that I mean to say is that every visitation of Nature does and should mean to us Nature's call to introspection, repentance, and self-purification.... I would even go so far as to say that even the recent earthquake would not be too great a price to pay, if it enabled India to cast out the canker of untouchability" (CWMG: 57: 318).

Here we may note how Gandhi views physical force are also affected by human action and *vice versa*. Thus what we find is that Gandhi articulates a position on the relation between physical and moral phenomenon. He wrote "I have long believed that physical phenomena produce results both physical and spiritual. The converse I hold to be equally true" (CWMG:57:164-5). This shows again his strong belief in the law of *karma*.

Finally, we see what Gandhi contributes to the notion of the law of *karma* which is the foundation of all Indian Philosophy in general and Hindu philosophy in particular. First of all, Gandhi's view on the law of *karma* differs to some extent with regard to rebirth than that of Hindu thinkers. As Jha notes, "In Hinduism, rebirth is, more or less, a metaphysical doctrine for explaining life prior to birth and after death. On the other hand, Gandhi gives a moral interpretation of this doctrine by emphasizing the pragmatic and ethical values of this belief. He believes that one is able to make the adjustment to life by believing this doctrine. It enables man to be loving, kind, moral and benevolent even in the midst of strife" (Jha, 1985: 82). Gandhi also emphasizes that doctrine of rebirth ensures that 'even a little effort in this life is not wasted' suggests that he informs us that life provides repeated opportunities for the man, who has not been able to fully realize himself in one life, to work again and again for self-development. In Gandhi's view, the law of *karma* is the law of moral continuity. He explains that our future will grow out of our present as our present is the product of our past. This is the reason Gandhi declares that law of *karma* is inexorable and impossible of evasion and hardly any need for God to interfere. For Gandhi, the law of *karma* gives a satisfactory explanation of 'what is' and 'what is going to be'. Gandhi believed in this theory and emphasized the metaphysical aspect of it. The individual, by his right-doing, can again enjoy freedom and liberation. In the light of this law of *karma*, Gandhi saw the importance of the present life and the necessity for moral life. The present life is the fruit of the past and the future will be the child of the present. However, for Gandhi, the moral significance of the law of *karma* appears to be more significant because it is consistent with his moral convictions. The realization that one's own *karmas* determine the future nature and status of an individual creates the future realization that man himself is the maker of his destiny. Gandhi thinks that such a realization will create a sense of responsibility in man.

Summing up

The law of *karma* is the foundation of all schools of Indian philosophy in general and Hindu philosophy in particular. It also serves as guiding principle of all social actions for the most of the Indians. The doctrine of *karma* is not only limited to ordinary human actions but it is related to the notion of rebirth, destiny, and liberation of human beings also. The term *karma* in classical Indian philosophies refers to multiple meanings in multiple contexts because of their difference in metaphysics. In spite of the disagreements in meaning and interpretations on the law of *karma*, the doctrine of *karma* is accepted by all Indian philosophical systems. All schools of Indian philosophy accepts certain assumptions related to the law of *karma*. First such assumption of the law of the *karma*, on which all schools of Indian philosophy agree, is that the world is linked together in the chain of cause and effect. The second assumption of the law of the *karma* on which all Indian philosophical schools agree is that there exists 'an eternal moral order in the universe'. Third, all schools of Indian philosophy schools agree that the law of *karma* implies all actions, good or bad, produce their proper consequences in the life of the individual. Fourth, all Indian schools of philosophy agree that *karma* is associated with earthly existence as well as with future. Fifth, all Indian schools of philosophy also agree that the law of *karma* is not limited only to human beings; it is also extended to the order and arrangement of the physical world. Sixth, all Indian schools of philosophy agree that law of *karma* does *not* mean fatality or determinism from which there is no escape. In spite of these commonalities among the different schools of Indian philosophy, they differ in interpreting it.

The Samkhya School views the *karma* through (*Hetu*), motive (*phala*) and substratum (*ashrya*) and object (*alambana*). *Nyaya - Vaisesika* believe that the law of *karma* is under the guidance and control of God the Supreme Being who creates the world in accordance with the law. They call it *Adrasta* (The unseen).

The *Mimamsa* School attempt to prove the Doctrine of *karma* with the help of its metaphysical doctrine of *apurva*. According to them, man enjoys the hits of actions performed in the present life with the help of *apurva*. The Vedantic thinker Shankara views the doctrine of *karma* from his famous view of *Brahma* and *Maya*. He argues that perfect knowledge consumes the seed of *karma* and makes rebirth impossible. Freedom from the subjection of the Law of *karma* is the end of human life. Within the Hindu philosophical traditions, most of them agree on three types of *karma—prarabdha*, *sanchita*, and *kriyamaka* which mean *karma* to be experienced in this lifetime, latent *karma* which we have not yet reaped, and *karma* that will result in our future lives, respectively. Saivite interpretation of the law of *karma* is that *karma* does not operate autonomously, but depends on the will of God, who acts as an agent and administrator of *karma*. On the other hand, according to Madhva, although God has control, He does not interfere with humanity's free will, and although He is omnipotent, He does not engage in extraordinary feats. Law of *karma,* according to Buddhism, is a dynamic doctrine and it explains the continuity of appearances in terms of the *karma*. The term *karma* in Buddhism is usually associated with the action that is 'tainted' with ignorance; ignorance and *karma* continue to determine each other and ensure that the agent remains trapped in an everlasting cycle of *samsara*. For Jainism, *karma* does not mean merely a 'deed' or 'work' or a mystical invisible force. In Jainism *karma* is conceived as a subtle matter, atomic particles, pervading the entire Universe in form of particles.

Gandhi's writings show like the traditional Indian philosophical thinkers, he believes in the existence of the law of *karma*. His belief in the law of *karma* is based on his extreme respect for Hindu beliefs and traditions and especially on his reading of *Gita*. Although Gandhi did not write systematically on the law of *karma*, his writings indicate that his views on the law of *karma* serve as bedrock in his entire philosophy of action. For Gandhi, *karma* is the 'process of creation', i.e. 'the process through which all beings come into existence'. He also relates *karma* to God and mentions that God is the 'sum total of *karma*' that 'impels men to do good things'. Besides, he also recognizes that *karma* is 'an unfathomable mystery'. For him, the law of *karma* is *also* 'inexorable' and 'impossible of evasion'. Moreover, he finds this law of *karma* 'independent' even to God although God laid down the law. He also affirms that aspect of Indian philosophical notion of the law of *karma* which means 'everything that happens is the effect of *karma*'. Gandhi also believed in the further life or re-birth and in the continuity of *karma* through successive births. He also believed in the incarnation, although his interpretation of the incarnation is radically different from the traditional Hindu views on the incarnation. Gandhi's view on the law of *karma* can be found out in his views on 'death', 'fate' and 'destiny'. Gandhi's belief in the law of *karma* can also be found in his writings on the correlation between means and end. In fact, his notion of means/end convertibility is the corollary of his conviction on Law of *karma*. Further, he also accepted that aspect of the law of *karma* according to which, human actions are responsible not only for individual virtues and vices but also for the physical calamities. He views physical force are also affected by human action and *vice versa*. Thus, he articulates a position on the relation between physical and moral phenomenon.

Gandhi's belief in the law of *karma* does not imply that he considers man's life and activities to be completely determined. For him, there is no antithesis between the law of *karma* and the freedom of will. In his view, the law of *karma* implies freedom, for it lays down that the man is the architect of his own destiny.

Further, in Gandhi's view, the law of *karma* is the law of moral continuity. He explains that our future will grow out of our present as our present is the product of our past. This is the reason Gandhi declares that law of *karma* is inexorable and impossible of evasion and hardly any need for God to interfere.

For Gandhi, the moral significance of the law of *karma* appears to be more significant because it is consistent with his moral convictions. The realization that one's own *karmas* determine the future nature and status of an individual creates the future realization that man himself is the maker of his destiny. Gandhi thinks that such a realization will create a sense of responsibility in man.

Notes

1. As we have seen in the previous chapter, Monima Chadha notes that there are five meanings of *karma* in Indian philosophy. *karma* is firstly understood as 'any act, being physical, mental, intentional, unintentional, moral or amoral' etc. Second, *karma* can be understood in a more restricted sense as 'any form of mental activity in any state of consciousness', this is 'not the action itself, but the intention of the action'. Third, *karma* is understood as 'as all acts that have moral value'. In the fourth sense, *karma* is taken as 'an imperceptible force or law shaping the destiny of all living beings'. This is known as the Law of *karma*. This is the context in which *karma* is generally understood in Western culture. Lastly and fifth *karma* is interpreted as the 'accumulated result (residue) of all acts during one's life'(Monima Chadha, 1998: iii).
2. Here it might be noted that animals, plants, and inanimate objects (which some schools of thought consider to be sentient) do not have the freedom to act consciously.
3. In this school of thought, the day of judgment by the God is not fixed. Nor it is in some remote future, but it is here and now. It is regarded that one carries with oneself every bit of our past. Further, no man can escape from the consequences of his own thoughts, words, and deeds either here or hereafter. There is, no doubt, room for repentance and forgiveness, but forgiveness is not a mitigation of God's justice, but only an expression of it. In the Indian philosophical system, it is argued that 'Dharma' is the right action, and '*karma*' is all kinds of action. If one deviates from 'Dharma' one gets the consequences of one's *karma*.

4. The Samkhya philosophy accepts reality as of two kinds—the purusa and the prakiti. One is being or the soul and the rest of them are other than the souls. The nature other than the souls is ever active and that has got its own three constitute characteristics of, Satva, Rajas and Tamas. Satva, Rajas and Tamas are the modes of activity. Satva is for balance or equilibrium which represents the noble qualities. Rajas indicates an energetic and active tendency. Tamas indicates the tendency of dullness or Inertia. All these aspects are there in nature in general.
5. For more detail visit www.newworldencyclopedia.org/entry/*karma*
6. For more detail visit www.newworldencyclopedia.org/entry/*karma*
7. There is a wider application of this view in Gandhi's paradigm. Since the soul is non-physical and spiritual in essence, Gandhi believes in the essential unity of mankind. For this, he offers the analogy of the sun and the rays. The rays of the sun are different but their source is the same. Similarly, there are many people but they possess the same divine spark, the soul, whose source is God. He also believes in the 'immortality of the soul'. He gives the analogy of the ocean. The ocean is composed of water, each drop is an entity and yet it is part of the whole, 'the one and the many'. Thus he concludes that 'in the ocean of life we are all little drops' (Prabhu and Rao, 2002: 478-9).
8. Especially, in Hindu philosophy, birth and death are the two forms of transformation of the human body. But this process of change does not affect the soul. Death is inevitable if there is birth. Birth is understood as the beginning of death. The existence of the present body or birth is self-evident. In the same way, rebirth, according to Gandhi, does not require any further proof. Gandhi seems to believe that Man is always chained in the cycle of death and rebirth. No one can escape from this cycle until moksha (salvation) is attained.
9. The notion of incarnation is directly related to the doctrine of *karma*. As Daniel notes, "The doctrine of *karma* is inextricably connected with the doctrine of reincarnation. The body being a garment of the soul, each life is one of the series of the incarnation of the soul in its journey through eternity, a chain beginning and ending in the amorphous ultimate. The *karma*, the accumulated good, and evil of each mortal lifetime determine the kind of body and life situation in the next incarnation" (Daniel, 1996: 78). Gandhi seems to assert this Hindu philosophical position. In Hindu tradition, the word incarnation usually indicates the ten incarnations of Vishnu, the God of preservation and sustenance.
10. One might note here Gandhi's conception of the psychology of human action. It requires the rejection of a conventional conceptual habit which makes us ascribe to ourselves greater knowledge and greater assurance than we actually possess. Thus he argues that individual has always control over the means but not over the end. This statement, as we may see, asserts a contingent truth about the extent and the limit of our free will, that the individual's capacity to determine what he can do in any specific situation

at any given time is much greater than his power of anticipation, prediction, and control over the consequences of his actions.

11. On 15 January, 1934, an earthquake shook Bihar and caused extensive damage. Gandhi declared that this earthquake was God's punishment for the sin of untouchability. He had no objection to the orthodox Hindus' suggestion that perhaps God was displeased with his teaching on untouchability: everyone had a right to interpret God's purpose as he pleased. For himself, he was absolutely certain that the devastation in Bihar was caused by men's sinful refusal to permit the untouchables into the temples. (Payne, 1969: 456).

References

Bharati, K.S. (1998). *Encyclopedia of Eminent Thinker*, Vol. 4. New Delhi: Concept Publishing Company.

Chatterjee, Satischandra and Dhirendramohan Dutta. (2015). *An Introduction to Indian Philosophy*. New Delhi: Rupa Publications.

Daniel, Mangalnat. (1996) *A Challenge and a Promise: Mahatma Gandhi's Philosophy of Man and Life*. Trivandrum: M.S. Publication.

Dasgupta, S.N. (1975). *A History of Indian Philosophy*, Vol. 2. Delhi: Motilal Banarsidass.

Dutta, Direndra Mohan (1953). *Philosophy of Mahatma Gandhi*. Madison: University of Wisconsin Press.

Gandhi, M.K. (1930). *Disocurse on Gita*. Ahmedabad: Navajivan. Retrieved from https://www.gandhiashramsevagram.org/pdf-books/discourses-on-gita.pdf

Gandhi, M.K. (1961). *In Search of Supreme*, Vol. I (ed. V.B. Kher). Ahmedabad: Navajivan. Retrieved from https://www.mkgandhi.org/ebks/in-search-of-the-supreme-I.pdf.

Gandhi, M.K. (1996). *The Essence of Hinduism*. Ahmedabad: Navajivan.

M.K. Gandhi, (2013). *The Story of My Experiments with Truth*. Ahmedabad: Navajivan.

Gandhi, M.K. (2014). *Ethical Religion*. Ahmedabad: Navajivan.

Iyer, Raghvan. (1967). "Means and End in Politics" in *Gandhi—His relevancy in our Time* (ed. G. Ramchandran and T.K. Mahadevan). Delhi: Kapoor Printing Press. Retrieved from https://www.mkgandhi.org/ebks/gandhi_relevance.pdf

Jha, Nirmala. (1985). *Law of Krama As Perceived by Gandhi, Aurobindo, Vivekanand, Radhakrishnan*. New Delhi: Capital Publishing House.

Mittal, K.K. (1990). *Various Perspectives on Karma and Rebirth*. Delhi University: Department of Buddhist Studies.

Monima Chadha. (1998). *Topics in Indian philosophy*. Churchill: Monash Philosophy.

Payne, Robert. (1969). *The Life and Death of Mahatma Gandhi*. New York: E.P. Dutton and Co.

Prabhu, R.K. and U.R. Rao. (2002). *The Mind of Mahatma Gandhi.* Ahmedabad: Navajivan.

Radhakrishnan, S. (1960). *The Hindy way of Life.* London: Unwin Book.

Radhiakrishnan, S. (1983). *Bharatheeya Darsanam (M), Vol. 1.* Calicut: Mathrubhoomi.

Swami Gnanananda Saraswathi. (1995). *Sankhya Darsanam.* Kanyakumari: Anandkudeeram.

Tilak, B.G. (1995). *Sri Mad Bhagwad Gita Rahasya.* Trichur: Sulabha Books.

The Collected Works of Mahatma Gandhi (CWMG) Vols. 1-100. New Delhi: The Publication Division, Government of India. Retrieved from https://www.gandhiheritageportal.org.

Conclusion

The study intended to explore Gandhi's philosophy of action. It attempted to examine, through a discursive journey of Gandhi's writings, that what elements really 'constituted' Gandhi's action, and how Gandhi's action was related to his metaphysics, epistemology, and ethics. Beginning with the abstracting and conceptualizing Gandhi's action, especially to his Satyagraha and Constructive Programme, it was noted that Satyagraha and Constructive Programme provided practical expression to his notion of truth and non-violence. In fact, these two powerful actions are motivated by the commitment and action to Truth thus they are Truth-in-action. Gandhi's notion of Truth and non-violence, serving as his metaphysics, also showed that they were not the static description of reality but dynamic and evolving in nature. This unique nature of his metaphysics indeed provided enough space to him for new avenues of action.

Examining Gandhi's metaphysics and its relation to his views on the action, it was noted that his notion of Truth, both the Absolute and relative, is not for academic interest or dry scholastic discussion but it strongly conveys one to engage in action. His Absolute truth serves as the guideline for the action; relative truth provides space for action in the form of experimentation. Non-violence or *ahimsa* as an activity and action also played the pivotal role in his metaphysical scheme and it is by means of non-violence or *ahimsa* Gandhi developed his philosophy of temporal action. Gandhi argued that one can comprehend Absolute truth only through non-violence. His argument is that the nature of Absolute truth is cohesive which symbolizes supreme love and pure conscience, thus, if one has to be in the conformity of Absolute truth, one cannot take the path which is against it. It means one cannot take the path of violence to have the glimpse of Absolute truth, as hate and other lower values are disintegrating forces. Further, violence against other is, in fact, violence against oneself as other is no other but one's own version. Thus, Gandhi argues that our action must be non-violent. The distinction between Absolute truth and relative truth was found only a working hypothesis for action in Gandhi's worldview. In fact, in the final analysis, there is no separation between them. Absolute truth cannot be comprehended as it is beyond our reason and experience, thus, one must depend on relative truth. For Gandhi, Absolute truth and relative truth are not the effect and cause rather they are in congruence with each other or there is an 'organic unity' between them. Thus in actual practice, the means and end become one. In other words, truth as an end and non-violence as means are actually the same. His notion of truth as 'inner voice' or conscience also invites one for heroic action. Moreover, very nature of Gandhi's metaphysics implied brave action which was not restricted to personal exercise in good faith but it incorporated the community and group action too calling for social and political action in the form of reconstruction or resistance.

The study also tried to understand Gandhi's metaphysics and its relation to his epistemology to have an in-depth view of Gandhi's action. Reconstructing Gandhi's epistemologically, it was noted that Gandhi's source and Absolute truth was Hindu scripture that was elaborated and reinterpreted by him to engage the individual in the given time and context. For Gandhi, Absolute truth is beyond our 'empirical' grasp and one must have 'faith' in it which was called by him as 'sixth sense'. For mundane and immediate action, Gandhi derived the notion of 'relative truth' which was empirical in nature. To realize Truth, Gandhi gave a very limited role to the 'sense perception' and found it 'deceptive'. Although he acknowledged 'reason' as 'an instrument of knowledge', yet he argued that 'reason' cannot be given the 'highest place'. For Gandhi empirical knowledge and reason are applicable in certain areas but there are areas where they cannot work. In such a case faith works. Arguing that faith is 'a living, wide-awake consciousness of God within', he suggested that 'faith transcends reason' when intellect fails. Most importantly Gandhi did not see reason and faith 'contradictory' to each other. His metaphysics and epistemology shaped his philosophy of action on a distinctive platform.

Gandhi's view of the action, derived from his metaphysics as well as epistemology, was logically bound to be moral in nature. He argued that action can be termed 'moral action' only if it is volitional, intentional, universal, practical, selfless and free from fear and compulsion simultaneously. If anyone of the above factors is lacking in any action it would not be a moral action in the Gandhian sense. He also argues that a moral action should be performed consciously, deliberately with the determined will, regardless of gain and loss, of life or death, without turning to look back, and ready to sacrifice themselves. It was also noted that in Gandhi's view 'action without knowledge is of no worth'. On the basis of *Gita*, he argues that there are three things that inspire action: knowledge, the object of knowledge and the knower. The most striking aspect of his interpretation is its inclusiveness/integration of action in relation to knowledge. Further, the concept of action that Gandhi borrowed from the *Gita* makes knowledge just one component of the totality of action. The need for knowledge was itself to be understood only in terms of its impact on action.

Action for Gandhi is not only the bearer of truth but also a means of self-disclosure as a precondition for discovering the truth. In his paradigm, self-disclosure invites one to take responsibility for one's self that further requires action for understanding self, self-discipline, self-restraint, and self-purification. As action is a means of self-realization in Gandhi's worldview, thus he argued that action must not spring from the motive of self-interest. The reason is: self-interested action is directed towards protecting and/or promoting individual welfare, thus, it violates the essential oneness of humanity and equality of human beings. As such, he argues, action must not be based on self-interest but on the welfare of others. Gandhi argued for self-less action, to develop a personal perspective that allows selfless action involving the subjugation of the empirical self.

On this basis, Gandhi's action invites the self to engage with others in the non-violent way. It is the responsibility by which the self is related to others in the form of action. Gandhi's notion of responsibility deconstructs the binary of responsibility to oneself and responsibility to other as the individual is not separate from others. He is the same as others. In his worldview, there are no others, there is only the self, or versions thereof. His notion of responsibility was based on individuals 'oneness with others', that was further based on his perception of the divinity of humanity, as he claimed that individual is 'part and parcel of the whole' and 'cannot find Him [God] apart from the rest of humanity'.

The study found that Gandhi's philosophy of action comprises three essential components—universal love, responsibility, and detachment. Offering and attaching special meaning to these terms, for him, 'universal love' is motive and intention of action, responsibility—both to oneself and others—, is a dynamic process by which action takes a shape and detachment shows the attitude towards the result of the action. For him, universal love cannot be possessive and suppressive of individuality. It has to be based on human dignity and the needs of existence, growth, and fulfilment. Gandhi's notion of responsibility is logically related to his theory of life/truth/love. Gandhi saw a life of truth/love as actively following an imperative to be engaged in the world, through responsibility, both in the term of reconstruction and resistance. Gandhi's notion/embodiment of responsibility is different from working out an *a priori* plan of ameliorating the suffering of others. Gandhi's engagement with others was always and at the same time turned towards an inner journey and it was more an exploration of his own being than removing the suffering of others with a set political-social agenda. His notion of responsibility was found 'radical' and 'infinite' in nature but not 'unrestricted'. His idea of responsibility also offers the critique of modern and prevalent response to human suffering. In his view, one is responsible not because one has a mission to spread the truth, and not because one is impelled to act by a sense of charity, but because other is suffering and that other is not separate from me.

As Gandhi seemed to be following the Indian philosophical tradition of action it was attempted to see how far he is near to or distant to Indian philosophy of the law of *karma*. It was noted that Gandhi advocates the efficacy of the law of *karma*. He recognized the law of *karma* as 'an unfathomable mystery', 'inexorable' and 'impossible of evasion'. He also affirmed that aspect of Indian philosophical notion of the law of *karma* which meant 'everything that happens is the effect of *Karma*' although he argued that the law of *karma* is 'independent' even to God although God laid down the law. He also described the metaphysical status of man in terms of his *karma*. He argued that every individual is unique because of his peculiar physical and mental inheritance. What an individual now is, the effect of his actions, habits, and thinking, feeling and speaking in the past. Man makes himself what he is through his diverse activities. Yet he interpreted the law of *karma* in his own way. He emphasized the moral significance of the law of *karma* which was consistent with his moral beliefs. The realization that one's own *karmas* determine the future nature and status of man gives rise to the further realization that it is the man himself who is the architect of his own destiny. He says that such realization helps man to create a sense of responsibility. It also informs that this helps man to realize the reality of Divine latent in him. Finally, the study concludes that Gandhi's philosophy of action is based on Gandhi's following premises/assumptions:

1. There are no two worlds as the material world (this) and spiritual (that or other) world. Thus, there can be *no* separate action for this world (*vayavharik karma*) and for another world (*parmarthik karma*). Hence, there is also no need for withdrawing from the world of everyday life to devote oneself to spiritual practices for the other world.
2. The action is unavoidable. Every moment, a human being confronts with the need to act. He, therefore, needs a code that could help him to determine his course of action. This code can flow only from the knowledge of the Supreme Law that governs the Universe. One needs to know the Law because the Law is unalterable, and its effect is inexorable. For Gandhi, this Law is Absolute truth.
3. The central objective of human life is self-realization. It means not only *to know* the truth but also *seeking* the truth i.e. to be in conformity with the higher law or Absolute truth. Thus, the individual has 'responsibility' and 'duty' to know and seek the truth. This responsibility and duty engage one in an active action.
4. As it is the 'duty' and 'responsibility' of the human being is to find the higher law/Absolute truth and live by it, therefore, one cannot ignore or withdraw from any field of human activity because the higher law is 'sovereign law', thus, it is everywhere. As a corollary, every mundane act, therefore, can be, and should be, made a spiritual act, through the conformity to the Supreme Law or Absolute truth.
5. As an act should be in accordance with the higher law or Absolute truth, and the Absolute truth is highest morality or ethics, thus, every act is bound to be moral in nature.
6. The conformity with the higher law comes directly through the action of service of humankind in general and to act or serve them who are in margin in particular.

7. To act for other or serve other is, in fact, acting and serving oneself as the individual self is not separate from others as other is no other but the version of self thereof. The self is related to other through duty and responsibility.
8. The motive and intention of individual action should be universal love as the Absolute truth also means universal love.
9. The action must be selfless in the spirit of detachment.

Bibliography

Allen, Douglass (ed.). (2008). *The Philosophy of Mahatma Gandhi for the 21st century.* Lanham: Lexington Books.

Anscombe, G.E.M. (1963). *Intention.* Oxford: Blackwell.

Austin B. Creel. (1972).'Dharma as an ethical category to freedom and responsibility', *Philosophy East and West.* 22.

Bharati, K.S. (1998). *Encyclopedia of Eminent Thinkers,* Vol. 4. New Delhi: Concept Publishing Company.

Brook A. (2004). *Kant's view of the mind and consciousness of self.* The Stanford Encyclopedia of Philosophy (Winter 2004 Edition), Edward N. Zalta (ed.). Retrieved from http://plato.stanford.edu/archives/win2004/entries/kant-mind/ on 23 -05-2017.

Borman, William. (1986). *Gandhi and Nonviolence.* New York: State University of New York Press.

Bondurant, J. (1957). *Conquest of Violence.* Princeton: Princeton University.

Bose, Nirmal Kumar. (1948). *Selections from Gandhi.* Ahmedabad: Navajivan.

Bratman, M. (1987). *Intention, Plans, and Practical Reason,* Cambridge, MA: Harvard University Press.

Chadha, Monima. (1998). *Topics in Indian Philosophy.* Churchill: Monash Philosophy.

Chatterjee, Satischandra and Dhirendramohan Dutta. (2015). *An Introduction to Indian Philosophy.* New Delhi: Rupa Publications.

Ch'en, Kenneth K.S. (1968). *Buddhism: The Light of Asia.* New York: Barron's Educational Series, Inc.

Dalton Dennish. (1993). *Mahatma Gandhi: Nonviolent Power in Action.* New York: Columbia University Press.

Daniel, Mangalnat. (1996) *A Challenge and a Promise: Mahatma Gandhi's Philosophy of Man and Life.* Trivandrum: M.S. Publication.

Dasgupta, S.N. (1975). *A History of Indian Philosophy,* Vol. 2. Delhi: Motilal Banarsidass.

Datta, Dhirendra Mohan. (1961). *The Philosophy of Mahatma Gandhi.* Madison: The University of Wisconsin Press.

Davidson, D. (1963). 'Actions, Reasons, and Causes' in *Essays on Actions and Events*. Oxford: Oxford University Press.

Desai, Mahadevbhai. (1946). *The Gospel of Selfless Action Or The Gita according to Gandhi*. Ahmedabad: Navajivan.

Diwaker, R.R. (1969). *Saga of Satyagraha*. New Delhi: GPF.

Frank Morales. (1999). *The Ontology of Self in Three Systems of Indian Philosophy: A Comparative and Veridical Analysis*. Retrieved from indunet.org/home/dharma_and_philosophy/vvh/vvhself.html.

Gandhi, M.K. (1930). *Discourse on Gita*. Ahmedabad: Navajivan. Retrieved from https://www.gandhiashramsevagram.org/pdf-books/discourses-on-gita.pdf.

Gandhi, M.K. (1945). *Gita the Mother* (ed. Jag Parvesh Chander). Karachi-Lahore: Indian Printing Works.

Gandhi, M.K. (1947). *India of My Dream*. Ahmedabad: Navajivan. Retrieved from https://www.idc-america.org/wp-content/uploads/2015/09/india_dreams

Gandhi, M.K. (1954). *Satyagraha in South Africa*. Ahmedabad: Navajivan.

Gandhi, M.K. (1955). *Truth is God*. Ahmedabad: Navajivan. Retrieved from https://www.mkgandhi.org/ebks/truth_is_god.pdf.

Gandhi, M.K. (1955). *My Religion*. Ahmedabad: Navajivan. Retrieved from https://www.mkgandhi.org/ebks/my_religion.pdf

Gandhi, M.K. (1958). *Hindu Dharma*. Ahmedabad: Navajivan.

Gandhi, M.K. (1959). *Message of Gita*. Ahmedabad: Navajivan.

Gandhi, M.K. (1961). *In Search of Supreme*, Vol. I (ed. V.B. Kher). Ahmedabad: Navajivan. Retrieved from https://www.mkgandhi.org/ebks/in-search-of-the-supreme-I.pdf

Gandhi, M.K. (1969). *All Men are Bothers*. Switzerland: Unesco. Retrieved from unesdoc.unesco.org/images/0007/000710/071082eo.pdf.

Gandhi, M.K. (1996). *The Essence of Hinduism*. Ahmedabad: Navajivan.

Gandhi, M.K. (2001). *Nonviolent Resistance*. New York: Dover Publication.

Gandhi, M.K. (2008). *Hind Swaraj or Indian Home Rule*. Ahmedabad: Navajivan.

Gandhi, M.K. (2013). *An Autobiography or My Experiments with Truth*. Ahmedabad: Navajivan.

Gandhi, M.K. (2014). *From Yervada Mandir*. Ahmedabad: Navajivan.

Gandhi, M.K. (2014). *Ethical Religion*. Ahmedabad: Navajivan.

Gandhi, M.K. (2015). *Constructive Programme Its Meaning and Place*. Ahmedabad: Navajivan.

Gergen, Kenneth J. (1991). *The Saturated Self*. New York: Basic Books.

Goflinan, Erving. (1951) "Symbols of Class Status." British Journal of Sociology, 11 (4): 294-304.

Guru, Gopal, and Sunder Sarukkai. (2012). *The Cracked Mirror*. New Delhi: Oxford University Press.

Hatfield, G. (2003). *Routledge Philosophy Guidebook to Descartes and the Meditations*, Routledge.

Iyer, Raghavan N. (2007). *The Moral and Political Thought of Mahatma Gandhi*. New Delhi: Oxford University Press.

Jameson, Fredric. (1984). "Postmodernism, or The Cultural Logic of Late Capitalism." *New Left Review*, Number 146: 51- 92.

Jha, Nirmala. (1985). *Law of Krama As Perceived by Gandhi, Aurobindo, Vivekanand, Radhakrishnan.* New Delhi: Capital Publishing House.

Juan Mascoró. (1965), *The Upanishads*, Delhi: Penguin Books.

Keith Ansell Pearson (ed.). (2006). *Nietzsche Reader.* U.K.: Blackwell Publishing Limited.

Mathai, M.P. (2000). *Mahatma Gandhi's World View*. G.P.F.: New Delhi.

Max Müller. (1879). *The Upanishads,* Part 2 (SBE15), see sacred-texts.com.

Mittal, K.K. (1990). *Various Perspectives on Karma and Rebirth*, Delhi University: Department of Buddhist Studies.

Mohanty, Jitendra N. (1997). 'Indian philosophy', in *Macropædia*, volume 21, 15th edition, *Encyclopedia Britannica*, Chicago

Payne, Robert. (1969). *The Life and Death of Mahatma Gandhi.* New York: E.P. Dutton & Co.

Nagler, Michael. (2014). *The Principles of Constructive Programme.* The Metta Center for Nonviolence.

Parekh, Bhikhu. (1989). *Gandhi's Political Philosophy*. London: Macmillan.

Parekh, Bhikhu. (1997). *Gandhi: A Very Short Introduction.* Oxford: Oxford University Press.

Parel, Anthony. (2006). *Gandhi's Philosophy and the Quest for Harmony.* New York: Cambridge University Press.

Peter Ackerman, and Jack Duvall. (2000). *A Force More Powerful: A Century of Nonviolent Conflict.* New York: Palgrave.

Prabhu, R.K. and U.R. Rao. (2002). *The Mind of Mahatma*. Ahmedabad: Navajivan.

Radhakrishnan, S. (1960). *The Hindy way of Life.* London: Unwin Book.

Radhiakrishnan, S. (1983). *Bharatheeya Darsanam (M), Vol. 1*. Calicut: Mathrubhoomi.

Sethi, J.D. (1994). *Gandhian Values in and 20th Century Challenges*. New Delhi: Publication Division Government of India.

Swami Gnanananda Saraswathi, (1995). *Sankhya Darsanam.* Kanyakumari Anandkudeeram.

Tilak, B.G. (1995). *Sri Mad Bhagwad Gita rahasya.* Trichur: Sulabha Books.

Ramin Jahanbegloo. (2013). *The Gandhian Moment*. London: Harvard University Press.

Roy, Ramashray. (1985). *Self and Society: A study in Gandhian Thought.* New Delhi: Sage.

Sinha, K.P. (1991). *The Self in Indian Philosophy.* Calcutta: Punthi Pustak.

Sharp, Gene. (1979). *Gandhi as a Political Strategist: With Essays on Ethics and Politics.* Boston. MA: Porter Sargent.

Singh, Dashrath (1975). *Gandhivaad ko Vinoba Kee Den* (Hindi). Patna: Bihar Hindi Granth Akadami.

Srimad Bhagvad Gita (1990). Mumbai: Bhaktivedant Book Trust.

Tellis, Allwyn. (2006) "*Mahatma Gandhi's Constructive Programme: Building a New India*" (Ph.D. Thesis) the University of Illinois at Urbana-Champaign, ProQuest.

Tercheak, Ronald J. (1998) *Gandhi: Struggling for Autonomy.* New Delhi: Vistaar Publication.

The Collected Works of Mahatma Gandhi (*CWMG*), Vols. 1-100. New Delhi: Publication. Division Goernment of India. Retrieved from https://www.gandhiheritageportal.org/

Unto Tahtinen, (1979). *The Core of Gandhi's Philosophy.* New Delhi: Abhinav Publication.

Varma, Ravindra. (2001). *The Spiritual Basis of Satyagraha.* Ahmedabad: Navajivan.

Velleman, J.D. (1989). *Practical Reflection.* NJ: Princeton University Press.

Index

Absolute truth, 24–26, 35, 38–42, 51–52, 102, 170–71, 174–75
Action
  kamya, 65
  love in, 122
  primacy of, 60, 66
  self-determined, 159
  self-interested, 172
  self-less, 172
  totality of, 67, 71, 172
Adverse fate, 70, 158
Ahimsa, 2–3, 8, 31, 33, 36, 47, 62, 86, 99, 121–22, 127–28, 170
Anasakti, 60–62, 64, 71, 125, 131, 134
Antyodaya, 99
Apurva, 148, 164
Atman, 40, 43–44, 78, 84–85, 87, 147, 153
Attachment, 62, 66, 71, 86, 121, 128, 131–32, 134, 136, 138, 144, 158

Bihar calamity, 161–62
Bondage, 60–61, 63, 132, 152
Brotherhood, 109
Buddhism, 79–80, 143, 150–51, 165

Charvaka school, 78–79
Community action, 1–2, 17
Compassion, 105, 119–20, 123
Consciousness, 26, 68, 76, 79–80, 82–83, 102
Constructive Programme, 1–2, 11–18, 33, 127
Corporate growth, 107
Cosmic spirit, 84, 134
Cowardice, 30, 130
Cultural life, 146

Delusion, 66, 152
Descartes, 80
Detachment, 61–62, 69, 118, 130–34, 136–38, 155, 160, 173
  attitude of, 132, 138
  selfless, 133–34
  spirit of, 60, 128, 132–33, 175
Devotion, 26, 30, 60, 65, 67, 132, 144, 154
Dharma, 5–7, 15, 39, 98, 112, 123, 145–46
Dialogical empathy, 111, 124
Divine Radio, 89

Earthquake, 161–62
Ecological relationship, 80
Ego-centrism, 8
Egotism, 110, 133, 153, 155
Empirical evidence, 52
Epistemological Basis, 38–39, 43, 45, 47, 53, 75
Epistemology, 38, 51–53, 56, 69, 71, 170–71
Esthetics of Gandhi, 118, 123, 125, 129, 131, 133, 135
Eternal truths, 39
Ethical
  relation, 124
  relationship, 98
  religion, 58, 85, 103
  responsibility, 125
Ethics of Gandhi, 75, 77, 79, 81, 83, 85, 93, 95
Evil karma, 150
Evil-doer, 9, 122

Faith versus reason, 45
Fasting, 93–94
Fearlessness, 29, 127

Gandhi Seva Sangh, 93
Gandhian responsibility, 130
Gautama Buddha, 79
Genuineness, 25
Gita, 35, 43, 46, 58–63, 65–71, 100–101, 127–28, 131–32, 135, 138, 142, 152, 154–55, 159–60, 172

Hallucination, 50–51
Heart of passions, 91
Hind Swaraj, 33, 98, 112
Hindu philosophical traditions, 39, 46, 84, 149, 164
Hindu philosophy, 39–40, 61, 145–47, 162–63
Hindu scripture, 39, 46, 52, 171
Hinduism, 39, 135, 138, 150, 153, 163
  historical, 135–36
  popular, 135–36
Human actions, 65, 98, 106, 112–13, 145–46, 161–62, 165
Human beings, 8, 16, 34–35, 83–84, 88, 107, 109, 113, 121–22, 127, 130, 134, 144–45, 151, 157
Human efforts, 70–71, 158

Indian Philosophical Schools, 143, 145–46, 160
Indian philosophical systems, 70, 142–43, 164
Indian philosophy of karma, 142
Individual growth, 107
Inner voice, 28–30, 36, 38, 49–51, 53, 171
Internal responsibility, 77

Jainism, 143, 150–52, 165
Jainism karma, 151, 165
Jivas, 85, 149–50, 152

Karm yoga, 59–60
Karma, 69–70, 98, 135, 142–58, 160–61, 163–66, 173–74
  administrator of, 149, 164
  anasakt, 59
  continuity of, 156, 165
  doctrine of, 143–44, 146, 148–49, 163–64
  fruition of, 70, 158
  inexorable law of, 154
  law of, 70–71, 129, 142–50, 152–66, 173
  negative, 144
  parmarthik, 174
  prarabdha, 70, 158
  residual, 151
  unchangeable Law of, 157–58
Karmayoga, 60, 160
Knowledge
  divine, 46
  empirical, 42, 53, 171
  factual, 42, 52
  final source of, 46, 53
  object of, 44, 67, 71, 172
  perfect, 68, 148, 164
  source of, 46, 49
  true, 26–27, 40, 68

Law of Karma, 148, 150–51, 160, 164–65
Law of Truth, 7, 26–27, 34
Love
  active, 122
  force of, 4, 106, 118–19
  mutual, 106
  perfect, 120
  philosophy of, 119, 123, 137
  supreme, 170
  true, 120, 128, 137

Marxism, 15
Material forces, 7–9, 18
Material sources, 7
Metaphysical belief, 7, 23, 35, 153, 160–61
Metaphysical scheme, 34
Metaphysics of truth, 38, 118
Moksha, 60, 85, 97, 100–101, 146, 149–50
Moral action, 9, 16, 56–59, 71, 172
Moral law, 40, 108–9, 160
Moral life, 106, 148, 163
Moral responsibility, 99–100, 102, 127, 129, 151
Multi-dimensional responsibility, 129
Nationalist movement, 11–12

Nishkaam-Karma, 60, 71
Non-duality, 77
Non-violence, 2–3, 9–10, 12–16, 18, 31–33, 35–36, 43, 62, 66, 69, 118–19, 121, 123, 127, 170–71
Non-violent society, 33

Oceanic circle, 14, 18

Partial truths, 42, 51, 157
Personal salvation, 134–35
Philosophy of self-transformation, 129, 138
Physical calamities, 161–62, 165
Political responsibility, 99, 112
Poorna Swaraj, construction of, 16
Primacy of reason, 46–47
Proximity, 8, 126
Purification, 25, 86–87
Purushartha, 101–2, 128–29

Ramanama, 92–93
Ramrajya, vision of, 130
Rational explanation, 43
Real knowledge, 68
Realization of truth, 30, 42, 52, 88, 94
Relative truth, 25–26, 32, 35, 38, 41–42, 51–52, 102, 170–71

Sadagraha, 2–3
Saivite interpretation, 149, 164
Samsara, 98–99, 144, 150–52
Samskaras, 155–56
Sanyasi, 102–3
Sarvodaya, 97, 99–100, 127
Sattva, 66
Satya, 2–3, 24, 39–40, 127
Satyagraha, 1–12, 17–18, 23, 33, 42, 97–98, 110, 122, 127, 130
Scientific truth, 50
Self
  correction, 76, 97
  discipline, 38, 86–87, 94, 101, 129, 172
  examination, 76, 97
  fragmented, 77, 81
  individual, 153, 175
  indulgence, 32, 137
  interest, 30, 58, 103, 111, 113, 136, 172
  love, 106
  post-modern, 81–82
  purification, 75–76, 86–88, 94, 97, 162, 172
  sacrifice of, 98–99, 110, 112
  sufficiency, 109–10
  transformation, 129, 138
  understanding, 94, 172
  universal, 85, 153
Selfish motives, 128, 133
Selfishness, 87, 103, 120, 135, 153
Selfless, 59, 71, 91, 137, 172, 175
  action, 65, 133, 172
  activities, 103, 135
  service, 97, 125–26, 128
  spirit, 35, 87
Social life, 16, 102, 106
Social organization, 14
Social restraint, 111
Sovereign Law, 6, 27, 174
Spiritual
  experience, 47–48
  life, 59
  pursuit, 92
  value, 89–90
Superstition, 92
Supreme Law, 31, 35, 174
Swadeshi, 97–98, 100, 126
Swaraj, 97–99, 103, 112

Tabula rasa, 80–81
Truth
  contextual, 26
  defined, 38
  empirical, 52
  eternal, 87
  ethics of, 69, 71
  force of, 5, 8, 10, 118
  identifying, 10, 18, 39
  perfect, 70, 154
  pursuit of, 3, 30, 32
  term, 24, 32
  test of, 26–27, 47
  universality of, 38
  votary of, 89
Truth-in-action, 4, 10, 18, 31, 170
Truth-in-Service, 11
Truthfulness, 24–25

Unison of Universal Love, 118
Universal love, 118–19, 121–24, 134, 136–38, 173, 175
Universal responsibility, 101, 125
Untouchability, 17, 123, 161–62
Upanishads, 77–78, 80, 146

Yajna, 60, 63–65, 71, 128, 132
Yervada Mandir, 26, 69
Yogi, 34, 65, 133